D. Robinson

The Environment
of Early Man
in the British Isles

Archaeology and Anthropology

This is the first in a group of books on Archaeology and Anthropology to be published by Paul Elek Ltd under the general editorship of J. V. S. Megaw, Professor of Archaeology in the University of Leicester

The Environment
of Early Man
in the British Isles

John G. Evans

Lecturer in Archaeology, University College, Cardiff

Paul Elek London

Published in Great Britain by
Elek Books Ltd
54–58 Caledonian Road
London N1 9RN

Printed by
Unwin Brothers Limited
The Gresham Press
Old Woking, Surrey, England
A member of the Staples Printing Group

ISBN 0 236 30902 1

For
Ottoline Atlantica

Contents

Plates

Figures

Preface

There is no book which describes the history of man's environment in the British Isles from his earliest appearance to the present day. Some, such as Dudley Stamp's *Man and the Land*[1] or H. J. Fleure's *A Natural History of Man in Britain*,[2] present a general approach but both are essentially geographies and do not discuss the evidence of environmental archaeology. The botanists, and in particular Harry Godwin[3] and Winifred Pennington,[4] have given us histories of the flora and vegetation, and these contain abundant detail on the general history of the environment; both recognize the importance of man. But for the archaeologist, the geographer or indeed for anyone wanting a short non-specialist introduction to the subject there is little, and certainly nothing describing the recent wealth of material which archaeology has revealed. It is the aim of this book to fill that gap.

The presentation of the data has not been easy, partly because many of the techniques of environmental archaeology are complicated and highly specialized, and partly because there are so many of them, encompassing practically all major branches of the sciences. What I have tried to do in most instances is to work from the specific to the general, first to examine the facts as presented by a single site, and then to try and fit them into the general scheme. In doing so I have introduced various techniques and concepts throughout the book as they have arisen. The main historical order of events has been adhered to, but nowhere is there a specific section describing the geography of the British Isles, although important aspects are discussed at intervals.[5] Nor is there a separate section on techniques.

In addition to the history of environment I have tried to look at the history of the subject of environmental archaeology. Again, the information is scattered and it is for the reader to fit the bits together into a coherent whole. Mention must be made of the pioneer work of F. E. Zeuner.[6] He figures little in this book because much of his research was done on the Continent but in setting up the Department of Environmental Archaeology at the Institute of Archaeology, London University, he laid the foundations for the present-day liaison between archaeologists and scientists, without which the past environment of man cannot be properly investigated.

Throughout the history of the study of man's environment there have been several shifts of emphasis in the importance of man himself. At first, man was thought to have had little impact in controlling plant

[1] Superior figures refer to Notes pp. 188–97.

and animal communities and the physico/chemical environment in prehistory. But between 1920 and 1940 there came about a gradual awareness of his great impact, in particular on the vegetation, and this has accelerated in recent years with the realization that even very small groups of hunter/gatherers can have an effect out of all proportion to their size (see pp. 15 and 23). But in the last few years there has been a different trend. How far, in effect, should we view man as different from any other animal species? If we view his relationship with the environment, and in particular with animal herds, not as aggressive but symbiotic, born of economic circumstance, then many of the problems posed by earlier workers on whether or not a particular episode of landscape change was humanly or naturally induced become irrelevant, even non-existent.[7] Unfortunately, from the practical point of view in discussing several aspects of environmental change, it has been necessary to distinguish between 'man' and 'nature' since the conceptual framework for doing otherwise in a book such as this does not yet exist.

In writing this book I have been much influenced by the ideas of several scholars, and in particular by the work of J. G. D. Clark. I am a firm believer in 'environmental determinism' and make no apologies for it. I have not, however, indulged at length on this aspect since the book is essentially a factual account, but I have allowed Clark's *The Stone Age Hunters*[8] to influence some of the broader outlines of this history. The book, however, is essentially an environmental history in which the facts about our human environment are presented. It is for others to take up these facts and work out how they fit in to man's history as a whole.

October 1974

Acknowledgements

I would like to thank the following for their permission to reproduce drawings and photographs; detailed sources are given in the relevant captions.

Methuen and Co. Ltd (Figs. 2, 17, 32); The Royal Society of London (Figs. 3, 13, 14, 15, 16, 18, 20, 63); Bristol University Speleological Society (Fig. 22); Department of Geography, Queen's University Belfast (Figs. 25, 45, 75); Cambridge University Press (Figs. 30, 33, 42, 46, 47, 53, 80); Oxford University Press (Fig. 36); Gerald Duckworth and Co. Ltd (Fig. 38); The Prehistoric Society (Figs. 39, 43, 44, 56, 58); The National Museum of Wales (Fig. 59); Council for British Archaeology (Fig. 67); Wiltshire Archaeological and Natural History Society (Figs. 68, 70, 71); Wm. Collins Sons and Co. Ltd (Figs. 69); Chateau Gaillard (Fig. 72); John Baker Publishers Ltd (Figs. 73, 74); Dorset Natural History and Archaeological Society (Fig. 77); George Allen and Unwin Ltd (Fig. 79).

C. Turner (Fig. 3); G. R. Coope, F. W. Shotton and I. Strachan (Figs. 13, 14, 15, 16); B. W. Sparks and R. G. West (Fig. 17); M. P. Kerney (Figs. 18, 20); E. K. Tratman, D. T. Donovan and J. B. Campbell (Fig. 22); T. Jones Hughes and F. M. Synge (Fig. 25); R. B. G. Williams (Fig. 26); J. G. D. Clark (Figs. 30, 32, 33, 42, 44); G. W. Dimbleby (Fig. 36, 33); I. G. Simmons (Fig. 38); S. Palmer (Fig. 43); A. G. Smith (Fig. 45); Mrs W. Tutin (Fig. 46, 47); J. Turner (Fig. 53, 63); C. Houlder (Fig. 56); R. Feachem (Fig. 58); B. Cunliffe (Fig. 67); C. Taylor (Figs. 68, 70, 71, 73, 77); J. Le Patourel (Fig. 72); M. Hooper (Fig. 76).

Aerofilms (Plates 1, 6, 11); J. K. St Joseph and Cambridge University (Plate 12); J. R. Pilcher and the Ulster Journal of Archaeology (Plate 2); W. H. Manning and the British Museum Quarterly (Plate 11).

I am grateful to Gaye Booth for printing some of the plates, to Gloria Powell for help with the line drawings, and to Pat Charlton for assisting with the arduous task of reading the proofs. Dr John Campbell very kindly read and commented on Chapters 1 and 2, and Professor Gordon Manley and Professor Leslie Alcock Chapter 7.

Geological Table

Quaternary	Pleistocene	
Tertiary	Pliocene Eocene	London Clay
Mesozoic	Cretaceous	Chalk (Flint-bearing) Greensand and Gault Clay
	Jurassic	Portland Limestone (Chert-bearing) Corallian Limestone Oxford Clay Oolite Limestone Lias Clay and Limestone
	Triassic	Keuper Marl
Palaeozoic	Carboniferous	Millstone Grit Carboniferous Limestone
	Devonian	Old Red Sandstone Limestone

The temporal relationship of the geological periods mentioned in the text, and their rock types.

1   The Hoxnian Interglacial

On the south side of the River Thames some 32 kilometres downstream from London is one of the most famous archaeological sites in the world—Barnfield Pit, Swanscombe (Fig. 1). Here, in ancient river gravels, the flint tools of Stone Age man have been collected for almost a century, together with the bones of numerous animals, some of which —lion, elephant, rhinoceros and bear—are now extinct in Britain. A number of types of flint tools are present at Swanscombe, but the finest and most sought after by collectors are the hand-axes.[1] These are not true axes in the sense that they were hafted and used for cutting, but rather general purpose tools which might be used for butchering, chopping, scraping and digging. They belong to the group of Stone Age industries known as Acheulian, named after the type site of St Acheul in the Somme Valley. But most exciting, has been the discovery, since 1935, of three skull fragments of man. At the same horizon there is evidence—in that a number of the flints appear to have been burnt— for the use of fire.

The industries at Swanscombe belong to a very remote period of man's history, in fact the very earliest at which he is certainly represented in the British Isles (Table 1).[2] The period is known archaeologically as the Lower Palaeolithic or Lower Old Stone Age.[3] Man obtained his living solely by hunting and gathering. Agriculture was unknown. Many dramatic environmental changes separate Swanscombe Man by more than 150,000 years from the development and eventual spread into Britain of farming communities—much of the land was twice engulfed under ice sheets; the sea twice fell to about 100 metres below its present level; and massive erosion and downcutting by rivers occurred, one result of which was to leave the Swanscombe gravels perched literally high and dry as a terrace some 25 to 30 metres above the flood plain of the present-day Thames. Geologically, the period in which these events took place is known as the Pleistocene or the Quaternary—or, more popularly, as the Great Ice Age. It constitutes approximately the last two million years of the earth's history (Table 1).[4]

Work at Swanscombe has been published recently as a monograph,[5] but there is still a great deal of information awaiting discovery by more refined techniques of excavation and scientific study. For example, in the last ten years, pollen has been extracted from the deposits for the first time, the mollusc fauna has been studied quantitatively and area excavation has led to a closer definition of the archaeological levels.[6] Indeed, evidence for ancient environments can be obtained from a

Table 1.   Time range of Palaeolithic industries in Britain in relation to the sequence of glacials and interglacials. (After Wymer, 1968)

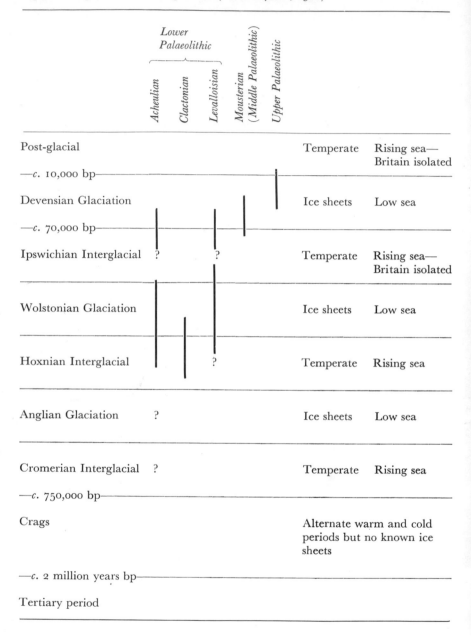

	Acheulian	*Clactonian*	*Levalloisian*	*Mousterian (Middle Palaeolithic)*	*Upper Palaeolithic*		
Post-glacial						Temperate	Rising sea— Britain isolated
—*c.* 10,000 bp—							
Devensian Glaciation						Ice sheets	Low sea
—*c.* 70,000 bp—							
Ipswichian Interglacial	?		?			Temperate	Rising sea— Britain isolated
Wolstonian Glaciation						Ice sheets	Low sea
Hoxnian Interglacial			?			Temperate	Rising sea
Anglian Glaciation	?					Ice sheets	Low sea
Cromerian Interglacial	?					Temperate	Rising sea
—*c.* 750,000 bp—							
Crags						Alternate warm and cold periods but no known ice sheets	
—*c.* 2 million years bp—							
Tertiary period							

whole variety of sources, and we may use Swanscombe as an intro-duction to some of these, and to the methods and concepts of environ-mental archaeology in general.

The deposits are largely of fluviatile, or water-borne, origin. They occupy a channel in the underlying geological solid—here sands and chalk[7]—and have a maximum thickness of about 13 metres (Fig. 1). Sands and gravels predominate, and there are two beds of finer loamy material. These sediments were laid down by a generally fast flowing river such as one sees in parts of upland Britain today (Plate 1) but which is not now such a familiar sight in the lowlands. Over the past 200 years, rivers like the Thames have been embanked to prevent flooding, and the flow of water controlled by locks and weirs (p. 179). Formerly their courses were braided, i.e. split up into several channels which meandered over a broad flood plain leaving a variety of deposits depending on the speed of flow—gravels and sands where the flow was fast and the water relatively shallow; finer loamy sediments where there was deeper quieter water. A multitude of different environments was created at the same point in time, and it is for this reason that the

Plate 1. The River Spey. An uncontrolled Highland Zone river.

stratigraphical sequences in the various gravel pits around Swanscombe are so difficult to match.

For agricultural peoples such a system of braided channels is wasteful of land, and artificial control has been imposed at various times in the past on river systems in the most heavily farmed areas of the country. But from the point of view of Lower Palaeolithic man such conditions were ideal. They provided tracts of open ground in an otherwise forested country with the obvious advantages of defence against predators such as the lion, and of concentrating herds of game such as deer, oxen, horse and elephant attracted to the river valley for water. The variety of habitats—open water, reed swamp, woodland

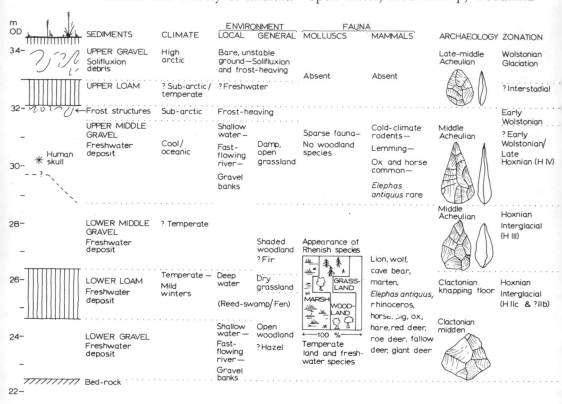

Fig. 1.   Swanscombe. Correlation of sediments, environment, archaeology and general zonation.

and, as we shall see, at one stage, grassland—together with the variety of game animals both large and small obviated the need for specialization in hunting and food-gathering techniques, and presented man with what was probably a relatively congenial existence.

The Lower Gravel and Lower Loam (Fig. 1) constitute a single depositional unit reflecting a change from fast-flowing shallow water to deeper quieter conditions. These local changes are a reflection of a more general trend at the time, that of a gradually rising sea level, to which almost the entire accumulation of deposits at Swanscombe is due. This process of build-up is known technically as aggradation and may be contrasted with the process of downcutting or erosion which takes place at times of low sea level. Aggradation to just over 30 metres OD led to the formation of the Middle Gravels, and it was in these deposits that the human skull fragments were found (Fig. 1).[8]

Before discussing the final episodes in the Swanscombe sequence—the deposition of the Upper Loam and Gravel—it is necessary to consider the faunal evidence in the earlier stages of the succession. The two main groups of animals used to reconstruct ancient environments are the mammals and the molluscs since both yield largely inorganic remains which are often preserved in near perfect condition.[9] Their identification from various levels can tell us what animal species were living at the time, and, by reference to their present-day habitats, they can give us an indication of the environments which obtained in the past. In the case of species now extinct, e.g. the straight-tusked elephant (*Elephas antiquus*), we can never be absolutely certain of their former habitats, but clues can be obtained from the other species with which they occur, as well as from certain anatomical details of their bones and teeth. For example, the number of cusps or plates on the grinding surface of the teeth of *Elephas antiquus* is far fewer than on those of the woolly mammoth, *Elephas primigenius*, which characterizes the colder periods of the Pleistocene (Fig. 2). This difference is directly related to diet: *Elephas antiquus* fed on the succulent foliage of forest trees, while *Elephas primigenius* was restricted to the tough fibrous plants of the steppe and tundra which needed a greater degree of mastication. The difference between the simple grinding surface of

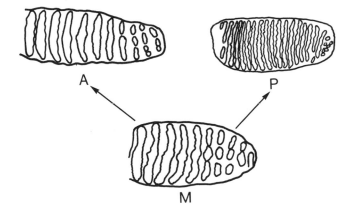

Fig. 2. Grinding surfaces of molar teeth of elephants. M, a generalized Middle Pleistocene form, *Elephas meridionalis*; A, a forest species, *Elephas antiquus*, the straight-tusked elephant; and P, a cold-climate form, *Elephas primigenius*, the woolly mammoth. (After Zeuner, 1958, Fig. 100)

cattle molars and the more complex pattern of those of the horse has a similar basis, reflecting the difference between a browsing and a grazing animal.

At Swanscombe, the mammals from the Lower Gravel and Loam reflect temperate climatic conditions in a generally wooded environment, but, as suggested by the presence of horse, with some open ground. Characteristic species of woodland are the marten, the pig and various species of deer. Further up the sequence in the Middle Gravel the fauna suggests a more open environment, there being an increase of horse and a decrease of elephant. A number of vole species of grassland habitats also appear, and just above the horizon of the human skull, the jaws and teeth of lemming—a species of completely open ground (steppe or tundra).

The molluscs indicate a similar sequence, but because of their smaller size they are more readily applicable to the detection of finer changes.[10] Two groups are present, namely those which were once living in the river (freshwater species) and those from dry land habitats (terrestrial species) which were swept into the river in times of flood and incorporated into the sediments. The freshwater species, as is to be expected, indicate a large body of well-oxygenated moving water. At the top of the Lower Loam and subsequently in the Middle Gravel a number of species of Central European (Rhenish) affinities appear. It has been suggested that this reflects the time when, due to the rising sea, the Thames and Rhine river systems became linked, and it is possible that the junction between the Lower Loam and Middle Gravel is of more than local significance. This, as we shall see, is suggested too by the archaeological content of the gravels.

Turning to the land molluscs, four main episodes can be recognized (**Fig. 1**). The first, during the deposition of the Lower Gravel and lower two thirds of the Lower Loam, constitutes a period of open woodland, probably dominated by hazel, with areas of reed swamp and fen. The second is an episode of deforestation when dry grassland species rose to 80 per cent of the fauna. There was then a return to wooded conditions, possibly of fir as suggested by species tolerant of extreme shade. Finally, in the Upper Middle Gravel, coincident with the influx of open-country rodents, a fauna devoid of woodland species and indicative of damp open grassland became present.

The molluscan and mammalian faunas thus indicate a similar sequence, but the land snails have enabled us to characterize more closely the nature of the woodland episodes, and have also shown up a remarkable feature—the temporary phase of deforestation in the upper part of the Lower Loam. To this we will return.

No fauna is present in the Upper Loam and Gravel. Instead we must rely on the character of the deposits themselves, and the indications are that, following the trend to open grassland conditions seen in the

Upper Middle Gravel, in at least part of the sequence a sub-arctic climate obtained. First, the upper few centimetres of the Middle Gravel and the entire thickness of the Upper Gravel have been thrown into a series of folds or involutions (sometimes known as cryoturbation structures) (Fig. 1), and this is thought to have been due to pressures exerted within the gravel by alternate freezing and thawing of the ground during periods of sub-arctic climate. It is certainly not a process which is going on today in temperate Europe. Secondly, the Upper Gravel is probably not of fluviatile origin but was most likely formed by downhill sludging under conditions of impeded drainage when the bulk of the ground was frozen all the year round (a condition known as permafrost), only the surface layers thawing out during the spring and summer. Thirdly, solifluxion deposits are generally made up of angular fragments of rock freshly broken by frost action, whereas in river gravels the pebbles are rounded due to the constant battering they receive on the river bed; and again, the Upper Gravel at Swanscombe conforms in this respect to a solifluxion deposit.

The origin of the Upper Loam is not clear. It may be 'loessic', that is it may be a result of wind-blown material under dry, very cold conditions, perhaps subsequently resorted. If on the other hand it is a freshwater deposit, then its deposition probably reflects a temporary rise of the sea after the recession during which the involutions at the surface of the Upper Middle Gravel formed. Subsequently no further aggradation by the river system took place. On the contrary, downcutting ensued leaving the surface of the deposits at about 33·5 metres above the present level of the sea.

To what are these changes of sea level due? To answer this we may now look at some of the broader implications of Swanscombe and try to fit the site into the British Pleistocene sequence as a whole. On at least three occasions in the past, ice sheets, similar to that which mantles Greenland today, formed over Scandinavia and the high mountain masses of the British Isles, and pushed their way southwards (Fig. 6 and Table 1). One result of this was the locking up of vast quantities of water which, under temperate conditions, would have been returned to the oceans. Thus the level of the sea fell (Fig. 17). During the intervening periods of temperate climate—known as interglacials—when the ice sheets melted, the level of the sea rose once again. But it is a curious fact that after each glaciation the rising sea did not return to its former high level but reached a maximum some distance below that of the previous interglacial. There is no adequate explanation for this phenomenon but from the point of view of Pleistocene geology it has led to the separation of successive interglacial marine deposits along the coasts and in the lower reaches of the major rivers. On this basis we can recognize the following interglacial high sea levels (see also Table 1):

	Height above present sea level (OD) (metres)
Post-glacial or Flandrian	0
Ipswichian or Last Interglacial	5–8
Hoxnian Interglacial	30–32

Each interglacial is named after a type site or area where deposits of that stage occur. Thus the name Flandrian refers to a stretch of the coast of north-west Europe, the names Ipswichian and Hoxnian to deposits at Ipswich and Hoxne in East Anglia. We at present are in a period optimistically termed the Post-glacial, but which may be an interglacial to be terminated at some stage in the remote future by a further age of ice. Hence the more realistic term Flandrian to bring it into line with the naming of earlier interglacials. The three glaciations to have affected the British Isles are named in a similar manner. These are, in order of decreasing age, the Anglian, the Wolstonian and the Devensian Glaciations (Table 1).[11]

The problem of correlating individual sites with particular glacials or interglacials must not concern us too closely but will be discussed at intervals in this and the succeeding chapter. Here it need only be said that on the basis both of their height above sea level and of the composition of their mammalian fauna the main body of the Swanscombe deposits is considered to belong to the Hoxnian Interglacial. The Lower Gravel and Lower Loam, and perhaps the Lower Middle Gravel, were laid down during a period of rising sea level, an event which took place in fully interglacial conditions as indicated by the temperate woodland fauna, both mammalian and molluscan. The Upper Middle Gravel was deposited during the final stages of this episode, with the open glassland fauna indicating a time at the end of the interglacial or even the beginning of the ensuing glaciation. The deposition of the Upper Loam, if of river origin, may reflect a temporary climatic amelioration for it falls within a sequence of cold climate deposits, resting on gravel which has been subjected to frost heaving, and overlain by solifluxion debris. Minor episodes of climatic amelioration of this kind are known as 'interstadials' if they fall clearly within a given glaciation—in this case the Wolstonian.

Three distinct flint industries of Lower Palaeolithic man occur in the Swanscombe deposits (Fig. 1).[12] The earliest of these, known as the Clactonian after the type site at Clacton-on-Sea in Essex, comprises chopper cores and flakes but generally not hand-axes. Clactonian artefacts are prolific in the Lower Gravel and are usually in a sharp condition indicating them to be virtually *in situ* as left by Palaeolithic man. During recent excavations two working floors were located, one on the surface of the Lower Gravel, the other within the Lower Loam.[13] The immediate environment of the Clactonian people was thus the sand and gravel beaches of the aggrading Thames, temporarily abandoned perhaps by seasonal low water levels or local variations in the braiding system. Game was abundant as indicated by the prolific faunal remains, and it is likely that many of these represent human food debris. Large herbivores were favoured, particularly the elephant, horse, fallow deer, red deer and wild ox (aurochs). Reed swamp and fen habitats were present locally while the general woodland background was probably mixed deciduous forest. The Thames flowed through a wild luxuriant landscape.

The subsequent hand-axe industries are divided into Middle Acheulian and Late Middle Acheulian on a typological basis. Early and Late Acheulian industries are not present at Swanscombe. Two similar stages of Middle Acheulian occur in the Middle Gravels, and here again the immediate environment was one of sand and gravel beaches in a constantly changing river system. But the general environmental background was different to that experienced by Clactonian man. Initially, in the Lower Middle Gravel, shaded woodland, probably of fir, obtained. Later, during aggradation of the Upper Middle Gravel, the environment became more open and the climate cooler. The fauna was less diverse than previously, only two species, the horse and the ox, being recorded as at all common, and we must envisage Middle Acheulian man at this stage—at the stage represented by the human skull fragments—as living in a more severe and specialized environment than that of his predecessors. The presence of charcoal and of flints possibly crackled and reddened suggests fire, although it is not clear whether this was of natural origin or was being directly employed by man.

The final stage of human activity at Swanscombe is represented by Late Middle Acheulian hand-axes in the Upper Loam. These include the famous 'twisted ovates', 'some of the most elegant hand-axes found in the Thames Valley'.[14] We do not know what the environment was like during the deposition of the Upper Loam due to the absence of any reliable indicators, but, if an interstadial, it was at best coniferous woodland such as obtains today in the Boreal forest belt of northern Europe, and at worst, if loessic, tundra with perhaps occasional birch woodland in sheltered places.

It is perhaps not without significance that the trend towards increasing climatic severity was paralleled by a trend towards greater perfection and elegance in man's ability to work stone.

Plate 2.   Stereomicrograph of pollen grains of *Fraxinus excelsior*, ash, × 2570.

Swanscombe has been used to introduce some of the ideas of environmental archaeology because of the very clear association between the
environmental and the archaeological evidence, and the long sequence
of both cultural and habitat change. From both these aspects it is a
classic site. But it is still mostly lacking in one of the most important
environmental indicators of all—pollen. Because of this we do not
have the detailed picture of vegetational changes at Swanscombe that
has been obtained from certain other sites of this age.[15]

Pollen is a fine powdery substance made up of myriads of tiny
grains.[16] Since each genus, and sometimes species, of plant produces
pollen grains of quite distinctive form, these can be identified when
viewed under the microscope at a magnification of about 300. Identification is based on characters such as size, shape, sculpturing of the
outer coat, or 'exine', and the presence or absence and number of
pores (Plate 2). The pollen of many species, in particular that of trees,

is airborne and thus widely dispersed. It is often produced in great quantities and if, when it settles, it becomes trapped in accumulating sediments, it may be preserved indefinitely due to the very resistant properties of the exine. The large number of grains produced and their microscopic size make pollen analysis a very suitable technique for the investigation of short-term vegetational changes as well as the more general trends exhibited during an interglacial.

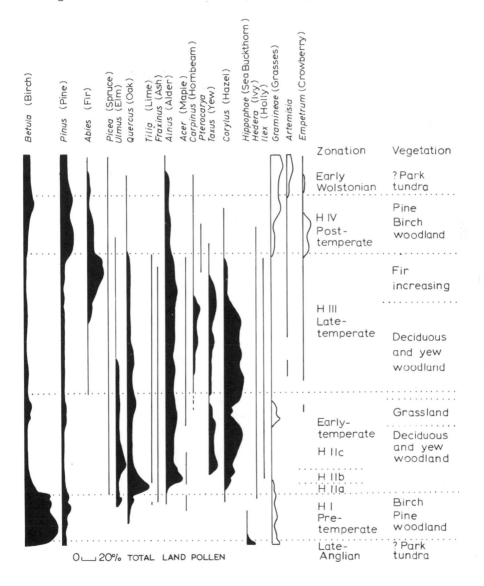

Fig. 3. Marks Tey. Generalized pollen diagram through the interglacial lake sediments. (After Turner, C., 1970, Fig. 15)

The most suitable conditions for pollen preservation are the complete exclusion of oxygen, thus preventing microbial decay, the absence of calcium salts, in particular lime, and the gradual and gentle accumulation of the deposits. With the exception of the gentle build up of the two loam horizons, none of these conditions is fulfilled at Swanscombe, and it is for this reason that pollen is virtually non-existent in the deposits. On the other hand, actively accumulating peat bogs and lake sediments often fulfil all these requirements, and a number of sites of Hoxnian Interglacial age, comprising ancient lacustrine deposits, have been investigated by pollen analysis. These include the type site at Hoxne in north Suffolk,[17] Marks Tey in Essex,[18] Nechells in Birmingham[19] and Gort in western Ireland[20] (Fig. 6).

Plate 3.   Boulder clay exposed in a river bank, Co. Clare.

The most complete sequence is that from Marks Tey (Fig. 3). This, and indeed all other interglacials in the British Isles, can be divided into four major climatic zones, as defined mainly by the type of woodland. Hoxnian zone I, or H I, is characterized by birch and pine, with a certain amount of open ground as indicated by the grasses; this is the pre-temperate zone. It is followed by the early-temperate zone, H II, in which warmth-loving trees successively invade—oak (H IIa), alder and hazel (H IIb), and yew (H IIc). H III, the late-temperate zone, sees the introduction of fir and hornbeam, possibly as a result of declining temperature, but also, perhaps, of deteriorating soil conditions. Finally in H IV, the post-temperate zone, pine and birch once more assume dominance and grasses reappear, heralding the onset of a further glacial period.

The Marks Tey lake sediments rest on boulder clay, or till, a heterogeneous unsorted mixture of particles of various shapes and sizes but consisting largely, as its name suggests, of boulders and clay (Plate 3). Deposits of this kind are of glacial origin, being laid down by an ice sheet or a glacier; in this instance, the ice sheet was that of the Anglian Glaciation. At the younger end of the succession, the uppermost clays of the lacustrine series contain plant remains of cold-climate type, and these belong to an early stage of the succeeding Wolstonian Glaciation. There is, however, no boulder clay overlying the deposits, the site being just south of the maximum extent of the Wolstonian ice (Fig. 6). Nevertheless, we have at Marks Tey a virtually complete record of vegetational change through an entire interglacial, sandwiched between two deposits of glacial type.

It remains to make a few comments on the detailed correlation of the Swanscombe and Marks Tey sequences. This is based largely on the work of M. P. Kerney and Charles Turner[21] on, respectively, the molluscs from Swanscombe and the pollen and other plant remains from Marks Tey (Fig. 3). Similar conclusions, although less detailed, had been reached by earlier workers through a consideration of the lithology of the deposits and their fauna.[22] The Lower Loam and Gravel are seen as having formed in the early-temperate zone, H II, and probably in H IIb and c. The formation of the Middle Gravels probably began in the late-temperate zone, H III, possibly during the high *Abies* (fir) substage, H IIIb, and continued into the post-temperate zone, H IV. The upper part of the Upper Middle Gravel with its frost structures may well be of early Wolstonian age, and it is possible that the Upper Loam reflects an interstadial. The Upper Gravel, a solifluxion deposit, is firmly placed in the Wolstonian Glaciation.

This is how environmental archaeology works. A site, in this case Swanscombe, may be important archaeologically but be devoid of certain environmental data—pollen. Other sites must perforce be investigated which, although of no immediate archaeological significance, can supply the missing environmental evidence. Correlation then ensues and a more nearly complete picture of the environmental background to the archaeological site established.

A very remarkable feature of both the Swanscombe and Marks Tey sequences is the period of deforestation and grassland which occurs within the early-temperate zone (IIc) (Figs. 1 and 3). At Marks Tey, the deposits had been laid down in what were considered to be annual laminae, and it was possible by counting these to estimate the duration of this phase of open country as being about 300 years. There seems little doubt that the Swanscombe and Marks Tey open-country episodes are contemporary—the close correlation between the two sequences strongly indicates that this is so. By implication, therefore, a common cause is to be inferred for both and we must now enquire into the nature of this. The first site at which this phenomenon was recognized was, in fact, the type site of the interglacial, Hoxne itself.[23] Hoxne, like Swanscombe, has long been famous as a Lower Palaeolithic site. It was here in 1797 that John Frere first recorded hand-axes 'as belonging to a very ancient period indeed' and as having been made by 'people who had not the use of metals'.[24] The hand-axes are little moved from their place of manufacture and lie close to the edge of the former interglacial lake. Current excavations by John Wymer are recording even clearer stratigraphic, occupational and environmental evidence, including completely undisturbed debris from the lakeside activities.[25] We are in effect dealing here with an Acheulian lakeside settlement, and pollen analysis shows that the occupation falls within the phase of open country in zone IIc.

The possible origins of this episode have been much discussed. Climate has been ruled out on the grounds that a marked shift towards either increased coolness or aridity would have had a more general influence on the forest composition and fauna as a whole. Nor do changes in water level give a satisfactory explanation, although they undoubtably occurred during the Hoxnian at a number of sites. The problem is in fact twofold: what caused the initial deforestation, and what prevented forest regeneration for a period of 300 years?

Fire is one possibility, and the one favoured by Charles Turner in his discussion of the Marks Tey and Hoxne evidence, for at both sites charcoal, either as microscopic particles or as visible fragments, was prolific in sediments of the high non-tree pollen phase. But, as Turner points out, it is difficult to envisage a fire 'on a scale necessary to affect both Hoxne and Marks Tey' at one and the same time.[26] The sites are some 57 kilometres apart, and now we have the evidence from Swanscombe too, 64 kilometres from Marks Tey in the opposite direction from Hoxne (Fig. 6), the possibility of a single major forest fire, covering a distance of at least 120 kilometres in what would have been essentially deciduous forest, seems all the more remote. Yet it is not an impossibility. Today, after prolonged periods of drought, coniferous and sometimes deciduous forest fires in the United States can be very extensive indeed.

But if not fire, or at least not naturally caused fires, can we invoke man as a causative agent? There are obvious difficulties here, not least of which are the supposed small size of the human population in south-east England—perhaps not more than a few hundred—and the supposed low level of culture at this stage, incommensurate with such sophisticated concepts as deliberate forest clearance, either by fire, felling or ring-barking, to create open spaces for such purposes as corraling game or aiding the chase. But we shall see when we come to discuss more recent hunting communities (p. 93) that man's impact on the forest could be on a scale out of all proportion to the size of his populations. In Australia, for example, the Aboriginal practice of burning is now invoked as an indirect cause for the extinction of the giant marsupials 20,000 years ago. Furthermore, we should not under-estimate man's skill, even in as remote a period as the Hoxnian Interglacial, in winning a livelihood by deliberate interference with his surroundings on a large scale, particularly when we have, in his stone tools, only a very biased impression of his technological ability—and some of these, as we have seen, are very fine. 'Many of the Swanscombe hand-axes . . . are superbly flaked and finished with a perfection which appears to exceed the requirements of bare necessity.'[27]

The maintenance of open ground is perhaps less difficult to envisage. All three sites, Swanscombe, Marks Tey and Hoxne, are close to water, and as such would have attracted large herds of herbivorous mammals. Once open ground had been created in the vicinity, the effects of grazing would have prevented the regeneration of woody vegetation and, if not too intense, enhanced the maintenance of grassland (p. 139). The attractions to Lower Palaeolithic man of such situations are manifest. It is interesting that pollen analysis of clay adhering to two teeth of *Elephas antiquus*, recovered from the deposits at Hoxne, showed the teeth came from the high non-tree pollen phase. The African elephant, today, is well known as a destroyer of trees both by defolia-tion and uprooting.

A major difficulty in studying the environment of Lower Palaeolithic man, and in particular of the Clactonian and Acheulian groups, is the extreme paucity of *in situ* camp sites or working floors, i.e. sites which are in a primary context completely undisturbed by later processes. Out of more than 1500 separate find spots in the British Isles only about six fall into this category,[28] and of these, four were found by one man—Worthington G. Smith.[29] In his undeservedly little-known book, *Man the Primeval Savage*, Worthington Smith describes how hand-axe

flakes, razor sharp and flint nodules ready for working were revealed
in situ during the extraction of deposits for brick-making high up on the
Chiltern Hills at Caddington in Bedfordshire in association with what
are probably lake sediments (Fig. 4). Unfortunately we know practically nothing of the immediate surroundings of the Caddington site.
Nor are we certain of its age, although an interstadial within the
Wolstonian Glaciation is a possibility; it may however belong to the
Ipswichian Interglacial. Another important site studied by Worthington Smith is at Stoke Newington in north London. One of Smith's
section drawings through the deposits is reproduced here (Fig. 5) to
show the detail with which he recorded the various layers, a drawing
made over 80 years ago.

It is sites of this kind, however rare they may be, which must be
studied by modern techniques, for although we may be able to construct elaborate sequences of environmental change from lake sediments
and ancient river gravels which can tell us something of the general
background to man's environment, these cannot provide the detail
unless tied in to actual archaeological horizons.

Nevertheless, taking the few Lower Palaeolithic working floors
which are known, and a number of other sites where the artefacts are

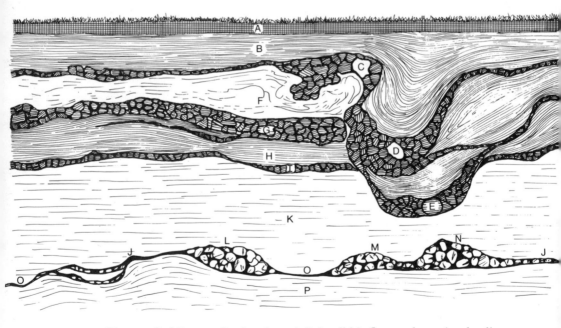

Fig. 4.   Caddington. Section through Palaeolithic floor and associated sediments.
A, topsoil; B, clay; C, D and E, gravel; F, clay; G, gravel with Palaeolithic
implements; H, clay with implements; I, gravel; J and O, Palaeolithic floor; K,
brickearth; L, M and N, artificial heaps of flint nodules brought by Palaeolithic
man; P, brickearth. (After Smith, W. G., 1894, Fig. 46)

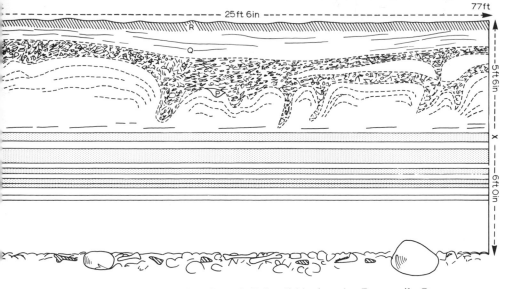

Fig. 5. Stoke Newington. Section through Palaeolithic deposits. R, topsoil; Q, mud; O, contorted drift; P, pocket of London Clay; N–B, sand and clay layers; A, gravel with animal bones and Palaeolithic implements. (After Smith, W. G., 1894, Fig. 140)

mainly in fresh condition and but little moved from their place o manufacture, together with the distribution of sites in the British Isles as a whole, we can make some general observations about the environment and habitat of Lower Palaeolithic man. In the main, it seems that his camp sites were in low-lying areas, close to water, either on river banks and shingle beaches, or at lake sides. This is certainly the case with those sites which are *in situ*, such as Hoxne, Caddington and the Swanscombe Clactonian, and with those where the artefacts are but little travelled.[30] It must be remembered that there has been considerable downcutting and erosion since the Hoxnian Interglacial, not only due to a drop in sea level and the associated changes in the base level of rivers, but also to processes peculiar to cold-climate environments, particularly solifluxion and glacial erosion (p. 55), and that in consequence the immediate present-day surrounds of sites like Caddington and Swanscombe, which are now high above the general level of the adjacent lowland vales and flood plains, give a very erroneous impression of their former situation.

Viewed as a whole, the distribution of sites is noticeably confined to lowland Britain (Fig. 6). There are no finds from Ireland, Scotland and northern England, and almost none from the West Country. Why this should be so is uncertain, and we are confronted here with a problem which will recur at intervals throughout this book. Is the distribution of artefacts and sites which we see today a genuine reflection of the distribution of a particular human culture, or is it an

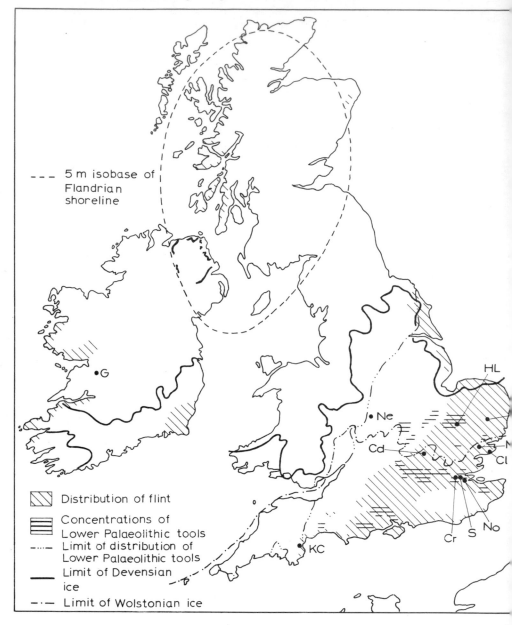

Fig. 6.   Lower Palaeolithic Britain. Distribution of artefacts (after Wymer, 1968, Fig. 109), and possible factors controlling this distribution. Hoxnian and Lower Palaeolithic sites: Cd, Caddington; Cl, Clacton; Cr, Crayford; G, Gort; H Hoxne; HL, High Lodge; KC, Kent's Cavern; MT, Marks Tey; Ne, Nechells; No, Northfleet; S, Swanscombe. Distribution of flint after Wymer, 1968, Fig. 4. The approximate northern limit of Pleistocene deposits with flint common is not shown but runs from the Humber estuary to the Severn and closely follows the northern limit of Lower Palaeolithic tools. (Shotton, 1968, Fig. 1)

artificial pattern, distorted by subsequent geological processes and environmental change, or by methods of collecting? In the case of the Lower Palaeolithic, deficiencies in collecting are unlikely, at any rate on a wide scale, although this cannot be entirely ruled out. So much archaeological work has been done outside their area of distribution (although, it must be admitted, not specifically in search of Palaeolithic sites) that it is hardly possible that no artefacts at all should have turned up had they been present. On a smaller scale, and within the general area of distribution, local concentrations and deficiencies may well be due to collecting techniques, and, in particular, to the way in which gravel and brickearth deposits have been worked by commercial enterprises. Prior to the invention of mechanical excavators and sorting machinery, gravel was dug and graded by hand, affording excellent opportunities for the recovery of artefacts. But since the last war this practice has ceased and recent large-scale gravel workings (e.g. in connection with the spate of motorway building in the last ten years) have produced practically no palaeoliths at all.

The main destructive geological processes which have been at work since the Hoxnian Interglacial and which may have been responsible for removing the artefacts of Lower Palaeolithic man are river erosion, solifluxion and glacial scouring. All three were most intense during periods of cold climate. The limits of the Devensian Glaciation ice sheet coincide closely with those of Lower Palaeolithic finds (Fig. 6) with the notable exception of the West Country. It is possible, therefore, that ice action has destroyed the evidence to the north and west of the present distribution although if this were so one would expect to find palaeoliths more often than we do in boulder clay. Also, the Wolstonian ice limits extended much further south (Fig. 6) and yet palaeoliths, particularly in East Anglia, are prolific in areas which it covered. Furthermore, deposits of Hoxnian age are known from as far afield as western Ireland in areas again covered by the Wolstonian ice sheet and which are yet devoid of artefacts.

Another factor which has led to greater erosion in the north and west of the British Isles is the phenomenon of 'isostatic uplift'. During a glaciation, the great weight of ice causes the land to be depressed. On melting, uplift ensues, to the extent that parts of Scotland, for example, have risen 12 metres in the last 6000 years. In the British Isles as a whole, the southern limit of this zone runs approximately from the Tyne through south Lancashire across the Irish Sea to the Wicklow Mountains (Fig. 6). North of this zone, river erosion during periods of temperate climate was more intensive due to continuous rejuvenation than it was in the south resulting in the removal of vast quantities of Pleistocene river gravel and lake sediments, together with any palaeoliths they may have contained. But the absence of artefacts from Wales, the West Country and southern Ireland—areas outside the zone of isostatic recovery—cannot be accounted for in this way.

On balance, therefore, it seems likely that the overall distribution of Lower Palaeolithic artefacts in the British Isles is a true reflection of the distribution of Lower Palaeolithic man. Conclusive evidence is still lacking, however, for his total absence in the highland and western regions which are less well explored and were more severely affected by erosion.

Turning to possible environmental limitations, the three most likely are climate, topography and raw materials for tools and weapons. Climate may have been a limiting factor in the case of the Late Middle Acheulian for we have seen that at this stage glacial conditions had come about. But previous to this, Middle Acheulian and Clactonian man were present in Britain during a period of more congenial climatic conditions when Ireland and Scotland were as inhabitable as they are today.

The effects of topographical control are hard to assess. We can only point out that outside Britain, highland Acheulian sites do exist.

The availability of raw materials, notably the occurrence of flint for hand-axe manufacture, is a third possible controlling factor. Flint occurs in three principle sources—the Chalk, Eocene gravels in the London and Hampshire basins, and Pleistocene marine and river gravels (Fig. 6). Flint from the Chalk, where it occurs as nodules in distinct bands (Fig. 54), is the most suitable from which to manufacture hand-axes, for the nodules are large and unaffected by the incipient fracture planes which occur in river gravel or beach flint, brought about by the constant battering they receive during deposition. But there is no evidence to show that flint was mined by Lower Palaeolithic man, and any chalk flint he used was probably hacked out of river-cliff or coastal exposures. The former were no doubt more widespread and apparent in glacial periods when rivers were actively eroding than they are today. Secondary sources of flint were less suitable due to their smaller size and the numerous fracture planes within them, but a compensatory factor was their greater abundance and more ready availability. Against the idea that raw materials exerted a control over Lower Palaeolithic man, F. W. Shotton has pointed out that flint-bearing chalk outcrops well beyond the limits of his distribution (Fig. 6), e.g. in Antrim and western Scotland, and that flint-bearing gravels occur in Aberdeenshire.[31] Moreover, Palaeolithic man was perfectly capable of utilizing other types of stone for his tools, and Shotton cites a number of examples of hand-axes made from stone coarser than flint. Indeed, outside Britain, and especially in Africa, hand-axes are most often of lava, basalt, granite or quartzite, rarely of flint except where abundantly available.

The Hoxnian Interglacial was a period of mild oceanic climate, perhaps even more so than that of today, the average temperature of the coldest month being not less than $-1 \cdot 5°C$ during the early-temperate zone. Mixed deciduous woodland, together with open grassland areas in river valleys, prevailed, the predominant trees being hazel, yew, alder, oak and elm. Herds of large herbivorous mammals were plentiful, and carnivores such as the cave bear, wolf and lion roamed the land. There seems to be no evidence that Britain was isolated from the Continent at any time during the interglacial (p. 66), but Ireland may have been cut off at some stage. During the late-temperate zone, the removal of nutrients from the soil may have reached a level at which it was seriously affecting the growth of certain of the more demanding tree species; the establishment of others more tolerant of poor soil conditions—notably fir and hornbeam—may have been directly attributable to this factor. Later on, climatic deterioration caused the replacement of the mixed deciduous forest by fir and pine. Plants and animals of open ground gradually became more abundant until finally a tundra environment obtained.

Immediately prior to the Hoxnian had been the Anglian Glaciation, and previous to this, Britain had witnessed a whole series of alternating periods of temperate and sub-arctic climate (Table 1). Geologically, these are best represented by the East Anglian 'crags', shelly marine deposits laid down in a shallow basin during the early Pleistocene. They end in the famous Cromer Forest Bed, a complex of estuarine and freshwater deposits whose upper levels contain abundant remains of plants and animals reflecting a period of temperate climate, known after the type site as the Cromerian Interglacial. Exposures of the Forest Bed can still be seen in cliff sections at various places along the Norfolk coast, notably at East Runton, where the deposits are overlain by till of the Anglian Glaciation. Claims for the occurrence of man-made artefacts from the Crag deposits have been made from time to time but none is convincing. The evidence has been reviewed by John Coles in an article dealing with early Pleistocene man in Europe as a whole.[32]

Until recently, the Hoxnian Interglacial has been considered as the earliest period for which there is certain evidence for man's presence in the British Isles. However, a reassessment of the context of a hand-axe industry from Kent's Cavern, Torquay, in Devon, has led to a reconsideration of this view.[33] The industry is possibly associated with three species of mammal considered to have become extinct prior to the Hoxnian, although it is not possible to be certain about this because the data come from old excavations carried out in the 1820s by Father John MacEnery and between 1865 and 1880 by William Pengelly. The species are a sabre-toothed cat (*Homotherium latidens*) and two voles (*Pitymys gregaloides* and *Arvicola greeni*), and if the asso-

ciation claimed by MacEnery and brusquely dismissed by his con-
temporaries is confirmed by further work, this site would rank among
the earliest Acheulian assemblages in Europe. Another interesting
aspect of the Kent's Cavern fauna is the dominance of cave bear
(*Ursus arctos*) (90 per cent). This, it has been suggested, reflects not a
natural assemblage but the result of specialized butchering activites by
Lower Palaeolithic man—an idea in direct contradiction to that of the
Acheulians as generalized hunters. However, as we shall see, hand-axe
industries spanned at least two interglacial/glacial cycles, and it may
well be that hunting patterns varied according to the severity or
congeniality of the climate. It is not possible on the evidence available
to say whether the Kent's Cavern assemblage belongs to an interstadial
in the Anglian Glaciation or to the previous Cromerian Interglacial.[34]

Going yet further back in time, we see the Pleistocene as the
dramatic culmination of a gradual cooling of climate in what are
today the north temperature regions of the world. Fossil plants in the
London Clay, an Eocene (see p. xvi) deposit laid down in the Hampshire
and London basins some 70 million years ago, indicate a tropical
climate with evergreen forests of a type now found in the Indo-Malayan
region. The Pleistocene, beginning about two million years ago, is
marked by fully temperate climatic conditions and a mammalian
fauna in which the species are forms either still living today or closely
related to them—horse, elephant, ox and deer. But the most characteristic feature of the Pleistocene was the rate and magnitude with
which climatic variation took place within the period itself, periods of
temperate climate alternating with periods of cold climate. In Britain,
the last three major cold periods saw the formation and spread of ice
sheets over much of the country.

The Pleistocene, too, saw the emergence of man, and it is not
improbable to associate his evolution with the environmental stresses
imposed by the deterioration of climate. Stone structures, possibly
rough wind-breaks, are known from Olduvai Gorge in east Africa
dating from 1·5 to 1·8 million years. A contributory cause may have
been the magnitude and rapidity of oscillations within the period,
leading to frequent migrations of population and the stimulus of
adaptation to unknown environments. However, the discovery of a
species of *Homo* at Lake Rudolph in Kenya dating to 2·8 million
years, and the very recent discovery from the Dessye region north of
Addis Ababa, Ethiopia, suggesting properly erect hominids at more
than three million years ago, suggests that the emergence of man may
have taken place in the period immediately preceding the Pleistocene,
known as the Pliocene (see p. xvi), and argues caution in invoking
the cooling climate of the Ice Age as being directly responsible for the
initial evolution of man.

In Britain, the traditions of Lower Palaeolithic archaeology and environment are founded largely on the terraces of the lowland rivers, with their deposits of gravel, sand and loam, and their mammalian and molluscan faunas. Ancient lake sediments also make a vital contribution through their preserved record of past vegetation, giving us the local ecological and broader climatic background. But when we turn to later peoples, and in particular to the highly developed blade-using communities of the Upper Palaeolithic, we find that it is cave sites which provide much of our information. This is not to imply that caves were the only sites exploited by Upper Palaeolithic man. But their special significance for us is that they provide, like river valleys, a ready catchment situation for environmental and archaeological data.

About 12 kilometres west-north-west of Kent's Cavern in south Devon is Tornewton Cave (Fig. 17).[1] It is one of a series in the Torbryan area which has been the subject of a detailed study by A. J. Sutcliffe and F. E. Zeuner, and the environmental sequence provides a useful introduction to cave stratigraphy. At the same time it picks up the story of man's environmental history from the point where we left it at Swanscombe and takes it into the final cold-climate episode of the Ice Age.

Tornewton Cave is situated in Devonian Limestone (see p. xvi) and opens onto the west side of a small dry valley. It was probably formed in the first instance by solution, ground water percolating through joints in the limestone and gradually enlarging them. Later, stream erosion and frost-weathering may have modified the shape of the tunnels and chambers.

The earliest deposit is a layer of laminated clay (Fig. 7), laid down in still water when the water-table was higher than at present. It is devoid of fauna and we are thus unable to determine the climate contemporary with its deposition. Above is (or was) a layer of drip-stone or stalagmite, Stalagmite V, the first of five to be laid down in the history of the cave. The deposition of this material takes place under conditions of high humidity. Water, charged with lime, trickles down the sides and over the floor of the cave, and, on evaporation, releases its lime content. As a climatic indicator, stalagmite is unreliable, since its formation depends so much on the local conditions inside the cave. It is favoured by a cool, moist temperate climate rather than one which is warm and dry; and it will not form under conditions of permafrost. By comparison with the underlying clay, the deposition of Stalagmite V

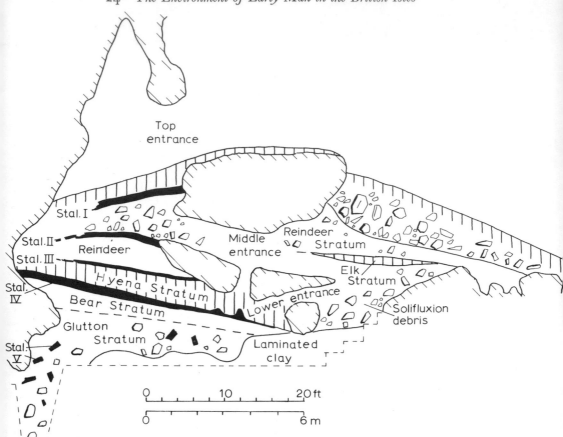

Fig. 7. Tornewton Cave. Section through the deposits. (After Sutcliffe and Zeuner, 1962)

reflects a lowering of the water-table and a change to the essentially terrestrial conditions which have persisted to the present day.

The material of Stalagmite V is not *in situ* but lies in a jumbled mass of broken fragments which have been incorporated into the subsequent layer. This has been caused by frost-shattering within the cave under severe cold climate conditions. A similar process can be seen taking place today near the mouths of frozen limestone caves at 3000 metres in the Pyrenees. The fragments of stalagmite in the Tornewton Cave lie in a matrix of earthy material which also contains shattered lumps of limestone from the sides and roof of the cave, together with numerous teeth and bones. The deposit has been sub-divided into a lower layer in which massive boulders are present and the matrix generally unsorted, and an upper, finer layer showing weak stratification. Both layers formed under a cold climate—the fauna confirms this—but conditions were probably harsher in the lower layer, which is essentially a solifluxion deposit. On faunal grounds the two layers cannot really be separated, but the occurrence of bones of at least two individuals of the wolverine or glutton (*Gulo gulo*) in the lower layer has led to its being designated the Glutton Stratum, while the predominant species in both layers, the brown bear (*Ursus arctos*), has given its name to the upper, Bear Stratum. Wolf, fox and cave lion are all common, and horse, rhinoceros (woolly?) and reindeer are represented by one or more individuals. The fauna definitely indicates a cold climate, the glutton for example being today confined to the forested areas of northern Europe, Asia and North America (Fig. 8).

The Bear Stratum is sealed by a layer of dripstone, Stalagmite IV, and there is thus no question of contamination between this and the layer above.

So far, the deposits and fauna have indicated cool temperate to permafrost conditions, and were probably laid down during the Wolstonian Glaciation. But the deposit immediately above Stalagmite IV, the Hyena Stratum, is of entirely different character and probably

Fig. 8. Upper Palaeolithic engraving of a glutton from Los Casares, Spain. (After Ucko and Rosenfeld, 1967, Fig. 77)

of interglacial origin. Much of the deposit consists of coprolites—fossil dung—and bones, and it is claimed that over 20,000 teeth of hyena have been recovered from this horizon. The original excavator of the cave in the late nineteenth century, James Lyon Widger, had good cause to name this the Great Bone Bed. It reflects a phase in the history of the cave when it served as a hyena den. The hyena (*Crocuta crocuta*) outnumbers all other species, the remains of at least 117 individuals being found in the recent excavations alone. Fox (9 individuals), wolf (5) and cave lion (5) are other carnivores which may have entered the cave voluntarily, but otherwise only a few specimens of about six other species were found. Some of these, notably the rhinoceros, *Dicerorhinus hemitoechus*—which is not the woolly rhino but a southern form—and the hippopotamus, together with the absence of horse, reindeer and glutton, very definitely indicate a warm climate of interglacial status.

Subsequently, it is difficult to tie in the deposits inside the cave with those outside the entrance which comprise the talus slope. But both groups reflect a range of climatic conditions colder than that of the Hyena Stratum, and probably belong to the Devensian Glaciation. There is a solifluxion deposit near the base of the talus slope, probably laid down under permafrost conditions. This is overlain by the Elk Stratum and the Reindeer Stratum which, as well as abundant bones of reindeer, contain horse and woolly rhino, all species characteristic of cool climates and open landscapes. Elk and red deer are present in the Elk Stratum suggesting milder climatic and perhaps wooded conditions—possibly an interstadial.

There is evidence, in the form of a few flint artefacts (p. 50) from the Reindeer Stratum that man was using the cave sporadically at this stage, and it is likely that many of the bones were brought in by him. For example, over 400 fragments of reindeer antler were recovered, but only seventeen teeth and parts of bones. Moreover, the antler fragments suggested human workmanship in that there were no straight portions of beam, just bases and fragments of irregular shape. It is well known that reindeer antler was one of the most important raw materials used by Upper Palaeolithic man[2] and it seems evident that we have here a shelter where antlers were cut up and the straight lengths selected for manufacture into tools and weapons (Fig. 21).

A further point of interest is the size of the antlers. Measurements suggest that they belong to young animals or females, but not to adult males. At the present day, bucks shed their antlers between November and March, while females and young do not do so until late spring or early summer. We can suppose, therefore, that the cave was occupied, or that reindeer were present in the area, only from the end of March on into the summer months, but not during autumn or winter. This is a matter of some considerable relevance to the way of life of Upper Palaeolithic man to which we will return (p. 52).

Overlying the Reindeer Stratum outside the cave is a deposit of rock rubble and earth, probably laid down by frost-shattering of the cliff above the cave entrance during a final episode of cold climate in the Devensian Glaciation. Inside the cave in an equivalent position stratigraphically is a series of stalagmite layers (I to III) and earthy rubble horizons. Both these and the rock rubble outside are overlain by the modern soil.

This then is the sequence at Tornewton Cave. It represents a cycle of initially cold climate followed by an interglacial and subsequently by a return to glacial conditions. The latter period was interrupted by a minor amelioration, the Elk Stratum.

The question now arises as to which interglacial is represented. We cannot use the height of the cave above sea level as we did in the case of the Swanscombe gravels, for the deposits at Tornewton (with the exception of the earliest water-lain clay) are terrestrial in origin and cannot be tied in directly to a sequence of river terraces. The main clue must come from the fauna, and we can compare that from Tornewton with faunas of known interglacial age elsewhere. Several indications suggest it belongs to the Ipswichian Interglacial.

Thus to return briefly to the Thames river terraces. Below the Swanscombe terrace, whose surface lies at about 32 metres above sea level, there is a second terrace whose maximum height is 8 metres OD. This is well represented at Trafalgar Square in London where, during the excavation of foundations for various buildings, interglacial deposits were revealed. Their height above sea level precludes any interglacial other than the Ipswichian, if we accept the Swanscombe deposits as of Hoxnian age (Fig. 9). The fauna from these deposits and

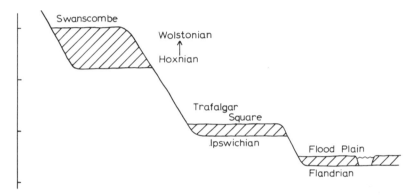

Fig. 9. Diagrammatic cross-section of the Thames Valley showing the relationship of the terraces mentioned in the text. Scale in 10-metre intervals.

several others of proved Ipswichian age differs significantly from that of the Hoxnian, and A. J. Sutcliffe has suggested the following characters to be typical of the Ipswichian:[3]

1. Presence of hippopotamus (absent from the Hoxnian).
2. Extreme rarity of horse (present in the Hoxnian).
3. Abundance of the rhinoceros, *Dicerorhinus hemitoechus* (rare in the Hoxnian).
4. Absence of the rhinoceros, *Dicerorhinus kirchbergensis* (present in the Hoxnian).
5. Abundance of hyena (apparently absent from the Hoxnian).

There are of course difficulties in dating deposits which are not directly superimposed, and we can never be certain when extrapolating data—whether it be altimetric or biological—from one site to another that our correlation is correct. With terraces, tectonic disturbance such as downwarping or compaction of the sediments may have ensued since deposition. This applies, for example, to the Hoxnian gravels at Clacton-on-Sea which today extend below sea level due to downwarping of the Essex coast. With faunal evidence it will be appreciated that in comparing the animals from a cave with those from a river gravel we are comparing faunas from different habitats, and that differences may be due to this factor alone. The Swanscombe fauna, for example, is dominated by herbivorous species, the Tornewton fauna by carnivores, and it is not surprising that the hyena is predominant in the latter. But bearing this in mind, there seem to be some differences which may have a chronological significance, and we do have the valuable deposits at Trafalgar Square in which hyena is present, making direct comparison with Swanscombe realistic. The key species is the hippopotamus which occurs in an Ipswichian context at several localities in England and Wales. Records extend west to the Gower Peninsula and north to the Victoria Cave, Settle in the West Riding of Yorkshire and Kirkdale Cave, Kirby Moorside, in the East Riding.[4] Yet there are no known examples of this species from the Hoxnian.

On Sutcliffe's criteria, therefore, the fauna from the Great Bone Bed or Hyena Stratum at Tornewton strongly indicates an Ipswichian age. Below are deposits of the Wolstonian Glaciation, and above of the Devensian.

At this point we may conveniently summarize the main periods of Pleistocene time whose environments we have so far considered.

Period	Climate	Horizon
Devensian Glaciation	Cold climate Interstadial Cold climate	Elk Stratum at Tornewton
Ipswichian Interglacial	Warm climate	Hyena Stratum at Tornewton Trafalgar Square terrace
Wolstonian Glaciation	Cold climate	Bear and Glutton Strata at Tornewton. Upper Middle Gravel (?), Upper Loam (interstadial?) and Upper Gravel at Swanscombe
Hoxnian Interglacial	Warm climate	Lower Gravel, Lower Loam and Lower Middle Gravel at Swanscombe Marks Tey and Hoxne lake beds
Anglian Glaciation	Cold climate	Acheulian at Kent's Cavern (?)
Cromerian Interglacial	Warm climate	Westbury-sub-Mendip

The climate during both the Hoxnian and Ipswichian Interglacials was similar to that of the Post-glacial. Even although the faunas were more exotic than those of today, with species of large mammal such as the lion, rhinoceros, hippo and elephant common, there is no reason to suppose that the subtropical climate with which these animals are now associated once obtained in Britain. The restricted distribution of these animals in the Post-glacial by comparison with their former more widespread range during the interglacials is probably due to factors other than climate (p. 73), and in particular to competition with man. Botanical evidence suggests that the Hoxnian Interglacial was more oceanic—wetter and milder—than either the Ipswichian or the Post-glacial. On the other hand, the Ipswichian Interglacial, as suggested for example by the paucity of evergreens and alder, was more continental, with warmer summers than obtained at any time during the Post-glacial. But these differences were probably slight—in the order of two or three degrees centigrade.[5]

Subsequent to the deposition of the Swanscombe river gravels, sea level fell, perhaps by as much as 130 metres, as the Wolstonian ice sheet gained in thickness and moved slowly southward over the British Isles. The 100-metre submarine contour—probably the approximate position of the coastline during the maximum of this glaciation—is shown in Fig. 17. Almost all of what is now England, Wales and Scotland was simply an extension of northern Europe, linked to it by low-lying marshy ground across the North Sea. The Orkneys, Inner Hebrides, the Isles of Scilly and Isle of Man were linked to the mainland, but the Shetlands and Outer Hebrides have probably been islands—albeit somewhat larger—throughout the Pleistocene. Similarly with Ireland. A deep channel separates most of the country from the rest of the British Isles, and it was mainly in the extreme north that a land bridge with Scotland existed. In the south, allowing for subsequent erosion, and using the 130 metre submarine contour, land bridges may possibly have existed at times. Of course, much of the area was covered by ice sheets which at their maximum extended beyond the western coastline of Ireland and the Outer Isles. The Irish Sea was filled with ice hundreds of metres thick which spread south to reach the Scillies and north Devon coast, while Scandinavian ice extended as far as East Anglia where we find erratic rocks of Norwegian origin in the boulder clays.

Then, during the Ipswichian Interglacial, the sea level rose. The main transgression took place in the early-temperate, mixed deciduous forest period (zone I II), and reached its maximum in zone I III at about 8 metres above present sea level.[6] It is likely that the Straits of Dover were first breached during this stage, and that previous high sea levels had not resulted in the complete isolation of Britain from Europe (p. 66). There is, however, no certainty on this point.

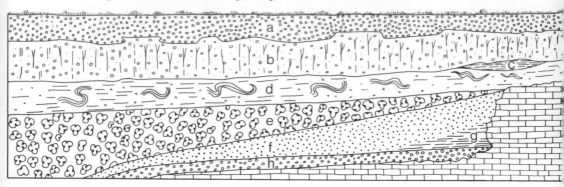

Fig. 10.   Sewerby. Section through the ancient cliff, beach and later deposits. a, solifluxion gravel; b, boulder clay; c, outwash sand; d, boulder clay; e, coombe rock; f, blown sand; g, coombe rock; h, beach gravel. (After Wilson, 1948, Fig. 27)

Along the south coast of Wales and the south and east coasts of England and Ireland there is abundant evidence for the Ipswichian Interglacial high sea level in the ancient beach deposits—gravels and sands—lying on a shore platform above the present influence of the sea, and overlain by deposits of Devensian age. One of the most spectacular sections is at Sewerby, near Bridlington (Fig. 10), where the ancient sea

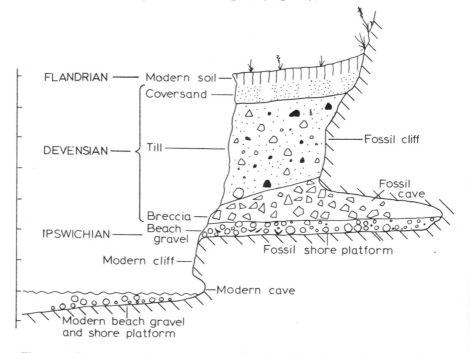

Fig. 11.   Gower coast. Diagrammatic section through ancient cliff, cave and associated deposits. Scale in 5-metre intervals.

Plate 4.   Bacon Hole, Gower. Section through scree (angular fragments) overlying interglacial beach deposits (rounded fragments).

cliff and shore platform have been cut transversely by modern marine erosion.[7] The beach gravel (h) contains bones and teeth of interglacial species (e.g. *Elephas antiquus* and hippopotamus) and is overlain by periglacial deposits and boulder clay (p. 57). Likewise along the south Wales coast, and particularly in the Gower Peninsula, there are magnificent cliff sections cutting through the cemented beach gravels of the Ipswichian sea (Fig. 11).[8] Water-worn pebbles and fragments of marine shells—winkles, limpets, dog whelks—rest on a platform at about 8 metres OD, providing a striking contrast to the overlying angular screes brought down by frost-shattering from the cliffs above (Plate 4). Here it is easy to visualize the former high level of the sea. Numerous caves carved out along planes of weakness in the rock by the erosive action of the interglacial sea extend back from the beach into the cliff. Some of these, notably Goat's Hole, Paviland, were inhabited by Upper Palaeolithic man. Today, another group of caves is being formed by modern marine erosion. May these too, at some remote time in the future, be abandoned by the falling sea of another glaciation?

The Acheulian hand-axe industries which first appear in the Hoxnian (or perhaps even earlier) continue, as we saw at Swanscombe, into the Wolstonian Glaciation (Table 1). They are possibly to be found too during the Ipswichian but the dating of many of these later sites is insecure, and their environmental contexts are not well known. All we can be certain of is that the Thames Valley and some of its tributaries such as the Kennet harboured Middle and Late Middle Acheulian industries in a river-beach environment similar to that at Swanscombe, and under a range of climatic conditions.[9] Other areas, particularly East Anglia, were also inhabited.

An important Wolstonian interstadial site is High Lodge, Mildenhall in Suffolk[10] where, as at Caddington, there are lake sediments, but here stratified between two sheets of boulder clay, both of Wolstonian age. There are three separate industries, an early crude flake industry, a later more elegant flake industry of Clactonian type, and the youngest a hand-axe industry. Thus the Clactonian, too, which first appeared in a mid-interglacial context, continued on into conditions of interstadial climate (Table 1), having presumably survived near-glacial conditions somewhere to the south.

Mention must also be made of the Levalloisian industry. This is characterized by a special method of obtaining flakes from carefully prepared cores, and the industry as a whole is geared to the production of flake tools, thus contrasting with the essentially core-tool industries of the Acheulian culture, although this distinction must not be overplayed. The industry is not certainly present in Britain until the Wolstonian Glaciation, when it appears in interstadial contexts (Table 1). Most famous is Baker's Hole, Northfleet,[11] a chalk quarry on the south bank of the Thames about 2 kilometres south-east of Barnfield Pit, where a working floor is overlain by coombe rock, a chalky solifluxion deposit. The site lies at about 13 metres OD on a river-cut bench and can be dated on altimetric grounds, therefore, to a late stage in the Wolstonian. Another important site is Crayford,[12] 8 kilometres west of Barnfield Pit. Here, there was a buried land surface with numerous Levalloisian flakes, some of which rested on the bones of the animals which man had hunted and killed. T. C. J. Spurrell, the discoverer of the site in 1879, succeeded in rejoining a series of flakes thus restoring the original flint nodule from which they had been struck. The floor was buried beneath brickearth, a loamy deposit of fluviatile origin (p. 63), laid down in the Wolstonian or during the Ipswichian Interglacial.

In general, the Levalloisian industries occupied a period of time from the Wolstonian Glaciation into the Ipswichian Interglacial when they flourished in the Lower and Middle Thames (Table 1). Their distribution is similar to that of the Acheulian industries—south-east England from the Wash to Hampshire, with most of the finds coming from river valleys or associated with ancient lake deposits.[13] There is evidence for the hunting of woolly rhinoceros, mammoth and other big game. The massive keenly sharp flakes produced by the Levalloisians were ideally suited to the skinning and cutting up of these animals.

No clear sequence of climatic and environmental change can be proposed for the period of Lower Palaeolithic occupation in the British Isles other than the general glacial/interglacial succession; the chronology, in particular of the Wolstonian, is poorly understood. Seldom can we tie in artefacts with deposits whose environment has been well studied, and this is especially true of certain Levalloisian sites whose status—whether interglacial or interstadial—is unknown. One is, however, left with the definite impression that Lower Palaeolithic man was a creature of either interstadial environments or, when living within an interglacial, did so, at least in Britain, during the early or late stage of such a period, rarely in the middle. The Swanscombe Clactonian is an exception. Can any of our Palaeolithic sites be securely dated to the Ipswichian Interglacial? Possibly Caddington, possibly Crayford. Yet we have a number which are certainly of interstadial age. And when man did live in the temperate zone of an interglacial, as at Hoxne and Swanscombe, he was doing so in an environment which had suffered a degree of deforestation. Of course, as argued by John Wymer,[14] the majority of our river gravels were probably laid down in a cold climate (p. 60), and since their content of artefacts seems in most cases to be derived, it is not surprising that few strictly interglacial sites are known. In addition, many interglacial sites are often deep water deposits, contexts which present unsuitable conditions for human settlement in the first place! But this is not the whole story, and until the detailed palaeontological work which has been done at, for example, Swanscombe and Tornewton is applied to many other sites, the environment of our Lower Palaeolithic cultures will remain obscure.

The Devensian Glaciation is the latest major cold-climate episode to have affected the British Isles. The record of climatic and environmental history is fuller than in previous epochs, and the various human industries can be tied into the sequence more satisfactorily. The glaciation as a whole lasted from about 70,000 to 10,000 bp (before present), but it must be emphasized that the period for which the country was actually glaciated was substantially less. The glaciation in the strict sense—i.e. the period when ice sheets covered the British Isles—lasted from 26,000/18,000 (depending on locality) to 15,000/ 10,000 bp.[15] Thus in South Wales, at the extreme limits of the ice sheet, the glaciation lasted perhaps only 3000 years (Fig. 17). In the Western Highlands of Scotland its duration may have been nearer 15,000 years. In this respect the term 'glaciation' is unsatisfactory— 'glacial' is more suitable—and it must be remembered that when one refers to a particular glaciation, a whole complex of different climatic and environmental regimes, both spatially and temporally, is implied— steppe, tundra and arctic desert, as well as the various interstadials which sometimes have birch and coniferous forests. The ice sheets and glaciers are but one of these.

One of the reasons for our greater knowledge of the sequence in the Devensian (aside from the fact that it is the most recent glaciation and its deposits are thus more likely to be preserved) is that we are able to date the various horizons by radioactive techniques. The most important of these is radiocarbon assay which can be used to date ancient organic material—bone, wood, charcoal, peat—with an age of anything back to about 75,000 years. The value of the technique is its use in making long distance correlations which are independent of site stratigraphy, altimetric data or faunal and floral assemblages.[16]

The main phases of the Devensian are shown in Fig. 12 and Table 2. The climatic deterioration marking the end of the Ipswichian Glaciation set in round about 70,000 bp. Sub-arctic conditions with tree-less tundra ensued for perhaps 5000 years or so, and then followed a period of milder climate known in Britain as the Chelford Interstadial after the type site in Cheshire. Here, a peat bed stratified between two layers of sand is dated to 60,800 bp. Pollen analysis indicates a cool climate with birch, pine and spruce forest similar to that found in northern Finland today.[17] Mean July temperature was perhaps about 16°C (being about 20°C today in Cheshire), but January temperature probably well below zero. The climate was more continental than that of

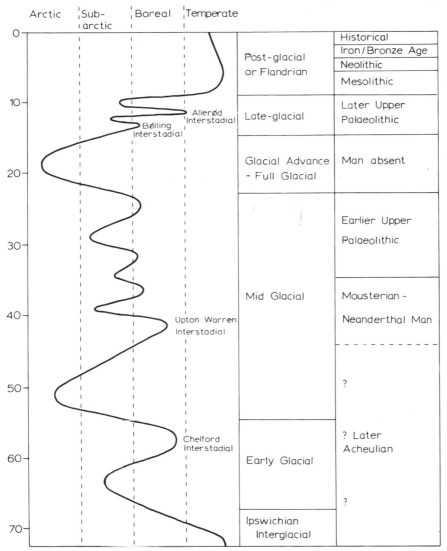

Fig. 12. Devensian temperature curve correlated with archaeological industries. Scale in 1000 years. (After West, 1968, Fig. 12.12)

today, a feature probably to be associated with the low sea level and weakness of ameliorating oceanic air streams.

Subsequent to the Chelford Interstadial, conditions once again deteriorated, and for over 30,000 years the climate was sub-arctic and the environment one of tundra over much of the British Isles. There is no good evidence for ice sheets or glaciers until the very end of this period. The mean temperature of the warmest month was not above 5°C, and during periods of extreme cold a mean annual temperature of less than 0°C prevailed. Several minor ameliorations took place, one of the best known being the Upton Warren Interstadial which is probably a complex of ameliorations beginning around 42,000 bp.

The Upton Warren report[18] is one of the classics of palaeoecology, a classic because of the great variety of techniques used to reconstruct the physical, chemical and biological environment of a small area of the English Midlands of over 42,000 years ago, and the success with which this was achieved. The interstadial takes its name from a small village to the south-west of Birmingham in Worcestershire, where gravel extraction has revealed thin organic bands in a river terrace of the Devensian Glaciation. One of the most exciting aspects of this site has been the recovery of the remains of plants and animals which are generally familiar to us. It needs little imagination when we see leaves and seeds, beetle wing-cases, fragments of spiders, the spines of sticklebacks and the bones of frogs, for a whole picture of life in these tiny Worcestershire ponds to unfold.

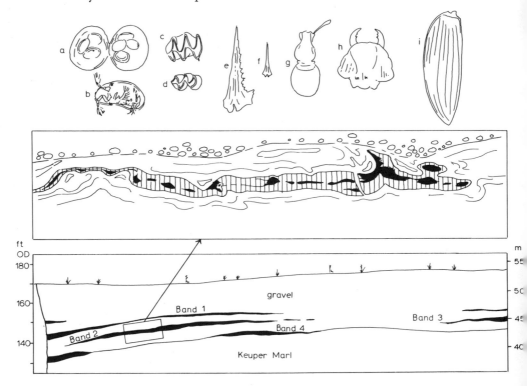

Fig. 13.   Upton Warren. Section through deposits, with some of the organisms extracted. a, *Pisidium*, opened, with two valves attached and unliberated young; b, ostracod (a modern example); c, lemming, molar; d, vole, molar; e, stickleback, pelvic spine; f, stickleback, dorsal spine; g, beetle, head and thorax; h, beetle, head; i, beetle, wing case. (After Coope *et al.*, 1961, Figs. 1 and 2, and Plates 19, 21 and 22)

The deposits are dated to the Devensian on altimetric grounds, and this is confirmed by radiocarbon dating of the organic bands. The vertebrate fauna includes cold-climate forms such as mammoth, woolly rhinoceros, bison (*Bison priscus*), reindeer and horse, as well as the teeth of an extinct species of lemming, *Dicrostonyx henseli*; the gravels from which this fauna comes are stratigraphically younger than terrace deposits of Ipswichian age containing hippo and *Elephas antiquus*.

The micro-fauna derives from the organic silt lenses which represent a succession of pools on the ancient flood plain (Fig. 13). Ecologically, the assemblages are something of a mixture, with both freshwater and terrestrial organisms present, but in general it appears that the pools were of still rather than flowing water, and that many of the terrestrial animals had either been swept in at times of flood, or had been incorporated incidentally, many of them being water-edge species anyway.

Conditions of preservation were excellent. This was not only due to the gentle processes under which sedimentation took place, but to the fact that since accumulation of the silt lenses the environment had remained totally anaerobic, i.e. free from oxygen, thus inhibiting bacterial decay. This accounts for the presence of organic material such as insect and plant remains, and is in contrast to the situation at Swanscombe where only inorganic fragments were preserved. Indeed, preservation was so good at Upton Warren that the shells of molluscs retained their outer protein coating, known as the periostracum. Many shells of the small-bivalve group of pea mussels (*Pisidium*) were still articulated (Fig. 13), and some of these, on being opened for the first time since death, were found to contain unliberated young.

The occurrence of a number of species which are today confined to coastal or estuarine situations, such as sea arrow grass (*Triglochin maritima*), and sea thrift (*Armeria maritima*), suggests a degree of brackishness in the water of one of the pools (Band 2). There are also a number of aquatic animals which normally live in water having a high salt content. One is *Cyprinotus salinus*, a small creature belonging to a group of animals known as ostracods. These have a superficial resemblance to the bivalve molluscs but are in fact crustaceans, related to the prawns and crayfish (Fig. 13). Another effect of the brackish environment was to bring about dwarfing in two species of freshwater mollusc, *Lymnaea peregra* and *Planorbis laevis*. Measurements of the latter (Fig. 14) showed that, by comparison with shells from Band 3 in which there was no brackish influence, they not only had fewer whorls but that specimens with the same number of whorls as those from Band 3 were smaller.

One cause of brackishness may have been extreme climatic continentality. In sub-arctic Siberia today, pools like those at Upton Warren are often saline due to the high evaporation caused by the very hot day-time July conditions. Another possibility is that salinity was brought about by natural brine springs which, even today (Fig. 79), are

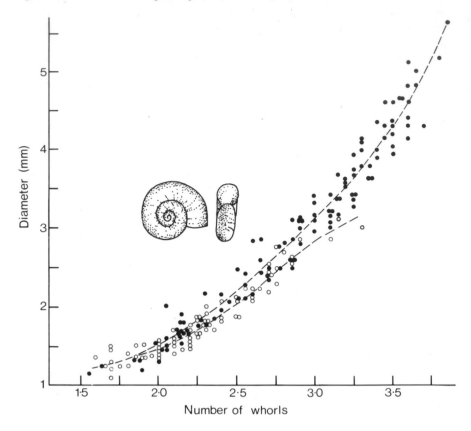

Fig. 14.   Upton Warren. Measurements of *Planorbis laevis* from Bands 2 (open circles) and 3 (closed circles). (After Coope *et al.*, 1961, Fig. 4)

a natural feature of this part of Worcestershire. Tidal influences can be ruled out since contemporary sea level was probably at least 50 metres below the site.

The most spectacular of all the groups extracted from the deposits are undoubtedly the insects. Insect remains have been known to occur in Pleistocene and archaeological deposits since the late nineteenth century, one of the earliest references being to 'large quantities of the horny coverings of insects like beetles . . . together with one or two brilliantly coloured elytra' in excavations at Lochlee Crannog, Ayrshire.[19] But the study at Upton Warren together with that from the earlier interstadial deposits at Chelford[20] were the first of a detailed kind to be made in Britain. Most of the species recorded at Upton Warren lived in damp situations amongst vegetation at the water's edge or were aquatic, living in the pools. The dytiscus beetles, carnivores which feed on tadpoles and small fish such as sticklebacks, indicate standing water. Large numbers of dung beetles of the genus

Aphodius, most of which feed on the dung of large mammals, confirm the local origin of the bones of bison and mammoth. These animals were probably attracted to the pools to drink and wallow; they may also have been attracted to them for their salt content. Flies and midges were prolific, and it is easy to imagine the clouds of these creatures which once swarmed over the pools harassing the bison and the mammoth in the warmth of the short sub-arctic summer.

Evidence bearing on the contemporary climate at Upton Warren is less easy to interpret, owing to the peculiar mixture of northern and southern species of insect present in the deposits. The bands of organic silt were affected by frost action (Fig. 13), being contorted into small festoons, and it can be assumed that winters subsequent to the laying down of each band were more severe than those of today. Some of the beetles are now confined to high latitudes in Scandinavia, occurring around and north of the Arctic Circle (Fig. 15), and the vertebrates too suggest a chilly climate. But other beetle species have a relatively southern distribution today (Fig. 16) which in many cases does not overlap with that of the northern group. The flora is similarly anomalous, with boreal and arctic–alpine elements in an assemblage which for the most part reflects temperate climatic conditions. Nor is this phenomenon

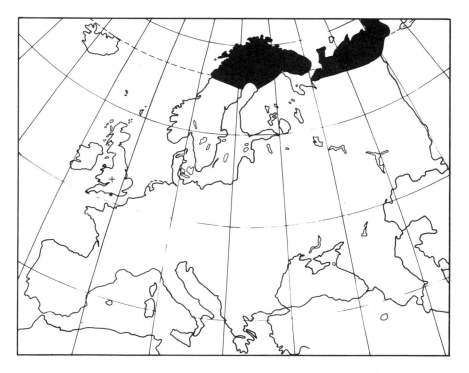

Fig. 15. Present distribution of the beetle, *Amara torrida*, found in Midland England during the Upton Warren Interstadial. (After Coope *et al.*, 1961, Fig. 5)

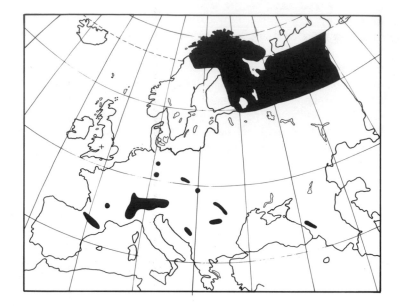

Fig. 16.   Present distribution of the beetle, *Amara erratica*, found in Midland
England during the Upton Warren Interstadial. (After Coope *et al.*, 1961, Fig. 7)

peculiar to Upton Warren. It characterizes plant and animal assemblages at the beginning and the end of the Devensian Glaciation also.
One possibility, which can be generally ruled out, is that of contamination, or mixing between layers reflecting different habitats and climatic
conditions. The problem is a genuine biological one. At Upton Warren,
the favoured explanation was that during the time represented by the
deposits there was a rapid amelioration of climate to conditions similar
to those in southern Sweden today, '. . . arctic species still persisting
against the inroads of the more thermophilous species coming in from
the south'.[21]

In considering the vegetation, there is a further anomaly, namely the
absence of trees and shrubs; any suggestion that the climate was so
cold as to inhibit the growth of trees is incompatible with the ground
flora and beetle evidence. In this case it was felt that grazing by large
herbivores, in particular bison and mammoth, prevented the growth
of woody vegetation, as did the bison on the prairies of North America
in more recent times. The open-country episode in the Hoxnian
Interglacial may be recalled as this too may have been caused by
overgrazing. At Upton Warren there may have been a rapid and unprecedented increase in the number of bison and mammoth brought

about by the ameliorating climate and more plentiful vegetation. The attraction of the brine pools may also have caused a greater concentration of animals in the area than occurred elsewhere. But there is also the point that salt spray is inimical to tree growth (p. 120) and this may have been a contributory factor.

There is no doubt that the floruit of the Lower Palaeolithic in Britain was the Hoxnian Interglacial, various interstadials of the Wolstonian and possibly the Ipswichian Interglacial. But there is some evidence to suggest the continuation of the Levalloisian and Acheulian industries into the early stages of the Devensian, e.g. at Ebbsfleet[22] in the Lower Thames, perhaps during the Chelford Interstadial. Otherwise, the Thames Valley and probably the rest of the area formerly occupied by man was deserted for much of the earlier part of the glaciation, not surprising in view of the severity of the climate.

Later, at a time broadly coincident with the Upton Warren Interstadial, people using bifacial tools similar to hand-axes, but smaller, less pointed and made on flakes rather than cores, appear at several sites in England and Wales (Table 2). They are related to the French Mousterian industries of *Homo sapiens neanderthalensis*, Neanderthal Man, and in Britain, as on the Continent, are found mainly in caves. Sites are known from Kent's Cavern[23] and one of the Torbryan Caves (although not Tornewton) in south-east Devon, Hyena Den by Wookey Hole in the Mendips,[24] Coygan Cave in south-west Wales and Pontnewydd Cave in north Wales.[25] There are also a number of open-air sites, notably Oldbury near Ightham in Kent, but at neither these nor the cave sites are the dates and environmental associations of the industries secure. It is only by analogy with the French sequence that the British Mousterian is considered to have occurred during the Upton Warren Interstadial, at a time when the climate was cool-temperate and the environment one of open grassy plains, perhaps with intervening stretches of pine and birch woodland in sheltered areas, and inhabited by herds of large mammals such as bison, reindeer and mammoth.

Climatic conditions similar to those at Upton Warren persisted in southern Britain for about 10,000 years, i.e. until about 30,000 bp. Then deterioration set in, culminating in the most dramatic event of the Devensian Glaciation—the formation and advance of the ice sheets (Table 2). At their maximum, probably around 18,000 bp, the ice reached the north Norfolk coast, the east Gower coast in south Wales, and to southern Ireland where there was also a local Kerry Mountain Glaciation (Fig. 17). Coastal sections showing glacial deposits are particularly dramatic in the Gower (Fig. 11) and on the Yorkshire coast, e.g. at Sewerby.[26] At the latter site (Fig. 10) (p. 30),

Table 2.   Palaeolithic man in the Devensian Glaciation.

Post-glacial		
——*c.* 10,000 bp———————————————————————————————		
Late-glacial		
Sub-arctic climate Zone III	Later Upper Palaeolithic cultures—	Modern man— *Homo sapiens sapiens*
Allerød Interstadial Zone II	Creswellian and Cheddarian	
Sub-arctic climate Zone I		
——*c.* 14,000 bp———————————————————————————————		
Full Glacial		
Main Devensian ice advance	Man absent from British Isles	
——*c.* 25,000 bp———————————————————————————————		
Mid Glacial		
Sub-arctic climate	Earlier Upper Palaeolithic cultures— Proto-Solutrean and Aurignacian	Modern man— *Homo sapiens sapiens*
——*c.* 30,000 bp———————————————————————————————		
Upton Warren Interstadial complex	? Mousterian culture	Neanderthal man— *Homo sapiens neanderthalensis*
——*c.* 45,000 bp———————————————————————————————		
Sub-arctic climate		
Early Glacial		
Chelford Interstadial	? Acheulian and Levalloisian survivals	? Neanderthal man
——*c.* 61,000 bp———————————————————————————————		
Sub-arctic climate		
——*c.* 70,000 bp———————————————————————————————		
Ipswichian Interglacial		

where raised beach gravels of the Ipswichian sea (h) are banked against a fossil cliff, a series of solifluxion deposits (e and g) and a layer of wind-blown sand (f) of periglacial origin are overlain by two sheets of boulder clay (b and d). The latter probably represent separate ice advances, but which need not be very separate in time. The sequence is overlain by a further solifluxion deposit (a).

Outside the limits of the ice sheet in what is called the 'periglacial zone', the sequence of events in the later part of the Devensian is represented by deposits in chalk dry valleys and on the plains at the foot of the escarpments of southern England. Valleys, or coombes,

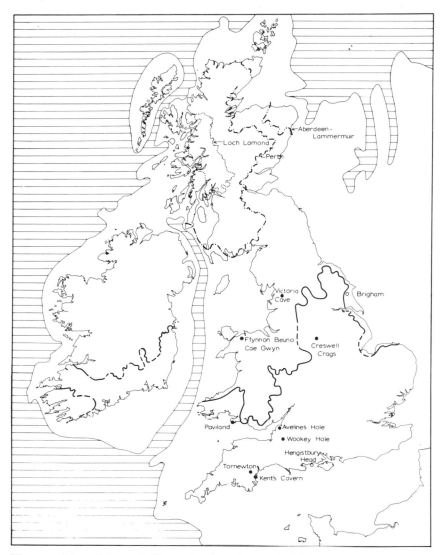

Fig. 17. Map of the main Devensian ice advance (solid line) and the three Late-glacial retreat stages. The approximate position of the coastline during the height of the glaciation is taken as the present − 100-metre contour. (After Sparks and West, 1972, Figs. 5.18 and 5.23) Some of the more important Upper Palaeolithic cave (closed circles) and open air (open circles) sites are shown.

are a characteristic feature of these escarpments lending to them drama-tic qualities particularly apparent in a setting sun. They often occur in clusters, and a good example is to be seen at Cherhill in north Wiltshire. The mode of formation of these coombes has been hotly disputed and there is still no general agreement as to their origin,[27] but one process which undoubtedly played a part was solifluxion. Debris of solifluial origin commonly occurs at the foot of chalk and limestone escarpments, at its coarsest comprising a jumbled mass of angular rock fragments in a finer matrix. Such material is known as coombe rock (p. 59).

At Holborough[28] in Kent where one of the best sequences exists (Fig. 18), coombe rock (a) is overlain by a silty deposit (b), or 'loess' of wind-borne origin. The latter formed during a period of cold, but drier, climate than that which obtained during the deposition of the coombe rock, probably during the height of the glaciation, coeval with the period of ice advance. Loess deposits are made up of silt, i.e. they have a particle size intermediate between sand and clay. They are generally of periglacial origin (but see p. 143). In Britain, thick beds of loess are rare due to the oceanic nature of the climate throughout the Devensian Glaciation by comparison with that in continental Europe, for a prerequisite of the formation of wind-blown deposits is a dry land surface from which frost-shattered rock flour can be whipped up and transported; and it appears that even in the most continental episodes of periglacial climate, conditions in this country were rarely dry enough for this to occur over a long period. Only in the extreme south-east are there deposits of any great thickness (p. 63), although isolated patches are recorded from as far west as Aberystwyth.[29]

Wind-lain deposits of a coarser, sand grade, known as 'coversands', are more common. These too are probably of an age equivalent to that of the ice advance. In the Netherlands, for example, coversands have been dated to between 26,000 and 13,000 bp.

The climate of the period of ice advance was, even in the area beyond the ice sheets, very cold indeed. Deposits of this age—mainly coombe rock and other types of coarse solifluxion debris, scree, coversand, loess and till—are rarely fossiliferous. There are few records of fauna or vegetation, and it is unlikely that many creatures or plants survived the rigours of the age. Man was virtually absent from Britain at this time.

An indication of the severity of climate is given by the occurrence of 'ice wedges', now preserved in the fossil state.[30] When active, these comprised tapering sheets of ice penetrating vertically into the ground for distances of up to 10 metres (and exceptionally more). They usually occurred in polygonal systems. Their formation took place by the contraction of frozen ground under conditions of extreme cold, and observations on modern systems in Canada suggest that a mean annual temperature of at least $-6°C$ was required. It has even been recorded that during the present-day Arctic winter the ground may be heard to crack open with a sharp report like that of a rifle shot. During the spring thaw, the cracks become infilled with water which subsequently freezes, and continuation of this process over several years may lead to the formation of a wedge of ice over 2 metres thick. At the end of the

Plate 5. The crossing of two ice-wedge casts, the fill removed, Broome Heath, Norfolk.

Ice Age when the climate ameliorated, the wedges melted and the cracks became infilled with fine sediments (Plate 5). Often, due to differences in texture between the fill and that of the surrounding parent material, fossil ice wedges show up clearly as vegetation marks from the air.

The final episode of sub-arctic climate, the Late Devensian or Late-glacial, lasted from about 12,000 to 8300 bc.[31] It is the latest period in the history of the British Isles for which there is evidence of massive physical erosion in strictly terrestrial situations—i.e. away from rivers and the coast—and for this reason deposits and erosion features of the period are common. It represents, too, the transition period between the extreme arctic desert conditions of the Full Glacial and the increase to temperate warmth of the Post-glacial or Flandrian. The Devensian ice was in retreat. Herds of animals—reindeer, horse and giant Irish deer—began to move northwards, and by 10,000 bc trees and shrubs—juniper, birch and pine—were becoming established.

In the north of the British Isles, three readvances during the general retreat of the ice are marked by 'moraines', huge banks of boulder clay and gravel, mounded up at the edge of the ice sheet. In order of decreasing age these are the Aberdeen–Lammermuir Readvance, the Perth Readvance and the Loch Lomond Readvance (Fig. 17; Table 3), and the latest of these is dated to between 8800 and 8300 bc.[32] After

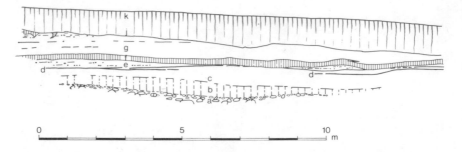

Fig. 18.   Holborough Kent. Section through Late-glacial deposits. a, coombe
rock; b, loessic chalk mud; c, chalk mud (zone Ia); d, Bølling Interstadial soil
(zone Ib); e, chalk mud (zone Ic); f, Allerød Interstadial soil (zone II); g, chalk
mud (zone III); j, Post-glacial ploughwash; k, modern soil. (After Kerney, 1963,
Fig. 9)

this, the ice sheet rapidly dwindled and finally disappeared as the
Post-glacial amelioration set in.

The sequence of events in the Late-glacial is now well established
(Table 3), and the Holborough section[33] already referred to provides a
reasonably complete record (Fig. 18). Here, a series of fine chalky
washes (c, e and g) overlies the Full Glacial deposits (a and b). They
are still essentially solifluial in origin in that they were formed by
downhill sludging of frost-shattered rock, but conditions were much less
severe and the sediments are finer and often layered. Intervening
organic horizons represent standstill phases when the climate ameliorated sufficiently for a continuous vegetation cover to form. These are
buried land surfaces or soils. There are two in the Holborough
sequence (d and f) and they have been dated by radiocarbon to about
12,300 and 9980 bc which equates them with two organic horizons
first recognized from sites in the Low Countries, known respectively as
the Bølling and Allerød Interstadials. The solifluxion horizons are
known as the Oldest Dryas (c in Fig. 18), the Older Dryas (e) and the
Younger Dryas (g) (Table 3), the name Dryas being taken from a
characteristic plant of the Late-glacial, *Dryas octopetala*, the mountain
avens.

The Holborough deposits are devoid of pollen but, like the Swanscombe Lower Loam and the Upton Warren silts, they contain the
shells of molluscs. These have been studied in detail by M.P. Kerney.[34]
The assemblages are totally terrestrial confirming the non-fluviatile, or
subaerial, origin of the deposits. Ecologically they are of open-country
character with grassland and scree-dwelling species predominant.
Climatically, a number of diverse elements is present, particularly in
the second, Allerød Interstadial. Here, although the majority of
species occur today in Scandinavia, and some beyond 70° north
(well north of the Arctic Circle), three species, *Abida secale, Helicella*

Table 3. The Late-glacial period.

	Glaciers	Periglacial zone	Fauna and vegetation
Post-glacial			
—8300 bc—			
Zone III— Younger Dryas	Loch Lomond Readvance	Solifluxion	Tundra
—8800 bc—			
Zone II— Allerød Interstadial	Climatic amelioration Ice sheets waning	Soil formation	Tree birch and pine woodland; much open ground. Elk and giant Irish deer Appearance of thermophile land snails
—*c.* 10,000 bc—			
Zone Ic— Older Dryas	Perth and Aberdeen– Lammermuir Readvances	Solifluxion	Tundra Appearance of horse and reindeer
Zone Ib— Bølling Interstadial		Soil formation	
Zone Ia— Oldest Dryas		Solifluxion	
—*c.* 12,000 bc—			
Full Glacial	Ice sheets	Aeolian activity and solifluxion	

itala (Fig. 19) and *Helicella geyeri*, are of west European affinities, totally absent from the Scandinavian mainland (Fig. 20). The situation is similar to that of the anomalous insect fauna at Upton Warren. But there is a difference. Species of both groups of snail are to be found living together at the present time. The odd feature of the fauna is not the persistence of cold-climate species in the face of

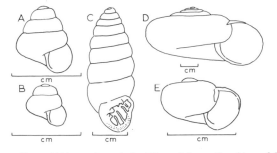

Fig. 19. Land snails. *Abida secale*, adult (C) and juveniles (A and B); *Helicella itala*, adult (D) and juvenile (E).

Fig. 20.   Present distribution of the land snail, *Helicella itala*, found in Britain during the Late-glacial. (After Kerney, 1963, Fig. 18)

approaching warmth, but the occurrence of three, and only three, relatively thermophile species long before many others of considerably more northerly range migrated into the area at all. But present day geographical ranges may be misleading. *Abida secale*, for example, flourishes at high altitudes in the Alps and is capable of surviving periods of intense cold in the order of $-10\,^{\circ}$C. It is also well adapted to life on bare ground, living in habitats in which diurnal and seasonal changes of temperature are extreme.

The Late-glacial sequence on the Chalk can be tied in to the record of vegetational and other environmental changes as established by radio-carbon assay, pollen analysis and the study of soils and sediments from other areas of the British Isles (Table 3). Three major vegetational zones (I, II and III) are recognized,[35] and further work has led to the closer definition of other aspects of the environment—soils, fauna and climate, and the link up in the north with glacial fluctuations. In Britain, the subdivisions of zone I are rarely recognized due to the weak nature of the zone Ic deterioration, and the Holborough site is an exception in this respect. Zone II, the Allerød Interstadial, saw the introduction of the elk (the interstadial in the Devensian deposits at Tornewton is probably of this age), and was the first zone to see the appearance of thermophilous land snails. Forest trees were present for the first time since the Chelford (or possibly the Upton Warren) Interstadial, the main species being birch with pine less abundant. But woodland as such was probably confined to sheltered situations, elsewhere there being tundra or park tundra. Zone III was a temporary but nonetheless dramatic deterioration during which renewed sub-aerial erosion took place. The Devensian ice sheet, by now a small remnant in the western Highlands, expanded briefly as the Loch Lomond Readvance, but by 8300 bc it had wasted completely, and all processes of terrestrial physical erosion had ceased.

At around 30,000 to 35,000 years ago the Mousterian industries developed into (or were replaced by) those of the Upper Palaeolithic, characterized by the use of flint blades. These are long thin parallel-sided flakes struck by means of a punch of wood, bone or antler (Fig. 21), and are far superior to the tool types which had gone before. These changes coincide with the development and spread in western Europe of modern man, *Homo sapiens sapiens*, and the abortion of the Neander-thalers. It is perhaps surprising that this change should have taken place at a time when, even in France and Spain, the climate was by no means equable. Man was dependent on shelter, whether artificial or natural, and not only as a protection from the sub-arctic winters of the Devensian Glaciation but from wild beasts as well. However, it was probably due to, rather than in spite of, these environmental limitations that such developments took place, just as we have already suggested that other major steps in man's progress may have been associated with an increase in the severity of the environment.

The key work on the British Upper Palaeolithic was written by Dorothy Garrod[36] almost fifty years ago, and has not been replaced. Most of our evidence comes from caves, although there are also some open-air sites (Fig. 17). There were two main episodes of occupation.[37] The Earlier Upper Palaeolithic is characterized by leaf-shaped points of flint (Fig. 21), associated with engraving tools (or burins), scrapers and simple bone points. It is thought to be related, and possibly ances-tral, to the French Solutrean, an industry of unsurpassed elegance in its flint work, and was present in Britain later than about 38,000 years ago but prior to the Devensian ice advance of *c*. 18,000 bp. It is represented

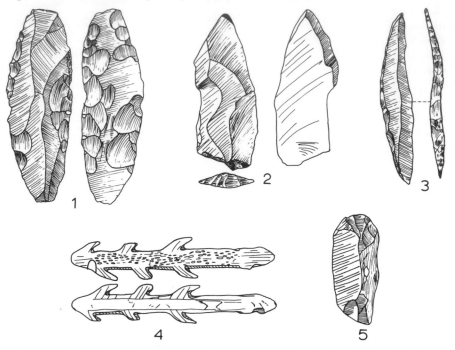

Fig. 21.   Upper Palaeolithic tools. 1, Proto-Solutrean (Earlier Upper Palaeolithic) bifacial blade, Kent's Cavern; 2, Aurignacian (Earlier Upper Palaeolithic) burin or graver, Paviland; 3, Later Upper Palaeolithic backed blade, Aveline's Hole; 4, Later Upper Palaeolithic harpoon, Aveline's Hole; 5, Aurignacian (Earlier Upper Palaeolithic) end scraper, Paviland. (After Garrod, 1926)

at several cave sites in Wales and England—Paviland in the Gower, Kent's Cavern, various sites in the Mendips, and indeed at all the main cave groups north to Creswell Crags in Derbyshire (Fig. 17). The contemporary climate was cold, but not as cold as it was to become in later millennia. Pollen analysis of cave deposits in the Mendips (Fig. 22) indicates a generally open environment with counts of less than 25 per cent for trees and shrubs—juniper, willow, crowberry and some pine and birch. The associated large mammal fauna from these sites included horse, reindeer, red deer, giant Irish deer, bison, woolly rhinoceros and mammoth as herbivores, and hyena, lion, wolf, fox and bear as carnivores.[38]

The Later Upper Palaeolithic, known as the Creswellian, or locally in Somerset as the Cheddarian, is characterized by backed blades —small flint blades with vertical retouch along one edge as in a penknife —burins and scrapers, together with a few well-made bone and antler tools (Fig. 21). It is the equivalent of the later stages of the French Magdalenian. The Creswellian occurred from early zone I, for example at Kent's Cavern, to zone III and may have continued on into the Post-glacial (p. 105).[39] The majority of sites are caves, in situations which can be considered as transitional between the upland and lowland territories of Britain, and they extend as far north as the Victoria Cave, Settle, in the West Riding of Yorkshire (Fig. 17). This is the industry which is represented in the Reindeer Stratum at Tornewton. In the Mendips, pollen analysis of cave deposits indicates values of between 25 and 40 per cent trees and shrubs, mainly birch and willow (Fig. 22). An environment of park tundra—scattered birches in a generally open landscape, but with denser woodland in the sheltered valleys and ravines—can be envisaged for much of Britain at low altitudes. A fauna similar to that prior to the Full Glacial was present with large herbivores predominant.[40] Horse and reindeer appeared early in zone I; elk was present by zone II,[41] and in Ireland, although not directly concerning us since Upper Palaeolithic man never reached that country, the Allerød period is characterized by the giant Irish deer.[42] But the mammoth, woolly rhinoceros, hyena and lion were all absent, for some reason not having been able to return to Britain after the glacial maximum.

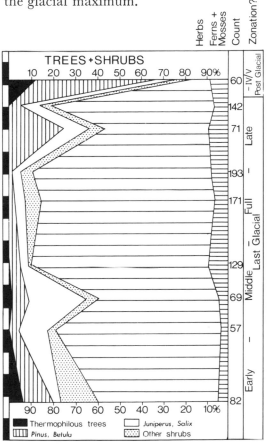

Fig. 22. Wookey Hole. Pollen diagram. (After Tratman *et al.*, 1971, Fig. 45)

We can thus see the Upper Palaeolithic cultures of Britain as occurring prior to and after the Full Glacial, but not during it.[43] Until recently it had not been possible to tie in Upper Palaeolithic artefact horizons with pollen spectra due to the unsuitability of cave sediments for pollen analysis. However, by the use of large samples of at least 50 grams (the normal sample size is 1 gram) and specialized techniques of concentrating pollen, John Campbell has been able to construct sequences from several sites. One of these, from Hyena Den, Wookey Hole,[44] is reproduced here, and although lacking in detail it does give the broad outline of the pattern of change in the Devensian (Fig. 22). The figure reflects the deterioration of climate in the early and middle parts of the glaciation with variations from temperate to sub-arctic conditions, the period of maximum cold in the Full Glacial when an environment of arctic desert prevailed, and the return to sub-arctic/temperate conditions in the Late-glacial.

In Britain, open-air Upper Palaeolithic sites are few, occurring sporadically in the south and east.[45] The fact that the majority of finds are from caves probably reflects a real distribution of these cultures, for under the climatic conditions which prevailed, shelter would have been at a premium. It is also felt that the distribution of sites reflects the exploitation, possibly on a seasonal basis, of upland habitats by people whose origins and more general environmental background were the lowlands of the North European Plain. Grahame Clark has vividly described how Upper Palaeolithic man was closely associated with large herds of herbivorous mammals, and in particular the migratory reindeer, an animal well adapted to the sparse and specialized habitats of the tundra.[46]

We saw earlier how evidence from Tornewton Cave indicated seasonal occupation by reindeer hunters in the spring and early summer. Evidence from open-air sites on the North European Plain, particularly in the Schleswig-Holstein area where reindeer bones are prolific, indicates a similar pattern. Further south, in France, analysis of reindeer skeletal remains suggests occupation of cave sites mainly during winter. On other sites, for example in the Dordogne, there is a clear year-round pattern of reindeer exploitation,[47] the reindeer having perhaps not always behaved as they do today in the far north.

In Britain, faunal evidence suggests horse often as important or even more important than reindeer for food and raw materials. Abundant herds of horse were probably available along the upland/lowland contact zone as indeed they would be today in the High Altai of Mongolia were it not for modern man.

The increasing specialization and technological skill seen in the flint, bone and antler tools of Upper Palaeolithic man, and culminating to some extent in the brilliant French Magdalenian of which the British

Creswellian is an offshoot, are probably a reflection of the sustained pressures of the specialized, and at times severe, environment of the Devensian Glaciation. The tundra vegetation, on which low temperatures and a short growing season were limiting factors, was not directly exploitable for food on a large scale by man, although seeds and berries were doubtless eaten. But the reindeer and the horse were ideally suited to it and it was through these animals that man's livelihood was largely gained. The enormous quantities of bone and antler, and implements made from them, which occur on British and European sites bear witness to the importance of these animals in the life of Upper Palaeolithic man. The specialization of these final Palaeolithic cultures may be compared with the generalized way of life practised by the Lower Palaeolithic big-game hunting communities of the interglacials. Living in the more equable climates and the more luxuriant environments of the Thames Valley, these people, at any rate during the climatic optimum of an interglacial, were not so strongly subject to the environmental pressures experienced by those of the Upper Palaeolithic. This sort of environmental determinism is often assumed, of course, and just as often questioned. The pressures of an interglacial, although different, may not have been any less severe.

In France, Spain and Russia the cultures are also famous for their cave art, of which Lascaux and Altamira mark the highest achievements. Most of the paintings depict the large herbivores on which man depended—the horse, wild ox, bison, mammoth and reindeer—although, curiously, the latter is not represented as frequently as might have been expected.[48] The reindeer is among the commonest animals represented in the food debris in Upper Palaeolithic sites, and the contrast with its low frequency in cave art may indicate an association between man and reindeer somewhat different from that established with the other large herbivores. A symbiotic relationship in which the reindeer obtained salt from man's urine and protection from predators has been suggested.[49] Deliberate herding could well have followed, and even domestication. In southern England and the Low Countries, Allerød Interstadial soils often have a high charcoal content indicative of widespread fires.[50] It is possible that these were deliberately started by man perhaps to aid in the herding of game or to encourage the growth of fresh grass and improve the animals' grazing grounds. The modern Lapps are a striking example of how useful an animal the reindeer can be. The animal may not have fulfilled all the same potentials for the Magdalenians, but the fact remains that in northern Scandinavia and Finland, domesticated reindeer are the main source of wealth to the Lapps, furnishing milk, meat, hides and sinew; in harness they can pull a sledge for 300 kilometres in a day, and are capable of drawing loads of up to 150 kilos.

The horse is another animal which may have been domesticated.

There is a carved bone head of this animal from St Michel d'Arudy with what appear to be indications of a bridle.[51]

In Britain we have no parietal cave art. This may reflect a genuine lack for there is no doubt that we are at the very limits of the Upper Palaeolithic culture province and our territories not exploited to the extent of those further south in Europe. Or it may be that with the more oceanic climate, paintings which were once present have since been washed away by a constantly moving film of water over the surface of the cave walls.

The ability to carve and engrave bone and antler was another great attribute of Upper Palaeolithic man which has left a wealth of material of the highest quality (Fig. 23), although unfortunately little in Britain. As well as animal representations there is a profusion of abstract markings and some of these, when they occur in regular groups of incisions (often on rib bones) have been interpreted as lunar calendars, notably by Alexander Marshack.[52] Some archaeologists are naturally sceptical of this idea,[53] but it is consistent with the practice of many living hunter/gatherer groups and might have helped predict, for example, migration times of reindeer, horse and birds.

The Later Upper Palaeolithic peoples endured in western Europe for over 4000 years. With their cave art, their carvings, their tools and weapons of extreme beauty, their sophisticated annual migratory movements and their possible near domestication of the reindeer and the horse they drew from western Europe and gave to it a fitness and a legacy which was not to be surpassed until the introduction of agriculture—and some would say never. The possible future of these communities had the Late-glacial environment been maintained is totally speculative. But there is little doubt that the Post-glacial amelioration of climate and the eventual spread of mixed deciduous forest drove the reindeer herds northwards and broke up one of the finest and most successful life styles ever known.

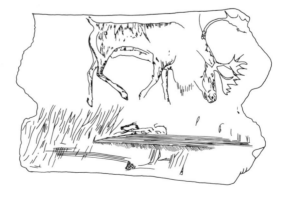

Fig. 23.   Upper Palaeolithic engraving of a reindeer, Kesslerloch, near Thayingen.

3 The influence of the Ice Age on the environment of Britain

The British Isles are situated in the north temperate climatic zone of the globe at the extreme western edge of the Old World continental shelf. The climate is mild, characterized by an absence of extremes of temperature and precipitation due to the ameliorating influence of the Gulf Stream. A great variety of rocks, ranging from soft clays to resistant granites, from limestones to acidic sands, underlies and gives rise to a varied surface relief. There is a corresponding variety of soil types, building materials and mineral resources. Intervisibility between islands and peninsulas makes for ease of communication, and the shortest sea crossing to Europe is not more than 35 kilometres. Under the present climatic regime the vegetation is, and always has been, rich, whether it be the mixed deciduous woodlands of pre-agricultural Britain or the lush grasslands of more recent times. The mild winters and warm, gentle springs make Britain one of the finest farming countries in the world.

It is not our purpose to describe the physiography, climate, vegetation and fauna of these islands, either as they stand today or in the geological past. This has been done admirably in a number of classic works all of which treat their subjects from a historical and inter-disciplinary point of view.[1]

What we cannot leave out, however, are those events of more recent origin which have taken place during the time Britain has been occupied by man, events which are associated more or less directly with the waxing and waning of the ice sheets. For although not strictly separable from earlier geological events, their closeness in time to the present day and the peculiarly dramatic effect they have had on the landscape endow these later processes with a significance disproportionate to the short time involved. The fact that they took place in parallel with the occupation of these islands by man—although he was not present continuously—gives them an added interest, and is very relevant to the theme of this book.

Glacier ice had both a constructional and destructional influence on the landscape, and the ways in which these processes operated have been discussed recently by Bruce Sparks and Richard West.[2] The most dramatic effects are to be seen in highland Britain where the freshness of the mountain corries and arêtes is a striking reminder of the nearness in time of the Ice Age. In the Cairngorm Mountains, isolated patches of snow are retained all the year round in a few localities, and it is not

Plate 6.   Wastwater. An example of a glaciated U-valley in the English Lake District.

difficult to imagine these, under conditions of slightly higher precipitation and cooler summers, swelling into permanent corrie glaciers. In the Lake District and other mountainous regions, valleys with U-shaped profiles are a characteristic feature (Plate 6). These were, in part at least, carved out by glacial action, and the steep-sided walls often over 100 metres high attest to the thickness of the ice. Fertile soils, developed on morainic material or later lacustrine sediments, now blanket the valley floors and have made possible enclaves of agriculture and settlement in what are otherwise regions of thin, impoverished soil and bare rock.

Along the west coast of Scotland a large number of sea lochs provides access to the hinterland. These natural harbours and route ways were formed, like the U-shaped valleys, by glacial erosion and have since become flooded by the Post-glacial rise of sea level. They are ana-lagous to the Norwegian fjords.

Beyond the immediate vicinity of the mountains, ice sheets brought about erosion over a wide area, particularly in upland Britain. We can thus sum up the destructional processes of glacial action as resulting in a diversification and lowering of the terrain.

The constructional effects of glaciation are various. The material scoured out by the grinding action of the ice, transported by it, and later redeposited is known as till or boulder clay (Plate 3). Often this material is deposited as banks lateral to or at the toe of a glacier and these are termed moraines. Terminal moraines, those at the toe of a glacier, may cause the damming up of the valley down which they came; in which case a lake is formed during the melting of the ice, and many of these, notably in the Lake District, remain today. Ground moraine, the material deposited beneath an ice sheet or glacier, although not imparting such marked topographical features to the landscape, has more widespread economic repercussions. The chalky boulder clay of southern Britain, where it overlies the London Clay, gives rise through its high lime content to a soil of greater fertility than soils derived from London Clay alone. Conversely, soil derived from sandy outwash material laid down beyond the edge of an ice sheet may be impoverished by comparison with that which would have developed on the underlying geological solid had this been exposed.[3] But such material is often a valuable economic commodity, being quarried to the same extent as lowland river gravels.

In some instances an ice sheet itself has dammed up a river, and again a lake forms. There is, for example, a series of such glacial lakes around the northern fringes of the North York Moors where ice sheets from the north have abutted against the escarpment, and another around the fringes of the Wicklow Mountains in eastern Ireland (Fig. 24) where the lakes were swollen with melt waters from the local mountain glaciers.[4] Where these lakes overflowed they cut vast gorges or 'glacial overflow channels' which today often provide major route-ways. The main Arklow to Dublin road passes through several such channels, one, the Scalp, being banked with 'boulders . . . random, raging, insensate chaos crashing to the valley floor in a jumble of wasted strength and spent violence'.[5] On drainage, the fine sediments of the lakes often provide good agricultural soils.

Differential melting of a glacier sometimes results in isolated lenses of ice remaining in rock debris or till long after the bulk of ice has gone.

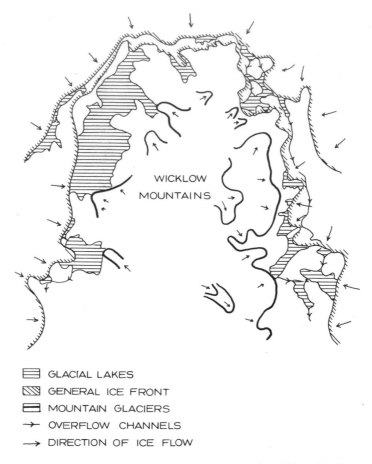

WICKLOW
MOUNTAINS

⊟ GLACIAL LAKES
⊠ GENERAL ICE FRONT
⊟ MOUNTAIN GLACIERS
→ OVERFLOW CHANNELS
→ DIRECTION OF ICE FLOW

Fig. 24.   Map of glacial lakes in the Wicklow Mountains. (After Charlesworth, 1937, Plate II)

When these eventually melt they leave hollows in the ground which vary in size from a few to some hundreds of metres across. These are known as 'kettle holes'. Often they have no external drainage, and as they generally occur in non-porous materials are usually filled with water, at least in the early stages of their history. Later they become infilled with clays and peat deposits, while the vegetation around the edges passes through a variety of stages—reed swamp, carr (a kind of damp swampy woodland in which alder is often an important species) and raised bog—and at the same time it encroaches on the open water, diminishing its area and eventually obliterating it (cf. Fig. 78). Kettle holes are important for two reasons. In the first place they make for variation in the landscape, and they provide a variety of habitats—drinking hollows for animals, refuges for wild fowl, a source of reeds for thatch and bedding, and a source of brushwood and withies when in the carr stage. Secondly, as units of sedimentation, they entrap and preserve a record of palaeontological and archaeological history. Many well known sites such as Ehenside Tarn, a Neolithic settlement on the edge of the Lake District,[6] are kettle holes. In Ireland there is a whole variety of infilled lake basins only some of which are kettle holes, others being simply irregularities in the surface of the till. Many have only been drained in the last century and previously provided refugia for a special type of island dwelling known as the crannog[7] (p. 181).

A glacial form which it is difficult to fit into the constructional/destructional classification is the drumlin. These are low oval mounds, smoothed by ice action and generally occurring in groups known as drumlin fields. Their make up varies from solid bed rock to pure drift. They impart marked characteristics to the topography of a region, reflected in Ireland, for example, by the striking correspondence between their distribution and that of the place-name element *druim*, a ridge (Fig. 25).[8]

Similarly in the periglacial zone, weathering was both constructional and destructional. Constructional processes brought about the formation of material such as scree and coombe rock largely through frost-shattering followed by downhill transport (Plate 3). Solifluxion has

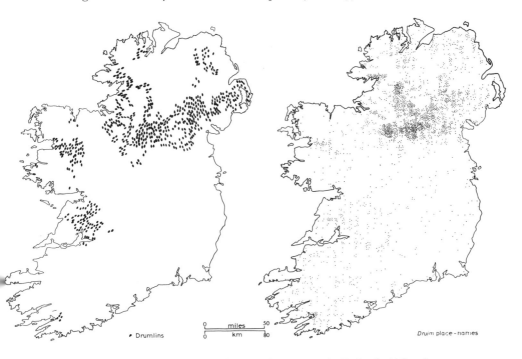

Fig. 25.   Distribution of drumlins and *druim* place-names in Ireland. (After Jones Hughes, 1970, Fig. 15.4, and Synge, 1970, Fig. 3.1)

·moved material hundreds of metres from its source, and distances of over two kilometres have been recorded. One of the most important effects of this process has been the removal of calcareous material from limestone escarpments onto the adjacent lowland clay plains. This has had a similar effect to that produced by the deposition of chalky boulder clay, in that the Gault Clay and Greensand, for example, at the foot of Chalk escarpments have become overlain by material of a higher calcium carbonate content, thus giving rise to more fertile soils. In addition, since the deposition of solifluxion debris depends not on fluviatile processes but on those of a terrestrial or subaerial kind, the deposits are usually built up to a height greater than that of the local flood plain level, and the land is thus better drained and not as prone to flooding. Such deposits are often known as fan gravels, and they provide land very suitable for agriculture.[9]

Among the more impressive results of solifluxion are the periglacial rock streams to be seen in certain parts of Britain. Most notable are those peripheral to the granite tors of the West Country and those made up of sarsen blocks in the valleys of the Marlborough Downs.[10] The sarsen rock streams derive originally from the plateau areas of the Downs where numerous boulders may still be seen strewn over the surface. Solifluxion of the frost-shattered and semi-liquid chalky subsoil carried these boulders off the hilltops into the valleys and many eventually reached the main river valley of the Kennet. It is interesting to compare an early map of the sarsens made by the antiquary A. C. Smith with that of their present distribution (Fig. 26).[11] Today their numbers are much depleted, most having been used as building or kerb stones.[12] Exploitation of sarsens began, however, long before the present era, for many of the spectacular prehistoric monuments of the area such as Stonehenge and Avebury are constructed of the larger stones.

The formation of fan gravels is often accompanied by localized erosion of the escarpment, and this process has given England some of the most dramatic lowland landscape features—the steepsided dry valleys or coombes.[13] These often occur in groups, and often below high points. They provide the focus for many prehistoric hillforts, and the defensive attributes of these clearly derive from the steep slopes of the coombes below.

The action of rivers in the periglacial zone is very intense due to the massive release of water from snowfields and frozen ground in the spring. Some authorities, notably John Wymer, would attribute virtually all major river gravel deposits to periods of cold climate, and it is true that their faunal content is more often than not of cold-climate type.[14] There are, of course, periods of flooding under conditions of temperate climate when the erosive and carrying powers of rivers assume massive proportions as they did, for example, in the

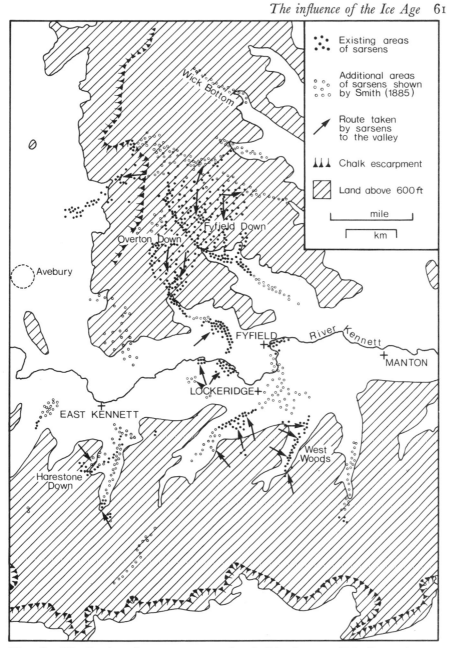

Fig. 26.   Distribution of sarsen stones on the chalklands west of Marlborough.
(After Williams, 1968, Fig. 4)

Lynton and Lynmouth disaster. But these are exceptional, at least in lowland Britain.

River gravel is a major economic concern. It is used extensively for road and building foundations, and for the manufacture of concrete and other constructional materials. It is also much needed as land for building on owing to its good drainage. Most gravel deposits occupy terraces above the present-day flood plain level and thus present the same desirable features for farming and settlement as do those of solifluial origin. Well-drained, fertile soils, nearness to water and the absence of flooding are essential aspects of the gravel environment, and these properties were recognized by prehistoric man. As a source of flint for the manufacture of tools and weapons, gravel has been exploited from the earliest times (p. 20).[15]

Flint is a fine micro-crystalline rock, almost a glass, which, as we have seen, can be readily worked with a punch or hammerstone into sharp-edged implements such as hand-axes, burins and backed blades. For manufacturing chipped stone tools, it is far superior to any other stone type found in the British Isles on the same wide scale. Primarily it occurs in layers in the Chalk (Fig. 54) but the weathering and destruction of this rock over the 70 million years since its deposition have led to the accumulation of vast concentrations of flint which, in our climate, is virtually indestructible by chemical weathering alone. Through the redistribution of these concentrations, not only by river transport but by solifluxion and glacial action, flint gravel is now to be found in many of the major river valleys of lowland Britain often well away from the Chalk (Fig. 6). Pebble flint occurs, too, along the east coast of Ireland, brought by glaciers from the Antrim or Yorkshire Chalk, and was probably a factor in the settlement of this coastline in Neolithic times. An erratic block of flint-bearing chalk has been found as far south as Kerry.

The extraction of gravel from river valleys has been carried on for over a century, at first by hand and later by a variety of mechanical processes. Today there is competition between gravel extraction companies and developers who demand land for building, competition which becomes particularly intense, for example, when new motorways are built in the vicinity of expanding urban areas. Where the gravel has been worked out, as it has in parts of the Thames Valley—notably in the Reading and Oxford regions—new landscapes have grown up. A few of the pits have been back-filled with refuse and industrial wastes and the land reclaimed for building or agriculture. But many have not, and are now flooded and used variously as bird sanctuaries and lidos for recreation. Others have been abandoned to dereliction.

In the past, many archaeological sites have been destroyed by gravel extraction, but more recently cooperation between archaeologists and extraction companies has led to the rescue of many by excavation. The surface remains of most prehistoric sites have, of course, long been destroyed by ploughing, initiated in some areas in Roman or medieval times (p. 168) .But through aerial photography, the subsurface features of these—the ditches, pits, wells and wall foundations—

have been revealed, often showing a palimpsest of occupation. A number of research committees and excavation programmes have been established to deal with archaeological sites faced with destruction, and much is now being saved.[16]

Palaeolithic sites cannot, unfortunately, be discovered by aerial photography since they comprise little but artefacts; nor can the rich concentrations of Pleistocene mammal bones which often occur associated with them. In the early days of gravel digging when hand sieving and grading were practised, palaeoliths and bones were readily recoverable, and many workmen were well aware of the interest and pecuniary value of these finds, an awareness which is reflected today in the mammoth and bison symbols used by some gravel companies. But the advent of mechanization changed all this, and the recovery of Pleistocene material is now a much less frequent occurrence.

In many parts of the Thames, the terrace gravels are overlain by thick deposits of loam which, because of their use in brick making, are generally known as brickearth. Their origin and composition is various. A clue to their mode of deposition is the relative proportions in the sediment of the various grades of particle—sand, silt and clay. Fluviatile sediments, such as the Lower Loam at Swanscombe, generally comprise an equal proportion of the three grades due to the relatively weak sorting powers of running water; technically such deposits are termed loams (cf. Fig. 60). Analysis of the Thames brickearths has shown that many of these are of this type, as is indeed indicated by their molluscan faunas.[17]

But other brickearths are more finely sorted, showing a preponderance of silt, and are essentially loessic. S. W. Wooldridge and D. Linton were the first to point out that such deposits were widespread in southern England.[18] They attributed their origin to the sorting action of wind during periods of periglacial climate when conditions were generally dry, at least for a part of the year (cf. p. 144). In Britain, the best pure loess deposits are in east Kent at Pegwell Bay and along the Sussex coastal plain. Otherwise they are rare. This is mainly due to the oceanic climate of these islands which hinders the formation of wind-blown deposits of all but the coarsest grades. Farther east, on the Continent, and particularly in central Europe where continental climatic conditions prevail, pure loess deposits are widespread, and were avidly sought out and settled by Neolithic communities in the fifth and sixth millennia bc.

The importance of Wooldridge and Linton's work was to demonstrate the way in which a thin loess mantle modified the parent material and made for a group of soils with structural and drainage properties intermediate between those of heavy clays and those of porous, free-draining chalk sands and gravels. More recently, analysis of seemingly pure chalk soils, showing no deposit between the surface humus horizon and the underlying bedrock, has demonstrated nevertheless that a loessic component is present.[19] And the former existence of a discrete layer of loessic drift, mostly now destroyed, over parts or even the whole of the Chalk is shown by the preservation of such material in cryoturbation structures under prehistoric field monuments, where protected from the ravages of later ploughing and weathering (p. 117).[20]

Northwards of the loess belt, between it and the edge of the former ice sheet, are coarser deposits known as coversands; these too are of periglacial, aeolian, origin. In Britain, coversands of Pleistocene age occur sporadically from Lincolnshire across to south Wales, Cardiganshire and the West Country. Their soils, however, unlike those derived from loess, are impoverished due to the poor water-retaining powers and high silica (quartz) content of the parent material.[21]

The impact of interglacial weathering on the Post-glacial landscape is not as marked or as widespread as that of the glacial periods. This is partly because the weathering processes which obtained in an interglacial were less dramatic and of a chemical rather than physical nature, involving the *in situ* alteration of rock into soil, and partly because the intense physical weathering of the Devensian Glaciation tended to remove all trace of previous soils and weathering processes. This is most noticeable in upland Britain where ice action and solifluxion were most intense. The bare rock areas of parts of north-west Scotland, even where gradients are gentle, are testimony to the erosive powers of the ice sheets and their recent presence.

But in parts of southern Britain, and particularly in the periglacial zone of the glaciations (Fig. 6), thick deposits of clays and loams which are in part of interglacial origin remain, imparting their properties to the present-day soils. These are best developed in flat and extensive plateau areas where they lie outside the influence of solifluial erosion and yet are too elevated to have been buried by processes of deposition. The deposit known as Clay-with-flints (Plate 7) which mantles large areas of the Chalk on the North Downs and Chiltern Hills is in part of interglacial origin, being the non-calcareous residue from the Chalk produced by weathering over long periods of time. It has given to these hills a character, environment and history very much their own. Unlike the thin well-drained soils of the Wessex Chalk, those of the Chilterns and North Downs are deep, clayey and often ill-drained, and they support not the characteristic sheep pasture of chalk country but shaded beech woodland. Evidence of prehistoric and early settlement, at least of farming peoples, is sparse,[22] and there was a sharp contrast in Buckinghamshire during the medieval period between the dense occupation of the Vale of Aylesbury and the almost deserted

Plate 7. Section showing pockets of Clay-with-flints overlying chalk bedrock, Gerrards Cross, Chiltern Hills.

Chiltern hinterland—the *deserta Ciltine*. The later importance of these areas, and the settlement pattern of isolated homesteads, is connected with the timber and furniture industries, and not with agriculture.

A fundamental attribute of the Pleistocene, and one which has contributed much to the evolution and development of man, is the element of change. Habitat change is a prerequisite for the success of any group of organisms as indeed has been argued in the case of Palaeolithic man. In the Post-glacial, the influence of the Ice Age in one form or another is seldom far off, and the development of certain habitats such as the infilling of lakes and kettle holes is a direct response to changes wrought initially during the Devensian Glaciation. In no aspect of the Post-glacial environment is this more strongly felt than in the rise and fall of the sea and the changing form of the coastline. From a low point of between −100 and −110 metres OD during the maximum of the Devensian, the sea has risen to its present level. We are not concerned here with the details of these processes—these will come later (p. 83)— only their general consequences.

During a period of depressed sea level, downcutting of rivers to a new base level took place, and fluviatile erosion as a whole was aggravated. As we have seen, this led to the abandonment, and in some cases the preservation, of old river terraces (Fig. 9) with all the attendant implications this has for later settlement, Pleistocene geology and Stone Age archaeology. In the upper reaches of a river, down-cutting was accompanied by headward erosion with the result that sources on either side of a watershed converged, and the watershed lowered. A similar process in coastal areas led to island formation, and it was probably due to river downcutting during times of low sea level that the chalk ridge between Calais and Dover was ultimately breached. The isolation of Britain from the Continent can thus be seen in terms not only of flooding during a period of high sea level, but also of erosion during glacial times.[23]

In the tidal reaches of rivers and along the coast, ancient cliffs, rounded by solifluxion and now vegetated, attest to former high sea levels (Fig. 11). Associated deposits of sand and gravel also occur, and these, like the river gravels, may have an important function in up-grading, or otherwise altering, the prevailing soil type of an area. The exact influence of these deposits varies, depending on their chemical and physical composition, their age, and their potential fertility by com-parison with the underlying rocks. In parts of the North Downs, for example, the Clay-with-flints is overlain by beach deposits of an early Pleistocene shoreline at a height of about 180 metres OD. In some respects the suitability of the soil for cultivation has been increased by comparison with that of the Clay-with-flints—its porosity and drainage are far superior, approaching that of the Chalk. But any advantages are offset by the chemically impoverished nature of the deposits, the soil being leached of most minerals other than quartz. This is probably a function of their extreme age.

Beaches of a much younger age are to be found in the area of isostatic recovery (Fig. 6). Some are of late Pleistocene origin, but the most recent are Post-glacial. They contain a variety of minerals which, together with the porous nature of the deposits, impart fertility and good drainage to the soils derived from them. Soils on the underlying boulder clay or acidic rocks, had these been exposed, would have been difficult to cultivate for long, supporting at best poor pasture or marshy ground. It is well known that significant groupings of archaeo-logical sites, particularly those of farming communities, lie close to or actually on soils of the raised beach deposits in northern Britain (p. 138).

That we have raised beaches and river gravels thus depends on a number of factors—downcutting by rivers during periods of low sea level, isostatic uplift in the north, and the fact that interglacial sea levels become successively lower. And in general, the later the deposits, the more suitable they are as farming land.

There are a number of important consequences of the rise of sea level which took place at the end of the Devensian. For Britain, isolation from the Continent around 6000 bc was the most significant; Ireland was probably cut off earlier on, the last marshy link between the Inishowen Peninsula and the Scottish mainland perhaps being breached in Late-glacial times. Many new islands, such as the Orkneys, were created, and the ratio of coastline to interior increased. The latter consequence may have been responsible for the expansion of hunting communities into the littoral habitat which appears to have taken place in the early Post-glacial, although it must be remembered that the rising sea flooded many coastal areas, submerging a whole range of Upper Palaeolithic and Mesolithic sites.

Drowned river valleys are an important consequence of the Post-glacial rise of sea level, particularly those of the south coast and south-west peninsulas. Examples are the Solent and Southampton Water, the Tamar, Milford Haven, the Shannon and the various long bays of south-west Ireland, some of which, like the sea lochs of western Scotland, have been glacially deepened as well. They provide natural harbours and navigable routes inland, and were probably in their present state by the mid Post-glacial.

Where wave action and erosion were insignificant, deposits of marine and estuarine clay were laid down by the rising sea. The East Anglian Fens, the Somerset Levels, Swansea Bay, Morecambe Bay, the Solway Firth and the Firth of Forth are among the most notable areas, and, like the kettle holes, but on a grander scale, they have added a temporal and spatial mosaic to the environment and have provided important catchment area for archaeological and palaeonto-logical material.

Minor changes of sea level and coastal configuration have continued well beyond the main period of marine transgression as is shown, for example, in the Scilly Isles by the presence of submerged megalithic tombs and field walls. In the north, the process of isostatic recovery is not yet complete, and although taking place now at a rate of only millimetres per year, it is a striking reminder that the consequences of the last Ice Age which technically ended 10,000 years ago are very real today.[24]

The deposits which we have discussed in this chapter are known as 'drift'.[25] The term was first applied in the early nineteenth century to superficial strata which were manifestly recent by comparison with the much older rocks of the geological solid. Their origin was thought to be largely fluviatile, a view which found much support from exponents of the Biblical Flood or Diluvial Theory, and which reached its peak in Dean William Buckland's *Reliquae Diluvianae, or Observations on Organic Remains attesting to the Action of a Universal Deluge*, published in 1823. This theory was contested by J. L. R. Agassiz, a Swiss naturalist whose work on the glacial phenomena of the Alps led him to put forward the Glacial Theory in his *Études sur les Glaciers* (1840) and *Système Glaciaire* (1847), a theory to which Buckland and other British geologists were soon converted. Two key factors in this theory were the similarity of fossil glacial landforms, such as the U-shaped valleys, to those which today are associated with active glaciers, and the discovery of far-travelled stones, or erratics, which could only be explained sensibly by ice transport. In Britain, rocks of Scandinavian origin occur in drift along the east coast, while in the west, fragments of granite from the small island of Ailsa Craig in the Firth of Clyde have been found as far south as Pembrokeshire and Cork.[26]

But while the propounding of the Glacial Theory by Agassiz showed remarkable deductive powers, and its acceptance by Buckland a mind open to new ideas, both men were inflexible in their adherence to the current views on the origin and antiquity of man. 4004 BC had been calculated on the basis of the Old Testament account of Genesis as the date of the creation of the world and man by Archbishop Ussher in 1636, and Buckland in particular, with his theological background, was reluctant to entertain alternative hypotheses. For example, in his excavations in the Paviland Cave on the south coast of the Gower Peninsula he discovered the skeleton of a young man in deposits of breccia, or cemented scree. The breccia he rightly recognized as the product of cold-climate weathering. The bones of the skeleton had been coated with red ochre and were in association with the skull of a mammoth, also recognized by Buckland as a cold-climate species, and of high antiquity. But Buckland was at pains to explain the human skeleton as that of a Roman-Briton, and the mammoth as having been dug up by the Romans and redeposited with the burial. Radiocarbon dating of the skeleton has now shown what had long been suspected, namely that the skeleton dates to the Upper Palaeolithic.[27]

Agassiz, in addition to his work on glaciology, was also a first class zoologist, best known for his studies on living and fossil fishes. But his views on the origin of species were opposed to those of the evolutionists. Rather did he believe in creation at centres isolated from each other, with related genera and species being linked by thought categories of a supreme intelligence. He was also a believer in the multiple origin of the races of man, a view which accorded well with the religious trends of the time. It was not until Darwin's *The Origin of Species by Means of Natural Selection* was published in 1859 that the biological climate of opinion was ready to receive the evidence of sites such as Paviland for the antiquity of man.

At about the same time, a new theory of geological processes was being formulated. Between 1830 and 1833, Charles Lyell, a pupil of Buckland's, published the three volumes of his *Principles of Geology*, a work which profoundly influenced Darwin in that it did away with the need for geological catastrophes and special creation, advocating instead the 'Principle of Uniformitarianism'. This stated, simply, that the formation of rocks and sediments had taken place by processes which are still operating today—'the present is the key to the past'— and it gave strong support to the acceptance of biological and genetic continuity in the fossil record which was to be a corner stone of Darwinism.

The importance and antiquity of the earliest discoveries of human artefacts in drift deposits, such as the hand-axe found in gravels near Gray's Inn Lane, London, about 1690 and the finds made by John Frere in the Hoxne lake beds in 1797,[28] were not fully realized at the time. It was not until the discovery in the 1830s by a French customs official, Boucher de Perthes, of hand-axes in the Somme gravels and their final confirmation in, significantly, 1859 by British geologists that the contemporaneity of man with the deposition of the drift was accepted.[29] And this was only made possible by the work of Lyell, Darwin and others in their elucidation of the true temporal structure of geological and evolutionary processes.

The trend to Uniformitarianism and evolution seemed absolute, and certainly the two theories gave strong support to each other. Evolution needed the temporal and biological continuum which Lyell's theory made possible. And from this came the concept of the 'zone fossil.' Rocks of a particular age over a wide area of the globe were seen to contain similar or identical species of animal or plant which could be placed in an evolutionary sequence, and the techniques of dating rocks in widely separated localities by means of their fossils thus grew up.

But in the Pleistocene caution is needed in the rigid acceptance of these views. In the first place, the time scale is much shorter than in other geological periods, while the degree of environmental change is greater. We cannot see the high cliffs of boulder clay along the Norfolk coast, or the U-valleys of Lakeland with their sheer rock walls, the granite trail from Ailsa Craig or the mighty sea lochs of the western Highlands without feeling the drama and immediacy of the Pleistocene ice. The ice sheets were a catastrophe which destroyed animals, plants and soils—whole landscapes—over thousands of square miles. Glacier ice and arctic desert alternated with periods of temperate climate. The fauna and flora migrated unceasingly across the European stage on which these geological events were enacted. Small wonder that Agassiz, as one of the propounders of the glacial theory, should adhere so strongly to the theory of Catastrophism.

The Pleistocene is unique too in that evolution of plant and animal species has been slow relative to the time scale involved. The main differences between successive interglacial faunas and floras are due to extinctions, particularly of characteristic pre-Pleistocene species, to slight climatic and environmental differences, and to chance. Evolution, as opposed simply to changes in the distribution and abundance of species, appears to have been virtually confined to the mammals. Plants, insects and molluscs show little or no change. The zone fossil principle, as originally envisaged, can only be applied to those groups which show a linear evolutionary development over the relevant time range. But in restricted areas, faunal and floral differences other than of an evolutionary kind can be used as an index of age so long as we are able to date such differences by independent means in the first instance.[30]

But although evolution is not common to all groups of organisms in the Pleistocene, in those in which it did occur, it did so with surprising speed. The voles show this best, due partly to their generalized structure and partly to their short generation interval. But larger mammals, particularly the prolific herbivores such as elephants, deer and hippos, also evolved. So too did man. And it is difficult to divorce these phenomena from those of faunal migration and change which were intimately associated with the catastrophic waxing and waning of the ice sheets. Pleistocene populations were constantly under environmental stress, a feature which, as propounded by Darwin, is a prerequisite of evolution, and it is possible that were it not for the Ice Age the degree of achievement which we see today in man could not have been attained. Catastrophism, faunal migration and evolution are fundamental aspects of Pleistocene biology and stand intimately associated as the processes responsible for the rise of those who now dominate the earth—the herds of man.

4 The early Post-glacial

The beginning of the Post-glacial was marked by a number of environmental changes, the most important of which was the rise of temperature. This led to a variety of other events such as the ultimate melting of the glaciers, the rise of sea level and the isolation of Britain from the Continent, isostatic uplift in the north, the cessation of frost weathering thus allowing deep soils to form, the spread of woodland and the incoming of warmth-loving fauna such as red deer, wild ox or aurochs, and wild boar. Climatic amelioration had, of course, been going on since the beginning of the Late-glacial (i.e. from about 12,000 bc) but was temporarily halted by the brief cold spell of zone III (8800–8300 bc). It was not until the end of this period that the Post-glacial really began.

Climate

Of fundamental importance is climate. As in the previous interglacials, the Post-glacial or Flandrian can be divided into four zones (Table 4) corresponding to a pre-temperate, an early-temperate, a late-temperate and a post-temperate stage. At present we are in the late-temperate stage, the post-temperate stage being hypothetical. There is no reason why the series of glacials and interglacials which Britain has previously witnessed should continue, but in view of the fact that we are in a period of deteriorating rather than ameliorating climate there is a strong possibility that a further glaciation will ensue. This classification has been proposed by Richard West[1] and is a formalization of a previous scheme put forward by the Swedish botanist von Post in which a threefold division of the Post-glacial was suggested. The first, or protocratic, stage was characterized by the appearance and spread of warmth-loving trees; the second, or mediocratic, stage by their predominance; and the third, or terminocratic, stage by their decline.

Other, more complex schemes have been put forward but all have recognized a fundamental attribute of the Post-glacial, the Climatic Optimum, a period when mean annual temperature in Britain was higher by two or three degrees centigrade than that of today. The evidence for this period is largely biological, resting on the fact that a number of species of plant and animal formerly had more northerly ranges.[2] An example is the freshwater tortoise, *Emys orbicularis*, whose present and past ranges are shown in Fig. 27.

This map was first published in 1907 by R. F. Scharff in his fascinating study *European Animals: their Geological History and Geographical Distribution*, and was considered by him as evidence for climatic change: '. . . after the Glacial period a milder climate prevailed, which induced southern species to travel north only to become extinct again on a subsequent change of climate'.[3] Another early recognition of the Climatic Optimum was made by the Irish naturalist Robert Lloyd Praeger through his study of the molluscs in deposits exposed in Belfast Harbour, published in 1896.[4] He pointed out that raised beach and estuarine deposits which had formed in the middle of the Post-glacial contained molluscan species today no longer present in the area and restricted to more southerly regions. Since then, botanical work and radiocarbon dating have refined our concept of the Climatic Optimum. For example, lime, the most thermophilous of our native trees, first appears in Britain towards the end of the seventh millennium bc and maintained a wide distribution for about 2000 years. During this time, tree belts were higher than today, deciduous forest extending to altitudes of 750 metres.[5] It has been shown too through the study of past distributions of species which are restricted by different aspects of climate that the Climatic Optimum was a period of increase in both summer and winter warmth.[6]

Table 4.   Post-glacial (Flandrian) zonation schemes compared.

Sparks and West (1972)		*von Post (1946) Iversen (1958)*	*Blytt (1876) and Sernander (1908)*	Pollen zones		
					Great Britain	*Ireland*
(Fl IV) (Post-temperate)		(Cryocratic)				
Fl III	Late-temperate	Terminocratic	Decreasing warmth	Sub-atlantic	VIII	IX
				—————1200 bc———		
				Sub-boreal	VIIb	VIII
				————3200 bc———		
Fl II	Early-temperate	Mediocratic	Climatic Optimum	Atlantic	VIIa	VII
				————5500 bc———		
Fl I	Pre-temperate	Protocratic	Increasing warmth	Boreal	VI	VI
				—7000 bc—		
					V	V
				————7500 bc———		
				Pre-boreal	IV	IV
				————8300 bc———		
Late-glacial					I–III	I–III

But not all changes in the distribution and abundance of organisms can be attributed to climate. An animal or plant living at the edge of its climatic range is in a delicate balance with the environment and needs optimum conditions in other factors—food, living space—if it is to survive. Alteration to the detriment of the species in *any* of these factors may cause a contraction in range having all the appearance of a response to climatic change when none in fact has taken place. In the Post-glacial particularly, man must be taken into consideration. Species of large mammal for example, such as the lion, elephant and hippo, have been absent from Britain throughout the Post-glacial although present during previous interglacials when similar climatic conditions obtained. Their absence is thought to be due to progressive extermination by man directly by hunting and for considerations such as safety, and indirectly by the destruction of suitable habitats through

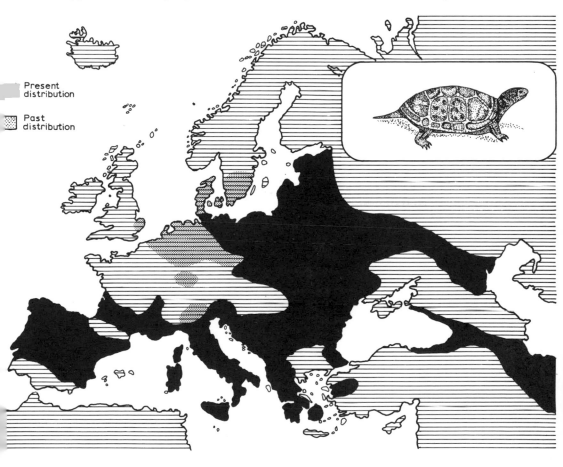

Present distribution

Past distribution

Fig. 27.   Present and past distribution of the freshwater tortoise, *Emys orbicularis*. (After Scharff, 1907, Fig. 57)

the creation of farmland. As James Ritchie has pointed out in his book, *The Influence of Man on Animal Life in Scotland*, published in 1920:

... since ... the animal world is no loose aggregate of living things, but a closely woven fabric of interdependent lives, man's crude meddling many a time brings in its train changes he little thought of, his snapping of a thread in the fabric deranges more than he could have dreamed, the pattern of the whole.[7]

Superimposed on the trend to increased warmth is a series of minor climatic setbacks, first recognized in the Alps from the evidence of pollen analysis and of moraines associated with the Alpine glaciers.[8] These may be a continuation, with decreasing intensity, of the Late-glacial series. They are characterized by the readvance of certain glaciers, a lowering of the tree line and an associated opening up of the landscape. Human agency has been ruled out due to the high altitude of the sites and the absence of contemporary settlement. These episodes have not been recognized for certain in Britain perhaps because the relevant high altitude sites have not been studied. Forest recession during the sixth and fifth millennia has been noted, for example at Stump Cross[9] in the Yorkshire Pennines, but it is not clear whether this is of climatic or anthropogenic origin, and if climatic, whether it is due to a decrease of temperature or an increase in rainfall, the latter leading to the formation of peat and the consequent destruction of woodland (p. 94).

Indeed, in a discussion of climate, rainfall cannot be divorced from temperature as a number of our climatic indicators are susceptible to the relative humidity of the atmosphere which is a function of both these factors. The early part of the Post-glacial (zone Fl I) is considered to have been relatively dry; towards the end of the zone a period of pronounced dryness is indicated by a fall in lake levels and the reworking by wave action of edge deposits. This took place between 6000 and 5500 bc at a time when the rise of temperature to the Climatic Optimum was beginning[10] (Table 5).

Subsequently, at the beginning of what is known as the Atlantic period (p. 79), there was a marked rise in precipitation coinciding with the rise of the sea to more or less its present level and to the flooding of the Straits of Dover. The two events are almost certainly related, the nearness of the sea and the establishment of total marine circulation around Britain leading to increased oceanicity of climate. Lake levels rose, the moisture-loving alder became abundant (Fig. 47) and a variety of semi-aquatic deposits, notably peat and tufa (p. 76) began to form or showed renewed growth (Table 5).

Peat is of considerable importance for Post-glacial stratigraphical studies. It consists largely of undecomposed plant material, although animal remains, notably insects, are sometimes found within it. In

Table 5.   Some important events in the Post-glacial.

Climate	Sea level	Scottish peat bogs	Forest vegetation	Archaeology
General Deterioration				
High rainfall Blanket peat formation	Stable	Upper Turbarian	Increase of ash, birch, hornbeam and beech Decline of lime	Iron Age, Late and Middle Bronze Age
—1200 bc—				
Low rainfall Wind-blown deposits		Upper Forestian	Increase of ash and birch	Early Bronze Age
—2000 bc—				
Declining warmth	Isostatic uplift in the north Stable in	?	Neolithic forest clearance Elm decline	Neolithic Introduction of agriculture
—3200 bc—	the south			
Climatic Optimum				
Warm and wet Blanket peat and tufa formation	Slight rise continues Breaching of Straits of Dover	Lower Turbarian	Mixed oak forest. Increase of alder Mesolithic clearances	Mesolithic communities Sauveterrian and Maglemosian
—5500 bc—				
General Amelioration				
Warm and dry	Main eustatic rise	Lower Forestian	Mixed oak forest with hazel and pine	
—7500 bc—	Low sea			
Increasing warmth	North Sea dry		Birch and pine	Maglemosian Creswellian survivals
—8300 bc—				
Late-glacial				Upper Palaeolithic

Denmark, and very occasionally in the British Isles (p. 165), the bodies of men and women complete with clothing, skin, hair and stomach contents have been recovered from the peat so excellent are the conditions of preservation. 'There is a strange power in bog water which prevents decay. Bodies have been found which must have lain in bogs for more than a thousand years, but which, though admittedly somewhat shrunken and brown, are in other respects unchanged.'[11] Preservation is due to a variety of factors. Waterlogging and the absence of oxygen, together with the often acidic, or sour, nature of the deposits prevent bacterial decay. In the case of the bog burials, a partial tanning of the skin through the release of tannin from the bog vegetation has also aided preservation.

Essentially there are two types of peat, topogenous and ombrogenous.[12] Topogenous peat forms in places of impeded drainage such as valleys, coastal flats and infilled lake basins, and its growth is controlled by the topography of the situation. This type of peat is a poor indicator of rainfall change as the water supply comes mainly from the ground, and factors such as sea level may influence the growth rate. Ombrogenous peat, on the other hand, forms in situations of high rainfall and its growth is controlled solely by precipitation. Topography is important only in so far as high ground engenders high rainfall. Otherwise it spreads over valley and mountain top alike, a feature which has given rise to the name 'blanket bog'.

In the Pennines and other upland regions of the British Isles, the growth of blanket peat originated at about 5500 bc and this is generally thought to indicate the onset of increased precipitation at this time.[13] But locally, as in the Cumberland lowland, ombrogenous peat was forming as early as 7000 bc.

Another type of deposit, the formation of which is climatically controlled, is tufa.[14] This is a chemical precipitate consisting of calcium carbonate (lime) which is widespread in the southern part of Britain and in Ireland, although not generally forming at the present day. Chemically it is indistinguishable from stalagmite (p. 23), the only difference being a terminological one, stalagmite forming in caves, tufa in the open air. Tufa is more suitable as a climatic indicator since it is free from the influences of the local humidity extremes which build up in caves. It forms under conditions of high rainfall and high temperature, and the optimum period for these in Britain was between 5500 and 3000 bc (Fl II), the Atlantic period. A key site is Cherhill in north Wiltshire at the foot of the Chalk downs.[15] Radiocarbon assay of charcoal below and above a tufa deposit gave a time bracket of 5280 ± 140 bc and 2765 ± 90 bc. But, as with blanket peat, we must not expect all tufa deposits to be synchronous. Unpublished radiocarbon dates from east Kent indicate that tufa was forming at the beginning of the Post-glacial,[16] and similar evidence is forthcoming from south Wales. At the other extreme, there are various places in the west of Britain where deposits resembling tufa are still forming today.

The local environment of tufa deposition was tree-shaded swamp as indicated by the land snails in which the deposits abound. The site at Cherhill is of added interest in that immediately prior to the deposition of the tufa the area had been occupied by a group of hunter/gatherer people who had left evidence of their occupation in the form of flint tools and animal bones. The swamping of the site, which resulted in the formation of the tufa and was a direct result of the rainfall increase, was no doubt responsible for the abandonment of the area by man. We find, too, at the base of the blanket peat in many upland parts of Britain profuse scatters of flint implements, and here again it is probable that the growth of blanket peat caused abandonment of favoured hunting grounds. But more of this later.

Short-term fluctuations of rainfall, possibly linked to those of temperature, also took place. The main evidence comes from standstill phases in the growth of ombrogenous peat. In a section through a peat bog these appear as bands of strongly humified material in which macroscopic plant remains are scarce (p. 145). Bacterial decay is the main destructive agent, and takes place during periods of dry climate when peat growth is thus retarded. Build-up is replaced by chemical and biological weathering which leads eventually to the formation of soil. Resumption of peat growth, leading to the formation of 'recurrence surfaces', takes place when conditions of high rainfall return.

Evidence of a more indirect kind for variation in the precipitation/ evaporation ratio in the early part of the Post-glacial has come from a study of lake sediments. The halogen, or salt, content of lake bottom deposits in the English Lake District is considered to derive ultimately from the sea in the prevailing rain-bearing winds. Marked fluctuations which have been recorded in halogen values are thought to reflect variations in oceanicity through time.[17]

Vegetation

The earliest work on vegetational history was done in Scottish and Scandinavian peat bogs, and was dependent entirely on the evidence of macroscopic remains.[18] James Geikie, one of the two Geikie brothers whose brilliant geological studies were both wide-ranging and precise, was among the first to describe the remains of forest trees preserved in the peat (Plate 8). He showed how these occupied two horizons which he called the Lower Forestian and the Upper Forestian and which consisted of silver birch and scots pine respectively (Fig. 28). They were separated by a zone of peat composed mainly of the moss, *Sphagnum*, and the sedge, *Eriophorum*, the latter a familiar plant in upland Britain and more commonly known as cotton grass. Above the Upper Forestian lay a further *Sphagnum* peat, and these two peat horizons were termed the Lower and Upper Turbarian, a word deriving from the Latin, *turbaria*, turf. (Turbary is the right to take peat from another's land.) At the beginning of the sequence, below the Lower Forestian, was a peaty horizon in which plants of open ground prevailed. Among these, low prostrate shrubs such as dwarf birch, *Betula nana*, and various species of willow, *Salix*, were conspicuous, together with the mountain avens, *Dryas octopetala*, a plant now generally confined to mountain ledges and crevices, and bare plateau

Plate 8.   Tree stumps exposed by peat cutting on Millstone Grit, Co. Clare.

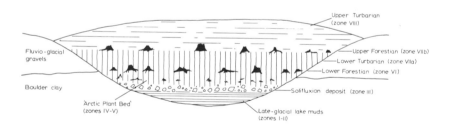

Fig. 28.   Generalized section through a Scottish peat bog.

areas such as the Burren (p. 140). This horizon was called the 'arctic plant bed' and was recognized as the transition zone between the glacial and Post-glacial periods.

At its most complete, the sequence was underlain by Late-glacial lake muds, glacial outwash deposits of sand and gravel, and, at the very base, boulder clay (Fig. 28).

Geikie's investigations took place in the later part of the nineteenth century. He was followed by F. J. Lewis and the Swedish botanist G. Samuelsson who correlated the Scottish sequence with the better-known scheme of Blytt (1876) and Sernander (1908) already established for Scandinavia (Table 4). In climatic terms, the Pre-boreal and Boreal periods of this scheme correlate with the period of increasing warmth (Fl I) and are characterized by the spread of various types of woodland into Britain (Fig. 47), first birch, then pine, and later a succession of more warmth-demanding trees—oak, hazel, elm, alder and, finally, lime. Many of the trees of the Lower Forestian were probably growing on drying bog surfaces towards the end of the Boreal period which, as we saw above, was a time of climatic dryness. The Atlantic period is equivalent to the Lower Turbarian and, locally, is marked by the destruction of woodland by peat growth. This was due to the pronounced rise in precipitation of the period which, in areas free from peat, and particularly in river valleys, brought about the spread and increase of alder. The period too roughly coincides with the Climatic Optimum (Fl II).

The Sub-boreal and Sub-atlantic periods reflect a similar sequence of dryness when woodland, this time largely of pine, spread over the drying bog surfaces, followed by deterioration to wetter, cooler, conditions when renewed peat growth took place. Both periods fall within zone Fl III, the period of declining warmth.

Pollen analysis has given precision to this scheme and the fine zonation of the Post-glacial which has often been used as a chronological yardstick (although now largely replaced by radiocarbon dating) is based on the relative abundance of different tree species as revealed by this method. In England, the zones are numbered IV to VIII and are a direct continuation of the Late-glacial zones I to III (Fig. 47). In Ireland, the zonation scheme is slightly different (Table 4).

The early vegetational history of the Post-glacial is represented at Star Carr[19] in the Vale of Pickering, north-east Yorkshire (Fig. 29). Here was discovered a camp site of early Post-glacial hunter/gatherers, situated on the slopes of a low hillock of glacial gravel by the edge of a former lake. The site is now covered by peat which has since been drained and converted into arable land. The human occupation horizon is dated by a single radiocarbon determination to 7538 ± 350 bc. This is a time when man was becoming adapted to a forest environment, and the term Mesolithic is usually applied to these

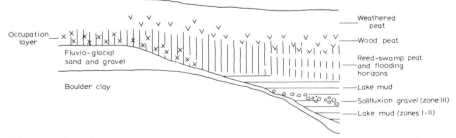

Fig. 29. Star Carr. Diagrammatic section through the occupation horizon and lake-edge sediments. (After Clark, 1954, Fig. 27a)

people[20]—people of Post-glacial age who had been forced to give up the specialized herd-hunting practices of the Upper Palaeolithic but who had not yet discovered or adopted the use of agriculture.

Star Carr was a camp site covering an area of about 250 square metres and consisting of a scatter of antler, bone and flint tools, the waste debris from the manufacture of these, and the bones of various food animals. A brushwood platform of axe-felled birch trees and branches bridged the gap between the settlement and the open water of the lake. This is the earliest example of artificially felled trees yet known. The occupation debris lay directly on solifluxion gravel of Late-glacial origin. The lake edge was bordered by reed swamp which continued to grow throughout the occupation of the site as was shown by the presence of reeds which had pushed their way up through the branches of the platform. Pollen analysis (Fig. 30) showed that the hillsides and drier parts of the vale were forested with closed birchwoods; pine had begun to establish itself and willows grew nearer to the water. But there was little evidence in the pollen record of human interference with the vegetation, in spite of the felling for the birchwood platform and the utilization of birch bark for resin—the latter for attaching small flint arrowheads to their wooden shafts. Just above the occupation horizon, however, the birch shows a temporary but nevertheless noticeable decline which may be a local response to man's activities on the site.

Until recently it has been felt that Palaeolithic and Mesolithic populations were too small either to exert any appreciable influence on the vegetation or indeed to require that such changes took place. But in the last ten years or so we have come to realize, notably through the work of G. W. Dimbleby, I. G. Simmons and A. G. Smith, that Mesolithic communities may indeed have altered their environment over a wide area.[21] In the case of Star Carr and other sites in the Vale of Pickering, A. G. Smith has argued that the rise of hazel and the

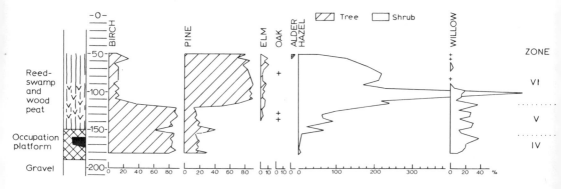

Fig. 30.   Star Carr. Tree and shrub pollen diagram. Shrub pollen as a percentage of total tree pollen. (After Clark, 1954, Fig. 27b)

decline of birch which took place at the horizon of human occupation is of anthropogenic origin. This is an important problem since the vegetational changes in question mark the zone IV/V transition and are generally felt to have been caused by climatic amelioration. At some sites layers of charcoal, possibly originating from forest fires, coincide with the expansion of hazel; and as Smith points out, hazel is a fire-resistant tree, springing up readily from burnt stumps. At Flixton in the Vale of Pickering the charcoal layer was overlain by sand and clay suggesting that burning was followed by soil erosion. Man cannot be seen as the sole cause of these changes because of the large number of sites from which they have been recorded where there is no evidence of human occupation. Where man was involved, he acted simply to increase the rate of change of processes already in operation.

There was considerable variation over the British Isles in the details of forest development during the early Post-glacial.[22] In England and Wales the Pre-boreal is characterized by birch with some pine (Fig. 30). During the early Boreal (zones V and VIa) pine rose to dominance and there are high values for hazel. The latter may have occurred as hazel scrub below the forest canopy or even as pure stands of hazel woodland; it is not possible to be certain about this. Oak and elm successively became important (VIa and b), and by the end of the Boreal period (VIc) lime had become a characteristic member of the forest. By this stage, pine and birch had become sparse, and the vegetation was of the mixed-deciduous-forest type familiar to us today. In Scotland the sequence is simpler. Birch alone predominates in the Pre-boreal and persists strongly, particularly in the north and west; some of the vestigial stands of birch which we see today in the Highlands may be direct derivatives from the early Post-glacial woodland. Birch, pine and hazel are the only common species in the Boreal period, oak and elm not becoming abundant until Atlantic times. Pine was an important element in eastern Scotland, but lime, the most thermophilous of our forest trees, was sparse or absent over large areas. Alder, as in the south, was a characteristic tree of the Atlantic period. The most noticeable features of the Irish sequence are the late rise to dominance of pine towards the end of the Boreal period, and the complete absence of lime.

Locally too there was variation in the forest composition from place to place. But it is difficult to work out vegetational structure from the pollen record due to the wide area from which the pollen 'rain' derives. As we saw above, it is uncertain whether hazel was occurring as an understorey in the early Boreal forest or as pure stands of woodland. But by considering their modern requirements we can make a few guesses about the distribution of some of the species. Pine, for example, was probably common on well-drained sandy soils and less frequent on the heavy clays of the English Midlands. It is a characteristic species of the drier parts of blanket bogs and occurs too in the transitional vegetation during the onset of peat formation above fen. The prevalence of pine stumps in peat deposits, as opposed to those of other trees, may thus be of local significance, and it is for this reason that pollen is preferable as an index of widespread vegetational change. On calcareous soils, elm, lime, ash and yew are favoured and it is likely that one or more of these thrived on chalk and limestone areas of southern and eastern England during the Atlantic period. Oak and hawthorn charcoals are frequent on Neolithic sites in these areas, and pollen analysis of chalk soils and of organic deposits adjacent to the escarpments has shown all the major forest trees to have been present.[23] But the beech, although today a characteristic tree of the downland, did not become widespread until the Iron Age. In Ireland, G. F. Mitchell has suggested that elm was growing in pure stands on lime-rich soils.[24]

One of the most significant results of pollen analysis has been the demonstration that much of the British Isles was once forested. This is a striking conclusion, particularly when we realize that it applies to such open and wind-swept areas as the North York Moors, the Pennines, the Outer Isles and the East Anglian Breckland. During the Atlantic period deciduous forest extended to at least 750 metres (2500 feet) above sea level on steep well-drained mountain slopes, and only above this did open habitats prevail.[25] Elsewhere, open vegetation was restricted to areas too unstable or otherwise not suited to the growth of trees, such as cliffs, active screes, reed swamps, growing bogs, river flood plains and gravel banks, and a variety of littoral habitats—shingle bars, sand dunes and the immediate coastal hinterland where salt spray inhibited tree growth. Grassland, so familiar a part of the British scene today, probably did not exist, apart from the montane type and that along the coast. The destruction of the Post-glacial forests and the creation of open ground was brought about largely by man, although the development of blanket bog and the Post-glacial marine transgression were no doubt contributory factors. When one sees the stumps of ancient forests revealed in the peat cuttings on bleak and desolate Rannoch Moor or a Connemara hillside the concept of vegetational change becomes very real (Plate 8).

But a fundamental defect of pollen analysis is that it is not generally applicable to calcareous deposits and soils. The reasons for this are not fully understood for pollen does occur in chalky deposits and is often well preserved; but it is never present in quantity,[26] and pollen analysts are wary of counting pollen in low concentrations due to the possibilities of differential destruction of the grains of certain species. As an alternative, the shells of land snails, which are often prolific in chalk soils and other lime-rich deposits, have proved very suitable.[27]

Through the analysis of these, as we showed in the case of the Swans-combe deposits, the general nature of the vegetation cover of a site can be determined. In Britain, the technique has been applied to the Chalk Downs, the Cotswolds and the shell sand areas of the west coast and Orkney, and faunas from Boreal and Atlantic deposits in these areas have demonstrated their formerly forested nature. This is a very significant fact in view of their importance in the settlement of early farming communities, but one to which, because of their very open nature today, it is difficult to accustom ourselves. We cannot unfortunately define the species composition of these woodlands but the very fact of their existence at all is remarkable.

The level of the sea

The frontispiece of Sir Charles Lyell's great *Principles of Geology* shows three columns of the ruined Temple of Jupiter Serapis near Naples, and high up around the columns at one level are numerous holes made by the marine stone-boring mollusc, *Lithodomus*. The zone affected is now well above the reach of the sea, and from this, Lyell deduced two changes in the relative level of sea and land since the construction of the temple. These changes are thought to have been due to up-and-down movements of land masses against a generally stable sea level, movements which are described as 'tectonic'.

In Britain, tectonic movements have taken place in the past and are still going on today as a result of two processes.[28] The first of these is confined to the southern part of the North Sea basin in which subsidence has led to the accumulation of marine deposits of Pleistocene age hundreds of metres thick. The cause of subsidence is unknown, but a side effect of the build up of these sediments is that they are becoming compressed, so that subsidence apart, downward movement of the deposits has occurred. Indeed, compaction of all marine deposits must be taken into account when assessing the height at which they were laid down. On the whole, compaction and long-term tectonic subsidence have affected southern and eastern Britain. But the younger deposits, those of Post-glacial age, have only been slightly affected; often, localized movements have been of more significance than those due to an overall subsidence of the land.[29]

The other tectonic process which has resulted in relative land/sea-level changes is isostatic uplift which has taken place in the north of Britain as a result of the loss of weight consequent upon the melting of the ice sheet. This has been greatest in the western Grampians (Fig. 6), and it can be seen that the Main Post-glacial Shoreline peripheral to this area has been uplifted to a maximum of 15 metres OD since its formation.[30] This shoreline is the '25-foot beach' of earlier writers, but the term is unsatisfactory owing to the variable height above sea level of the beach. It was probably formed during the Atlantic period when the main eustatic rise of sea level had been attained (see below). Earlier shorelines, of Late-glacial date, are known, the most pronounced of which is of zone III (Loch Lomond Readvance) age. Of more recent origin, is a series of beaches lying at a lower level than the Main Post-glacial Shoreline. And tide-gauge records show that the process of isostatic recovery is still going on at a rate of 2 to 3 millimetres per year.

But the most widely represented sea-level change in the British Isles is the world-wide eustatic rise which took place as a result of the return of water to the sea on the melting of the Pleistocene ice. The isolation of Britain from the Continent, the formation of numerous islands, the deposition of thick beds of estuarine clay, the drowning of river valleys and the submergence of coastal forests were the main results of this important event, and pollen analysis of estuarine clays has shown that the major rise took place in the late Boreal and early Atlantic periods. A key area is Swansea Bay on the south Wales coast[31] where estuarine clays and silts with interbedded peaty horizons extend to −18 metres OD. Locally, the succession reflects a series of alternating estuarine and terrestrial environments on which is super-imposed the more general, secular, rise of the sea. The sequence is overlain by peat of Atlantic and Sub-boreal age.

In the area of isostatic recovery the succession was naturally more complex. With the melting of the ice, the Late-glacial shoreline was uplifted and peat formed in lowlying areas. For a long time, the uplift of the land kept pace with the rising sea, and there was little submergence. But late in the Boreal period, inundation took place (Fig. 31), and this is the time when the carse clays of the Firths of Tay, Forth and Clyde were laid down. Carse is a Scottish term for the alluvial riverside plains which border the tidal reaches of the major rivers and which were uplifted by the continuing isostatic recovery late on in Atlantic times when the rate of eustatic rise had

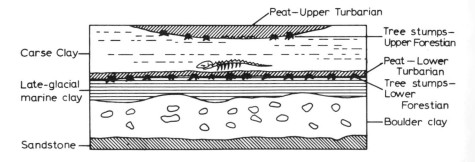

Fig. 31.   Section through Blair Drummond Moss, Perthshire. (After Lacaille, 1954, Fig. 26ii)

slowed. It was at this time too that the beach deposits of the Main Post-glacial Shoreline were formed, and vertical sections through these frequently show an upward transition from estuarine clay to beach shingle. The classic example is that described by Lloyd Praeger from Belfast harbour.[32] The beach material is often derived through longshore drift, for often the nearest rock outcrops are many miles away, and it can be seen as the final depositional stage in the succession to the terrestrial state.

These sequences have given us some of our most spectacular instances of environmental change. In Blair Drummond Moss, for example, a peat bog some 4 kilometres west of Stirling in the Forth

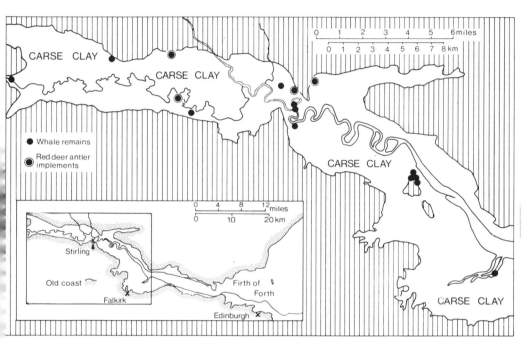

Fig. 32. Distribution of whale remains and red deer antler implements in the Forth estuary. (After Clark, 1952, Fig. 64)

Valley,[33] boulder clay is overlain by marine clays of the Late-glacial sea (Fig. 31). This is succeeded by a land surface which represents the early Post-glacial emergence, and *in situ* tree stumps indicate the forested nature of the area at this time. Of Boreal age, this horizon is equivalent to Geikie's Lower Forestian. A thin layer of peat overlies the tree stumps, and then follows a thick deposit of carse clay in which are preserved the bones of whales. Many skeletons have been found in the carse clay of the Forth, animals no doubt stranded by the falling tide when far from the open sea (Fig. 32), and J. G. D. Clark has shown how Mesolithic man probably took advantage of these occurrences for perforated antler implements, one of them an axe mounted on a long wooden handle, have been found in intimate association with the skeletons.[34] Tree stumps of the Upper Forestian overlie the carse clays at Blair Drummond, indicating the continuation of the Post-glacial emergence. There is a prehistoric trackway at this level, in a similar stratigraphical position to those in the Somerset Levels (p. 145). Moss peat brings the succession to an end.

The recovery of blocks of peat or 'moorlog' in trawl nets from the bed of the southern part of the North Sea containing the remains of terrestrial plants and insects is clear evidence for the former presence of land. Pollen analysis of moorlog samples indicates a Pre-boreal and Boreal age for this land surface which is now known to have extended as a lowlying, marshy, plain from the east coast of Britain to Denmark and southern Sweden (Fig. 17). A dramatic discovery, made by the master of the fishing vessel *Colinda*, was a lump of moorlog dredged up between the Leman and Ower sand banks and found to contain a Mesolithic barbed point of bone—convincing evidence of the former presence of man on this extension of the North European Plain, long since submerged by the rising waters of the Post-glacial sea.[35]

Fauna

The rise of temperature and the destruction of the grassland and other open-landscape habitats of the Ice Age by the spread of woodland had a profound impact on the fauna. The reindeer, the giant Irish deer and the arctic fox were exterminated, and the horse very much reduced in numbers, to be replaced by warmth-loving and forest forms such as the roe deer, red deer, elk, wild boar and aurochs. Higher temperatures and increased habitat diversity made for a more varied fauna than that of the Late-glacial, and a return to the conditions of the previous interglacial periods. But some of the more exotic large mammals, notably the elephants, the rhinoceros, hippos and the lion, did not re-enter Britain or indeed Europe although quite capable of surviving the British climate of Atlantic times, and this must be seen as due to the effect of man in the world as a whole (p. 73).

In addition to the changes in species composition and diversity induced by climate, vegetation and man, the transition from tundra to forest brought about changes in the structure of the fauna and its distribution in space and time. A considerable quantity of leafy foliage which had hitherto been available to animals at ground level now existed high out of reach as the forest canopy, unobtainable to cattle and other browsing animals. There was also a reduction in the amount of ground space available to animals in that a large area was now occupied by the trunks of trees and impenetrable undergrowth.

Grazing land was not merely reduced in area; what remained was broken up into discrete patches—on mountain plateaux, river flood plains, etc. (p. 82)—separated by vast tracts of forest. Per unit area it is difficult to assess the effect of these changes on the size of the animal populations by comparison with those in the Ice Age, particularly in view of the opposing forces of the rising sea and the waning ice sheets, the one making for less land, the other for more. But it is probable that the large migratory herds of herbivorous mammals, which were the key to man's livelihood in the Upper Palaeolithic, were not to be seen again in Britain until the introduction some 4000 years later of the flocks and herds of immigrant transhumantic farming communities. Thus although the amelioration of climate and the absence of ice sheets presented a more equable environment for man than that of the glacial period, radical changes in hunting techniques and life style were necessary. The easily culled herds of reindeer had been replaced by more diffuse populations of red deer and aurochs, animals too which were far less receptive to man's presence and thus less easy to exploit. A greater range of animals existed and these included not only the large land mammals, but smaller woodland creatures such as the marten, polecat and squirrel adapted to life in trees, a whole variety of forest canopy birds, and aquatic animals such as fish, water fowl, beaver and otter.

Man

Man responded to these changes variously. He adapted his methods of hunting to the pursuit of individual animals rather than herds and began to make greater use of the bow and arrow. He widened his range in the quest for food and became less specialized, pursuing a greater variety of animals than in the Ice Age. It is inevitable too, although we have little evidence for this, that a more varied plant diet was exploited than was possible in the sub-arctic tundra.

The earliest forest-dwelling Mesolithic culture in Britain is the Maglemosian, named after the type site of Maglemose (literally 'big bog') in Denmark. It is classically associated with forest, marsh and reed-swamp habitats, and, as far as we can tell, adapted readily to the changed environment of early Post-glacial times. The equipment (Fig. 34) consisted of small flint blades or microliths, some of which were mounted as composite arrowheads, engraving tools, or burins, used for working bone and antler, and the bone and antler tools themselves—mainly barbed projectile points. Chipped flint axes make their first appearance in the archaeological record, and these were used for dealing with timber.

The best-known Maglemosian site is Star Carr[36] where the main animals exploited were red deer (80 examples), roe deer (33), elk (11), ox (9) and pig (5), a fauna reflecting the prevailing forest vegetation. Other animals present were the pine marten, hedgehog, hare, badger, fox, beaver and domestic dog.[37] The latter is the earliest record of a domesticated animal in Britain, preceding by some 3500 years the introduction of other domesticated animals—cattle, sheep and pig—into Britain. It was probably used by Mesolithic man in hunting. The elk is characteristic of these early Post-glacial times, although hunted too in the Late-glacial,[38] but becomes rare by the Atlantic period. A number of antlers of this animal had been made into perforated mattock heads, one of which was found with the wooden handle still attached. It is not known what these were used for but it is likely that they served in the grubbing out of roots from the soil.

Star Carr was occupied during the winter and spring. This is indicated by the presence of red deer and elk antlers which had been cut from the skull, for it is only during this part of the year that the antlers are fully grown. Elk shed their antlers in January, red deer in April (Fig. 33), after which they are eaten by the deer unless immediately collected by man. Thus the presence of two elk skulls with the pedicels of shed antlers but no signs of new growth, and of shed red deer antlers further confirms the season of occupation. One may compare this with the evidence for summer occupation at Tornewton Cave in the Upper Palaeolithic as shown by a study of the reindeer antlers.

At Thatcham,[39] a Maglemosian site in the Kennet Valley, Berkshire, the animals included wild cat and horse. The latter is an unusual record for a Mesolithic site and was probably present as a rare survival from the open environment of the Late-glacial. Dog, beaver, pine marten, elk, roe and red deer, wild ox and pig were all present in addition to a variety of water fowl. It is probable that the beavers were building dams, for the occupation at Thatcham was on the edge of a former lake whose existence is hard to explain solely on local topographical grounds.

Other Maglemosian sites include a number in the tributaries of the Thames in Hertfordshire and Buckinghamshire, notably Broxbourne in the Lea Valley, and localities along the Colne. Mesolithic axes are recorded from Pembrokeshire, Cornwall, the Marlborough Downs of Wiltshire and various sites in the West Riding of Yorkshire. Their general distribution is thus essentially southern and eastern, being largely confined to the Lowland Zone of Britain (see p. 147) and in particular to wooded valleys. The British sites represent the western extreme of the Maglemosian culture province which extended across the then dry North European Plain to Denmark and as far east as Estonia. Classically, sites are of Pre-boreal or early Boreal age, occurring at a time prior to the full development of mixed deciduous forest. But Maglemosian influence has been seen in later cultures of probable

Atlantic age, such as those of the Sussex Weald (p. 103), and, at the other extreme, may find its origins in the Late-glacial period as suggested by a recent find of two bone points from Lancashire, in association with the skeleton of an elk.[40]

This then is the environmental background to the early Post-glacial hunting communities of Britain—a warming climate, a rising sea with yet marshy extensions to the east and links with Europe, an increasing variety of game and plant food, and the spread of all pervasive forest—conditions quite different from those experienced by Upper Palaeolithic man. These changes may have had a very great psychological impact

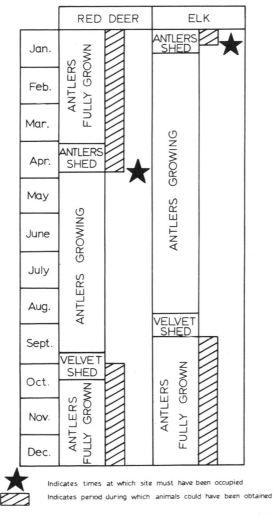

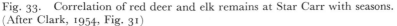

★ Indicates times at which site must have been occupied

▨ Indicates period during which animals could have been obtained

Fig. 33. Correlation of red deer and elk remains at Star Carr with seasons. (After Clark, 1954, Fig. 31)

on man, the equable conditions and diversity of habitats and food supply both obviating the need for specialization and also retarding development. Can we see in these Mesolithic peoples an echo of the Clactonian culture of long ago when man also lived in an equally congenial environment—the river valleys of southern England with their abundant herds of game? But as pointed out above (p. 53) the pressures of an interglacial (in this case the Post-glacial) environment may not have been any the less severe, and the sheer fact of having to adapt to them at all must have imposed a challenge. Nevertheless, it is a fact that not only in Britain but in Europe as a whole Mesolithic man has left little of artistic wealth. We have few clues to his beliefs, and burials, apart from a few examples such as the horrible nests of human skulls at Ofnet in Bavaria, are rare. There is nothing of the brilliance of the Upper Palaeolithic hunters living as they were in the stimulating landscape of the Ice Age, nor anything of the vital urgency with which later farming communities were to settle and cultivate the lands of western Europe and the British Isles.

5 The impact of man on the environment in mid Post-glacial times

The distribution of Mesolithic axes in Yorkshire is essentially a lowland one, peripheral to the high mass of the Moors (Fig. 34).[1] These tools are characteristic of Maglemosian industries, and, where stratified, occur in situations now covered with valley peat as at Star Carr and Thatcham. Their association with a forest environment and their use in felling trees, lopping branches and as woodworking tools in general seems undoubted.

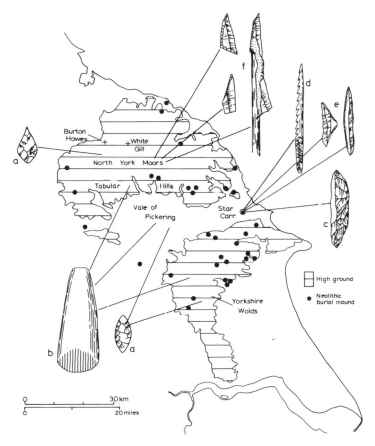

Fig. 34. Map of Yorkshire showing the distribution of various Mesolithic and Neolithic artefacts and of Neolithic burial mounds. a, Neolithic leaf-shaped arrowheads; b, Neolithic axe; c, Maglemosian axe; d, Maglemosian barbed bone point; e, Maglemosian microliths; f, Sauveterrian microliths, two reconstructed in wooden haft.

But on the high moors of north-east Yorkshire another group of industries, also Mesolithic but of different character, occurs. These lack the heavy axes, and contain instead a profusion of microliths. The name Sauveterrian—after the type site in France of Sauveterre-la-Lémance— has been applied to them, and they are considered to date from about 6000 bc.[2]

At White Gill, 380 metres above sea level on the North York Moors, microliths, long flint blades and a few larger tools such as scrapers, knives and gravers occur stratified beneath a thin layer of peaty raw humus (Fig. 36).[3] The latter is similar to peat in that it is largely organic, but its formation takes place in an aerobic situation in which bacterial activity is inhibited by the acidic state of the vegetation rather than by waterlogging. It is characteristic of grass-heath communities. Beneath the microlith level is the Post-glacial mineral soil consisting of the parent geological solid (in this case sandstone) weathered by frost action and chemical processes, and into which organic material is incorporated to form humus. This sequence of bedrock, mineral soil and raw humus (sometimes overlain by true peat), with Mesolithic flints at the junction of the mineral soil and raw humus, is one which occurs in a large number of upland situations, not only in the North York Moors, but in such areas as the Pennines, Dartmoor and parts of Wales. No such sites, however, have been found in Ireland.

The main technique which is applied to these upland Mesolithic sites to elucidate their environmental background is pollen analysis, but the methods and problems are different from those we have

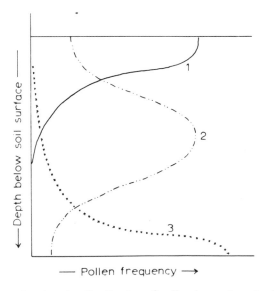

Fig. 35.   Diagram showing the distribution of pollen in a mineral soil. 1, recent pollen; 2, pollen of intermediate age; 3, ancient pollen.

previously met in the study of peat and lake sediments. In these latter deposits, pollen is stratified in the layers of sediment or peat as they are laid down, and there remains fixed. In soils, on the other hand, the pollen becomes combined as part of the humus and moves slowly down through the profile.[4] There is a certain amount of blurring in the pollen record with grains of different ages becoming incorporated at a single level (Fig. 35); but the broad pattern is a true representation, nevertheless, of vegetational changes which have gone on at the surface of the soil. Another important difference is that pollen in soils is generally local in origin, deriving from vegetation close at hand, whereas the pollen trapped in peat and lake sediments comes from a wider range. This means that the use of soil pollen diagrams for dating or zoning is not easy, particularly if a site is in open country where the representation of tree pollen is negligible. The main value of soil pollen diagrams is in giving precise information about a particular locality, and this is of crucial significance in the study of the environment of man whose habitat requirements and influence on the landscape are so often local. Our knowledge of the intricacies of soil pollen analysis in this country is almost entirely due to the pioneer work of G. W. Dimbleby.

The importance of the pollen sequence from White Gill (Fig. 36) is first, the demonstration that this part of the North York Moors was once forested, and second, that the process of deforestation leading to the present-day bleak and windswept landscape was initiated by hunting communities at a time long before agriculture was introduced into Britain. Each species in the diagram is represented by a double

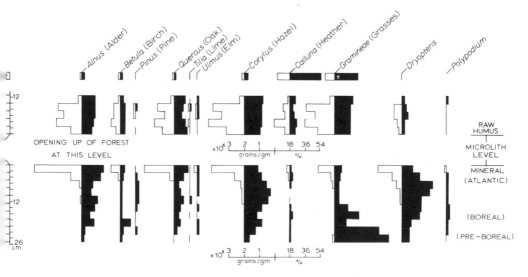

Fig. 36. White Gill, Stony Rigg, pollen diagram. The symbol in the grass curve indicates cereal pollen. (After Dimbleby, 1962, Fig. 30)

histogram, the left side being the absolute frequency of pollen, the right side the percentage of total pollen plus fern spores. In the lowest level, grasses predominate indicating an open landscape, probably of early Post-glacial (Pre-boreal) age. Trees soon become important, and a period of mixed deciduous forest with hazel and ferns as significant elements in the succession ensues. The decline of pine and rise of alder towards the surface of the mineral soil implies a mid Post-glacial (Atlantic) age for this horizon. The flint industry is thought to belong to this period and is comparable in this respect to similar industries elsewhere in Britain which have been dated by radiocarbon to the fifth millennium bc.

The pollen record in the raw humus above the microlith level indicates opening up of the forest. Grasses rise from 8 per cent to 20 per cent and heather shows a slight increase. These changes are not considered to have been caused by climate since the diagnostic species, elm and lime, which are susceptible to climatic deterioration, remain unchanged. Nor is there any development of blanket bog in the area which might have caused the destruction of trees. An anthropogenic cause is much more likely, and in the absence of heavy axes in the tool assemblages of the contemporary human cultures, fire is held to be the main agency. This is supported by the slight increase of birch and hazel, species which are fire-resistant, and indeed which generally spread into areas cleared by fire today. Further evidence of fire, and of woody plants, is the presence of charcoal of oak, alder, birch and hazel at the level of the microliths.[5]

We have already mentioned the fact that temporary periods of forest recession took place in parts of Europe during mid Post-glacial times (p. 74). In Britain, the decline of woodland in the Atlantic period is often associated with processes of soil deterioration and the inception of blanket bog growth. Pollen analysis on Kinder Scout in the southern Pennines showed that peat growth on high plateau areas had begun by the Boreal/Atlantic transition and was to be associated with the trend to high rainfall at this time.[6] At Stump Cross[7] near Grassington, also in the Pennines, Mesolithic flints were recovered from the organic filling of an ancient pool. Abundant charcoal was collected from the same level, and dated by radiocarbon to the mid fifth millennium bc. The pollen record indicated a generally forested environment but with open country beginning to take over above the microlith level. There was a sharp rise of hazel (evidence of fire?), an increase in grasses and heath plants, and an overall rise of non-tree pollen. It was considered by D. Walker who investigated this site, that the trend to openness was caused by the engulfing of the forest by blanket bog as a reaction to the increase in precipitation of the Atlantic period.

This view has been challenged by Dimbleby[8] who would see both the leaching of nutrients from the soil and the growth of blanket bog as products of human interference with the vegetation. Trees act as a drainage system for the soil, a full grown oak liberating several gallons of water per day by transpiration from its leaves, water which is brought up in the first place by the tree's root system (Fig. 37). Severance of this cycle is seen as leading to waterlogging of the soil, and thence to peat formation. In addition, trees bring up from the sub-surface layers nutrients, and in particular calcium compounds, which are ultimately returned to the soil in the leaf fall. Calcium is an important agent in binding the soil crumbs and in thus maintaining soil structure. Once this cycle is broken, the soil would have begun to degrade, especially if on poor parent material. A contributory factor may have been local compaction of the soil by herds of animals thus

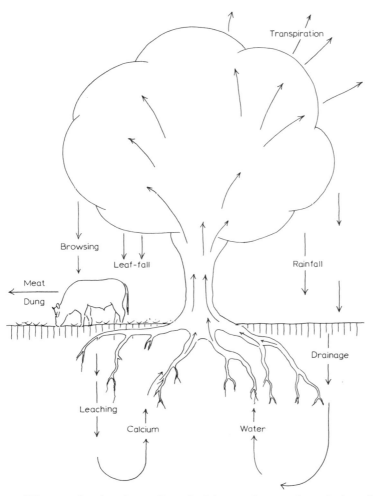

Fig. 37. Diagram showing the cycling of calcium and water through the soil in a wooded environment.

leading to the formation of a perched water table, for one of the reasons for forest clearance at these high level sites may have been to create open spaces in which to corral game.

The special effect of fire is to alter the composition of the forest. Fire causes soil impoverishment by dissipating as gases and water vapour quantities of organic matter which, like calcium compounds, helps to bind the soil particles and maintain its structure. Large amounts of energy are lost as heat and light. The vegetation which recolonizes burnt ground is generally less demanding in its nutrient requirements than that of mixed deciduous forest, species like birch, pine and various heaths being predominant, and as such is of little value in upgrading an impoverished soil. The litter is poor in nutrients, and resistant to decay, often building up as a thick layer of raw humus as at White Gill. Moreover, this type of vegetation is itself more liable to burn. The processes of soil degradation and accompanying impoverishment of plant communities are thus interlinked and cumulative. Once started, a chain reaction sets in which, in extreme cases, may lead to total soil erosion or its burial beneath blanket peat.

Another protagonist of these views is I. G. Simmons who, again using pollen analysis, has demonstrated the possibility of clearance by fire during late Boreal to Atlantic times on parts of the North York Moors and in Dartmoor.[9] Simmons has suggested various reasons for the opening up of the forest using as a guide the practices of recent hunting groups, notably the North American Indian. For example, although nomadic, these people had temporary or semi-permanent villages which necessitated clearings of between 40 and 60 hectares (about 100 to 150 acres). Hunting was made easier by the burning of woodland in autumn and spring, flushing out and aiding in the corral-

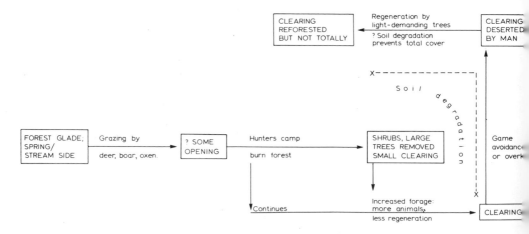

Fig. 38.   Proposed mechanism for the sequence of clearance by Mesolithic man in upland areas. (After Simmons, 1969a, Fig. 4)

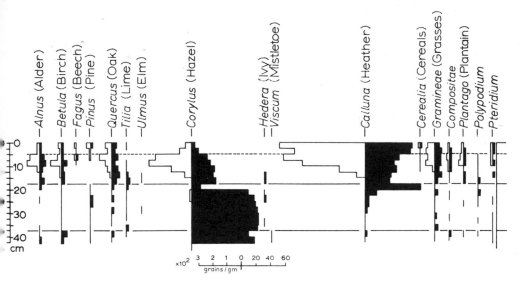

Fig. 39.   Iping, pollen diagram. (After Keef, *et al.*, 1965, Fig. 1)

ing of game. The psychological attributes of open ground may have been important in making for a freer and more invigorating chase, although in Mesolithic Britain, hunting took place not on horseback but on foot, probably aided by dogs. Burning by the Indians in the Hudson River and Lake Champlain regions was also carried on in order to improve the growth of grass (cf. p. 53). A similar practice goes on today in moorland areas of Britain, many of which are now given over solely to grouse shooting. The burning off of old heather plants in autumn every few years favours the growth of fresh succulent shoots, of value in rearing the young birds.

A possible mechanism for the sequence of clearing by hunting communities has been proposed by Simmons (Fig. 38). Forest glades around springs and streambanks are seen as initial nuclei of open ground, created by animals coming to drink. The dual attraction to Mesolithic man of both water and game in these areas was probably exploited, and their enlargement by burning a logical follow up which in turn would have attracted more animals. Game avoidance of the area or overkill by man may then have led to desertion of the clearing and subsequent regeneration of woodland. The extent to which the latter process resulted in a total return to the state of mixed deciduous forest depended on the degree to which the soil had been degraded. With upland sites in exposed situations and where rainfall was high, regeneration may hardly have occurred at all, as seems to have been the case at Stump Cross and parts of the North York Moors. On Dartmoor and other areas in north-east Yorkshire, regeneration was partial.

But even in some lowland heath areas, once heather was established it remained the ecological dominant to the present day. A good example is the Mesolithic site at Iping Common in Sussex.[10] The flint industry here is of Maglemosian type and occurs as a layer about 30 centimetres below the present surface. Pollen analysis (Fig. 39) suggests a Boreal age, with a local environment of hazel woodland. Heather became important late on in this period (at *c.* 20 centimetres) indicating the replacement of the woodland by heath, and this could hardly have taken place without some biotic influence such as fire or grazing. Subsequently, heather remained predominant on the site, even although mixed deciduous woodland developed in the area as a whole. This is seen as possible evidence for a local, but nevertheless, permanent effect of Mesolithic man on the vegetation.

An anomaly at Iping which is not at first easy to explain is the presence of the flint artefacts 30 centimetres deep in the soil. What processes were involved in their burial? In the first place, the break in the pollen sequence between 18 and 23 centimetres suggests a 'buried surface' at this level, the material above having been deposited, probably by wind action, subsequent to the heather-dominated vegetation. Areas of broken ground were no doubt prevalent—perhaps caused by overgrazing by cattle and deer—for wind erosion cannot take place from a totally vegetated land surface.

But we still need to explain the presence of flints 13 centimetres below this buried level, probably the level of the ground surface in Mesolithic times. The main agency involved was almost certainly earthworm activity. Charles Darwin[11] was the first to draw attention to the prodigious activities of these animals, and to point out the part they played in burying human artefacts and indeed whole sites. Fig. 40 is Darwin's drawing of a section through one of the fallen 'Druidical stones' at Stonehenge, demonstrating how earthworm burrowing has caused it to sink into the ground by 15 centimetres. The two species involved are *Allolobophora nocturna* and *A. longa*. They may number over a million to the hectare, and the weight of worms below the surface of a field may equal the weight of cattle above. These two species eject their castings onto the surface; disused burrows are constantly collap-

Fig. 40.   Section through fallen stone at Stonehenge. (After Darwin, 1881, Fig. 7)

sing causing subsidence. The two processes—surface accumulation and underground collapse—result in the burial of objects too large to pass through an earthworm's gut, the maximum capacity of which is 2 millimetres. The burial of the flints at Iping from the ancient surface into the soil can thus be explained in these terms.

But there is a further difficulty. The two species of *Allolobophora* which eject their casts onto the surface only live in soils which are rich in nutrients and in which the rate of decomposition of organic matter by micro-organisms is rapid. Such soils are termed base-rich, and the main type in the British Isles is the 'brown earth'. At Iping, however, the soil today, in common with many other heathland areas, has none of these characters. Raw humus is accumulating at the surface and decomposes but slowly; the body of the soil is leached of nutrient bases—calcium and iron; and earthworms are absent. This type of soil is known as a podsol (Fig. 57), and its main characteristics are a pale, leached horizon just below the surface humus, from which bases and organic matter have been removed, and a layer of redeposited iron and humus lower down. It seems clear, therefore, that if we accept the position of the flints as evidence of former earthworm activity we must postulate a change in soil type from a nutrient-rich brownearth to an impoverished podsol. That such a change has taken place is supported by the paucity of pollen in the lowest levels of the soil for, as already discussed (p. 82), pollen preservation is poor in base-rich soils. The change in soil type evidently took place *after* the deposition of the flints but *prior* to the ultimate deposition of the high quantities of hazel and heather pollen between 18 and 23 centimetres, for the strongly graded pollen frequency curves of these species clearly demonstrates the absence of faunal mixing.

The age context of the industry at Iping is late Boreal, with the deposition of the wind-blown sand on top of the Mesolithic land surface taking place in Atlantic times. The importance of the site is obvious. Here is evidence for the destruction of hazel woodland leading to a heath environment, accompanied by soil deterioration and, later, by wind erosion—all being brought about by hunting communities in the sixth millennium bc.

The most recent contribution to this study of the influence of hunting communities on the habitat has been made by A. G. Smith.[12] Just as Dimbleby has questioned the natural origin of such processes as soil leaching, forest recession and blanket bog formation, Smith has expressed doubt concerning the purely climatic origin of the vegetational changes which characterize the boundaries of the pollen zones in the first half of the Post-glacial. Thus while radiocarbon dates show a general synchroneity, and while regional differences such as the late rise of pine in the north and west and the early presence of alder in Ireland can be explained in terms of climatic differences across the

British Isles, there are many local divergences in the pattern of vegetational succession which do not appear to have a climatic origin.

It is a fact, of course, that ever since the broad sequence of Postglacial forest history was worked out, people have sought to explain all or parts of the succession in terms other than of climate. Some have urged that soil development was important, the weakly developed soils of the early Post-glacial being unable to support the more nutrient demanding trees such as oak, elm and lime. This view was strongly advocated by the late W. H. Pearsall, who was of the opinion that the introduction of successive tree species was closely linked to the development of increasingly rich soils, established in the first instance by the pioneer species birch and pine.[13] Differences of migration rate must also be taken into account.

A. G. Smith first explored these problems in terms of the concepts of threshold and inertia.[14] 'Threshold' was defined as the value of a combination of environmental factors which had to be attained before a particular vegetation or tree species could become established. During a period of climatic change, the threshold for a particular vegetational change would be crossed at different times in different parts of even a small area as well as in the country as a whole. At one extreme, localities of favourable microclimate or soil type might harbour species which were generally absent as a major component of the vegetation; at the other, a detrimental climatic change, such as a short-term temperature drop, might be registered only in those upland areas where susceptible species were close to their temperature threshold (cf. p. 73).

The concept of 'inertia' is not unrelated. A closed climax forest inhibits the establishment of new species; it is inimical to change. And this will be greatest where climatic and other environmental conditions are most favourable. For example, the Mesolithic sites where clearance phenomena are most pronounced are those either in upland situations or on base-poor soils. The few sites in the Vale of Pickering which showed any response at all were uninfluenced in the long term, rapidly recovering their natural state—that is, with the exception of hazel.

We have already discussed (p. 81) the rise of hazel which marks the zone IV/V transition, and suggested that this may, in part at least, be of anthropogenic origin (Fig. 30); and Smith argues that the prevalence of hazel during the Boreal period may too have been engendered by the continued use of fire.[15] It is perhaps significant that the hazel maximum in the Post-glacial falls at a much earlier stage in relation to the climatic succession as a whole than in previous interglacials.

The purely climatic origin of the vegetational changes at the Boreal/Atlantic transition has also been questioned, largely on the grounds that they are so often exactly synchronous with layers of wood charcoal and Mesolithic flint artefacts. The onset of the Atlantic period is marked by a rise in alder and a decline in pine which in ecological terms is generally held to indicate a rising water table leading to the creation of new areas into which the alder could spread, and where it replaced the pine. In parts of the north and west, alder was present early on in the Boreal period although at a low level of abundance, it being prevented from spreading widely by climatic dryness and the inertia of the Boreal forest. Disruption of the latter by man—and Smith cites several examples of the utilization of pine—would encourage the spread of alder without the need for a climatic shift.

A secondary hazel maximum occurring around the Boreal/Atlantic transition, and occasionally coinciding with an increase of herbaceous pollen, is perhaps further evidence for widespread human interference with the vegetation at this time.

But there are strong arguments for maintaining the traditional explanation of the Boreal/Atlantic transition. In the dry climate at the end of the Boreal period, lake levels fell and the surfaces of fens and marshes dried out. Man was compelled to spread onto these areas of freshly exposed lake-edge sediments and drying organic soils in order to reach water and exploit the receding marsh and fen habitats rich in game. It would also not have gone unnoticed by Mesolithic man that these newly created areas of open ground presented just those favourable habitat conditions which at other times he sought to achieve by artificial means. The advantages of these marginal zones between major ecological communities, sometimes called 'ecotones', is well known, and we should not be surprised to see them being colonized as they were created.[16] Man was not only forced to spread onto them; he was desirous of them as well.

The corollary to this of course is that when the increase in rainfall took place at the beginning of the Atlantic period, it was these same areas which were most affected by flooding or the growth of peat or tufa. The Mesolithic sites were buried under lake clays, peat and tufa, and thus preserved. Occupation sites of a date earlier than this period of ultimate dryness at the end of zone VI were further from the lake or bog margins and thus not in such favourable situations for preservation (Fig. 41). We should not wonder, therefore, that so many of our known

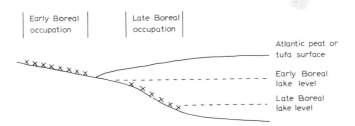

Fig. 41. Diagrammatic section through a Boreal lake-edge situation.

Mesolithic sites fall at major zone boundaries; there were no doubt many others but these have been destroyed by later processes of erosion through not being so securely buried.

A measure of the complexity of the situation is that exposure of damp soils suitable for colonization by alder may have been brought about by a lowering of lake levels as induced by climatic dryness!

In the case of the upland microlithic sites, many of which appear to fall at the Boreal/Atlantic transition, there is frequently a nonconformity at the mineral soil/peaty humus junction. Much of the surface raw humus, and its pollen, may have been lost through burning or erosion.

We cannot be certain as to the relative importance of man in the vegetational changes of the early Post-glacial, whether they be the local episodes of deforestation or the more widespread and fundamental changes in the composition of the forest. Perhaps, in fact, we should not be so rigorous in our division between human and natural factors. Man after all is simply another animal, living in groups, or herds, controlling and being controlled by the environment as it evolves. Perhaps if we accepted this more readily, many of the problems raised in the above discussion would be automatically resolved. But there seems little doubt that fire, the axe and grazing herds, the latter perhaps in some kind of loose symbiotic relationship with man,[17] are factors which must be taken into account in any consideration of the development of the habitat at this early stage.

In Britain, Mesolithic man comprises several groups, or cultures, defined by material equipment and habitat. The earliest of these are

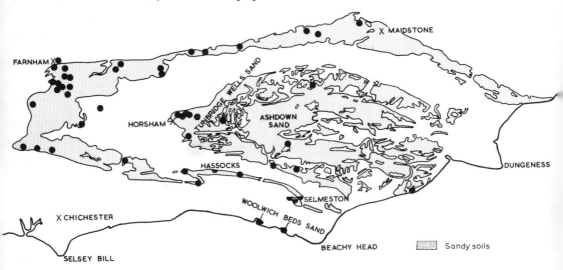

Fig. 42.   Map of Mesolithic sites in the Sussex Weald. (After Clark, 1932, Map II)

the Maglemosians who, at Star Carr, come closer to the previous Upper Palaeolithic communities in many respects than to later Mesolithic groups. By contrast there are the Sauveterrian industries whose artefacts often occur in upland situations, areas which are now moor or heath.[18] Assemblages of artefacts dating from the Boreal/Atlantic transition often show a mixture of traits from these two cultures, as for example in the case of Cherhill.[19] Features of a third group, considered to reflect the continental Tardenoisian, were also incorporated, in particular the use of the chisel-ended, or tranchet, arrowhead, specifically designed for immobilizing birds and other small game (Fig. 52).[20] In the north of Britain, and especially along the coasts of the North Channel, groups of people known as 'Strandloopers', who subsisted to a considerable extent on shellfish, are represented by the Larnian and Obanian industries.[21] These fall relatively late in the Mesolithic of the British Isles, the very earliest date for the Irish industries being about 5750 bc.[22] Typically these industries lack axes and microliths, but are characterized by long subrectangular pebbles, sometimes called 'limpet scoops', whose probable function was as pestles or the removal of limpets from rocks.

In considering the relationship of Mesolithic man to his environment, two problems must be borne in mind. The first concerns the distribution of artefacts in relation to soil type or geology. For example, a map published by J. G. D. Clark in 1932 shows a positive correlation between the distribution of flint artefacts in the Sussex Weald and areas of light sandy soils (Fig. 42).[23] The explanation of this in ecological terms has never been easy, although it can be argued that the vegetation of these areas was more readily cleared and the resulting grassland more suitable for grazing animals than that of the intervening tracts of heavier clay (cf. p. 165). But it is now known, through careful and extensive fieldwork, that the distribution of artefacts is not as closely linked to soil type as was previously thought, and that the preponderance of finds from the sandy areas is related to ease of discovery, at any rate in part.[24] Sandy soils are susceptible to degradation, loss of plant cover and wind erosion. Considerable quantities of sand are lost, and heavier objects such as flint artefacts become concentrated—a process known as deflation. Because of this, and because of the frequent exposure of the soil surface, the artefacts in these soils are readily uncovered. An additional factor is that these areas, being unsuitable for agriculture, have a high amenity value and are more likely to be casually visited by collectors. Similar conditions do not obtain on the heavier soils or in valleys. In the latter, where accumulation and burial, rather than deflation, are more general, there is little doubt that many Mesolithic sites await discovery.

The second problem is less easy to define. It concerns the real status of a single Mesolithic site, and the significance in cultural terms of the various industries and environmental distributions which we have described. The industries of the Weald which have just been mentioned range over a wide area of southern England, an area which roughly coincides with the distribution of artefacts made out of a material known as Portland chert (Fig. 43).[25] Chert is a stone similar to flint but with a mat rather than shiny surface. It occurs as layers of nodules in limestone, and the variety at Portland Island, Dorset, was particularly favoured by Mesolithic man. It is also abundant in beach gravels. Richard Bradley has suggested that its widespread distribution, and the fact that concentrations are to be found only on the largest sites, indicates barter or trade at annual gatherings of different groups or families. We know, for example, that Star Carr was visited on several occasions, and the range of radiocarbon dates for sites such as Morton in Fife and Thatcham[26] suggests a similar continuum of, possibly seasonal, occupation. Such an idea provides a useful anticipation to the 'causewayed enclosures' of later, farming communities.[27] It also emphasizes that an individual site may perform a specific function in the livelihood of a tribe, serving only one of a number of different activities carried on in different habitats and at different times of the year. The sites, for example, on Portland Island itself are in an unsatisfactory locality in that the resources of the immediate hinterland were probably limited. At the time of occupation (*c.* 5200 bc)[28] the sea level was close to its present height, and the site already an island. Wild animals—boar, red deer and aurochs—were probably few and would have been hunted rapidly to extinction. Nor was the coast particularly rich in shellfish, apparently the staple food of these people, the cliffs being steep and sandy bays few. A possible *raison d'être* for these sites was the chert, a desirable raw material and one which appears to have been distributed by barter over a wide area. If it were the case, then, that Portland Island was a factory site, unsuitable for life as a whole, it is likely that occupation was seasonal. For part of the year, the inhabi-

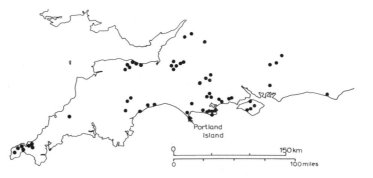

Fig. 43. Distribution of Portland Chert artefacts in southern England. (After Palmer, 1970, Fig. 1)

tants probably forsook their industrial and strandlooping activities and moved inland to obtain their living by other means, in different environments, and probably with different assemblages of artefacts.

We can apply these concepts to some of the more fundamental distinctions recognized in the Mesolithic period. Thus the environmental and artefactual differences between the Maglemosian and Tardenoisian groups 'may well represent different facies of a single population exploiting a variety of territories'.[29] This view has been strongly advocated by Eric Higgs who emphasizes that a Mesolithic, or indeed Palaeolithic, site represents only one of a number occupied by a group of hunters. Throughout the year, a range of territories may have been exploited, each presenting different economic and environmental circumstances.[30] This conception of the life of hunter/gatherer communities finds a parallel in the annual migration cycles of recent North American Indians—seashore in summer, deep woods hunting camps in autumn and winter, and rivers in spring. Also to be noted is the practice of such communities to break up into different sized groups—large in winter, small in summer—for different seasonal activities.[31]

But in Britain there is a chronological difficulty in applying this model in that Sauveterrian industries are scarcely present before the seventh millennium bc. A possible solution to this paradox is that the early Maglemosian groups as represented at Star Carr, a site which was certainly occupied on a seasonal basis, reflect a continuing Upper Palaeolithic hunting tradition, and perhaps lived largely on the land between Britain and Denmark which was maintained as open ground by the marshy and swampy conditions. Only when this area was flooded by the rising Post-glacial sea would these people have taken in the upland regions of the Moors and Pennines. Can we perhaps see the cultural transition between the Palaeolithic and Mesolithic as a result of the rising sea and as taking place at around 6000 bc rather than as a result of the earlier temperature rise at 8000 bc? This is certainly an exciting possibility.[32]

The Strandloopers, too, may be considered as seasonal variants of contemporary inland groups. Shellfish introduce an element of stability into a hunter/gatherer economy, for the 'feast-or-famine' situation resulting from the seasonal availability of most plants and animals does not apply.[33] They are as nourishing as a meat diet if eked out by vegetable food, they contain large quantities of glycogen, and need not be added to by other animal flesh. They also contain the valuable vitamin A. Moreover their abundance per unit area is greater than that of any other food animal. The main drawbacks to a strandlooping mode of life are the monotony and the fact that shellfish populations are rapidly depleted if exploited continuously.[34]

It was not only in Britain, but in the world as a whole, that a strandlooping mode of life was adopted in the mid Post-glacial. Previously, although Palaeolithic groups had eaten shellfish, there had rarely been any special emphasis on this source of food. It is possible, as already stated (p. 67), that the absence of earlier shell middens is due to their having been submerged under the sea, and it is certainly the case that even within the Mesolithic period the major strandlooping sites are found associated with the maximum development of the Main Post-glacial Shoreline in the north and west (Fig. 6). If, however, this association is not altogether due to the submergence of earlier sites, we can argue that its origin was a normal consequence for coastal dwellers living against a background of population increase and environmental change. The relative increase of coastline to land area, caused by the rising sea, may have been a contributory factor. A correlation has frequently been made between the inception of strand-looping and the spread of forest, the restriction of open areas available for hunting, and the extinction of the game animals familiar to Upper Palaeolithic man. Open coastal sites may have been sought out too by Mesolithic man in a subconscious craving for the treeless environment of former times.

On a seasonal basis, the same factors apply. 'Shellfish, as a main article of food, were eaten for lack of something better rather than from choice—perhaps in bad seasons, in winter or when in unfamiliar surroundings, so that the better potentialities of the place had still to be learned.'[35] They may have been eaten during the exploitation of a coastal site for raw materials; during winter when plant food was scarce; and perhaps during the red deer breeding season, for we can suppose that Mesolithic man well understood the life cycle and habitats of these animals and would not disrupt their populations unduly. It is also possible that during the winter months when foliage was in short supply, herds of herbivores moved to the coast to feed on seaweed and the maritime pastures. The littoral habitat had its attractions not only for man but for animals too, and once again we can see the possibilities of a symbiotic relationship arising. The development of domesticated cattle from the wild aurochs against such a dual background of trans-humance and open country is certainly plausible and has indeed been suggested as a possibility by Peter Jewell.[36]

But the origins of agriculture as a whole in the British Isles must be seen firmly in terms of introduction by alien groups rather than of indigenous development. The earliest farming settlements were in south-west Asia and arose in the ninth millennium bc at a time when the British Isles and northern Europe were still in the final throes of the Ice Age. Notable sites are Zawi Chemi Shanidar in northern Iraq where selective herding of sheep and the autumn killing of young animals was taking place around 8650 bc, and Jericho in Palestine

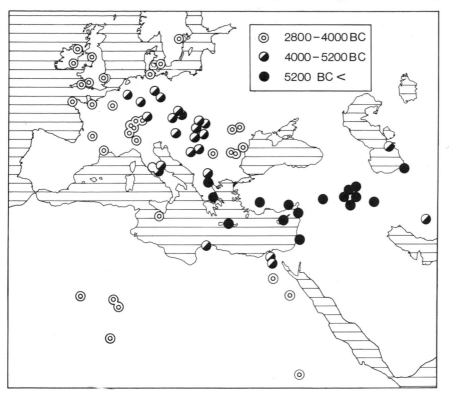

Fig. 44.   The spread of farming settlements into Europe. (After Clark, 1965, Fig. 2)

where the reaping of cereals—although whether wild or cultivated is uncertain—was going on at about 8850 bc. Goats were domesticated at the latter site prior to 7000 bc. From these early centres, agriculture spread out in various directions, but most strikingly into central and western Europe (Fig. 44).[37]

It was only possible for agriculture to evolve in south-west Asia because of the presence in the area of the wild progenitors of the animals and plants which were to provide the basis for the new economy. But it is not irrelevant to point out that without the necessary environmental conditions, the hunting and food-gathering existence of the Upper Palaeolithic inhabitants would probably have continued. The exact order and mechanisms by which the various domesticates and cultigens arose is not at all clear but open-country conditions of dry grasslands or park habitats and a climate becoming increasingly dry were clearly favourable both to the growth and development of cereal grasses and the continuation and intensification of the Upper Palaeolithic herd-hunting practices. There was no intervening forest phase between the end of the Ice Age and the beginnings of agriculture, and there was consequently little or no development of Mesolithic cultures in the area. The Neolithic can be seen as a direct continuation of the Upper Palaeolithic, not only temporally, but, in some respects, economically as well. The uniqueness of the European Mesolithic age becomes more apparent. It is perhaps also pertinent that north of the European deciduous forest belt where, because of the low temperatures and short growing season, crop cultivation is impossible the Upper Palaeolithic has persisted, and is seen today in the hunting and herding mode of life practised by the Eskimos and Lapps.[38]

This view of the origins of agriculture is not universally accepted. D. R. Harris, for example, would see 'the most favourable conditions for plant domestication among those generalized gatherer/hunter/ fisher populations of forest and woodland margins'.[39] Nor is the theory of a drying climate at the end of the Ice Age in south-west Asia wholly established as fact.[40]

The earliest evidence for farming communities in the British Isles comes from northern and eastern Ireland, the English Lake District, and southern England where radiocarbon dates indicate that settlement began in the middle of the fourth millennium bc. In Ireland, relevant sites are Ballynagilly, Co. Tyrone, where the foundations of a Neolithic house have been uncovered,[41] Newferry, Co. Antrim, where a polished Neolithic axe (p. 124) and hearth were found,[42] Ringneill Quay, Co. Down, a midden site containing the bones of domesticated cattle, sheep and pig,[43] and two middens in Co. Dublin—Dalkey Island and Sutton.[44] The age of these sites is comparable with that of a brief phase of forest clearance at Ballyscullion in the Lower Bann Valley as indicated by pollen analysis and radiocarbon assay,[45] and dating to the mid-fourth millennium bc, and of another at Fallahogy,[46] Co. Londonderry, of similar age. The latter site is an elegant example of the

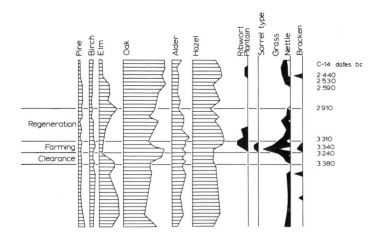

Fig. 45.   Fallahogy, pollen diagram. (After Smith, A. G., 1970b, Fig. 5.9)

influence of Neolithic man on the vegetation (Fig. 45). Essentially there were three successive attacks on the forest vegetation. The first was extremely slight, marked by a fall in elm pollen and a peak of bracken and sedges; grasses increased only slightly. The second was more pronounced, and can be subdivided into three stages, clearance, farming and regeneration of woodland. Of the forest trees, only elm was affected in the clearance phase; grasses increased, and weeds, such as stinging nettle, appeared. The cultivation phase is marked by an increase in the pollen of weed species, in particular ribwort plantain, *Plantago lanceolata*. Total regeneration then ensued. The third episode of deforestation resulted in more widespread clearance, but again the elm was affected more than other trees.

The main difference between these and the clearance episodes previously discussed is the, apparently, selective exploitation of elm. This phenomenon, known as 'the elm decline', was widespread not only in Britain but in much of western Europe as well. It is such a consistent feature that it was used from the first to mark the zone VIIa/b (Atlantic/Sub-boreal) transition in the pollen record. Originally it was attributed to a drop in temperature, and it will be remembered that we have already put forward evidence for short-term cool periods within the earlier post-glacial (p. 74). On the whole this idea is not now favoured, mainly because other cold-sensitive trees such as the ash are not similarly affected; indeed the ash appears to increase in the Sub-boreal (Fig. 47). An alternative hypothesis, put forward by the Danish botanist J. Troels-Smith, attributes the elm decline to the utilization of elm leaves for cattle fodder by Neolithic man at a time when grasslands as we know them today were virtually non-existent.[47] This theory has much to recommend it—for example, the preservation of bundles of elm branches in the waterlogged conditions of Swiss Neolithic lakeside dwellings, and the continued use of elm leaves for cattle fodder by primitive peoples today. Neither of these hypotheses requires there to have been a reduction in the number of trees, but simply in the pollen output, and in some instances, although not at Fallahogy, it is indeed true that the elm decline is accompanied by changes in no other species of plant.

But where, in addition, opening up of the forest and the introduction of light-demanding plants occurs, additional processes are implied. At their most simple these may be an intensification of the intial stages of the mechanism we proposed for the Mesolithic clearances—the concentration of herds of animals around springs, riverbanks and lakesides, selective browsing on elm, and the gravitation to these areas of human groups. In the absence of cereal pollen or other artefacts diagnostic of farming, it is difficult to decide whether these temporary clearances are the work of Neolithic or Mesolithic man; and if Troels-Smith is right in postulating the existence of Neolithic communities with an economy based entirely on cattle, albeit domesticated, the distinction between this and the Mesolithic herd-hunting type of economy which may well have obtained in parts of the British Isles becomes very slight. This is particularly so in north-east Ireland where the chronological overlap between the two groups of communities—native hunter/gatherers and immigrant farmers—was in the order of half a millennium. An overlap of this duration itself perhaps implies that the Mesolithic economy in the area was firmly established and that of the incoming Neolithic peoples was little different. Humphrey Case describes the environmental attractions of the area to early man: 'Within and around . . . the Cretaceous exposures . . . the tills, cliff-screes, beaches and river-valleys held massive and abundant flint, unsurpassed in surface exposures elsewhere in Ireland or Britain. Fish in . . . rivers, lakes and coastal-waters . . . game, wild fowl, timber, withies and reeds . . .'. The Larnians had a 'potentiality for stable and productive existence like that of the Magdalenians . . . Their influence on the succeeding Neolithic may . . . have been strong, even decisive'.[48]

This process of fusion may be seen at Dalkey Island on the south side of Dublin Bay where Larnian flint tools occurred with bones of sheep and domestic ox,[49] and it is relevant that many other similar sites are coastal.

Thus both archaeologically and environmentally there may have been no clear distinction between the Mesolithic and Neolithic communities of the fourth millennium bc; nor should we try to define one. There has perhaps been too strong a tendency in the past to ask the wrong questions with regard to these early episodes of forest utilization. Rather than enquiring too closely into the cultural status of the people who brought about these changes in the vegetation and soil, we should perhaps define them in terms of the changes themselves. There is no doubt that a wide variety of land-use phenomena took place, and while some aspects of this variation may be attributed to differences of aspect, soil, climate, etc., from site to site, others may be of fully cultural significance. The precise definition of these changes, their accurate dating and their classification into groups—in fact their treatment as artefacts—would go a long way to furthering research into the way of life of these early communities.

A different view on the origin of the elm decline has been put forward by G. F. Mitchell.[50] He has suggested that while initially the elm was pollarded for its leaves, later on, selective felling took place because the elm was growing on the better, more calcareous, soils which were required for the cultivation of cereals. A prerequisite of this hypothesis is that the elm was growing in relatively pure stands, a view by no means universally held. Nevertheless, such conditions may apply to areas where a strong contrast exists between base-rich habitats along stream courses and the impoverished soils of surrounding moorland

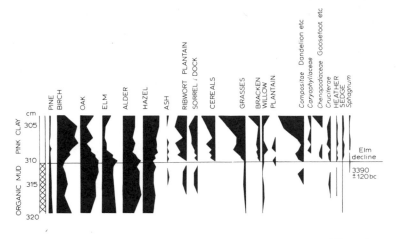

Fig. 46. Barfield Tarn, pollen diagram. (After Pennington, 1970, Fig. 11)

areas as has indeed been described by W. H. Pearsall.[51] Such a hypo-thesis, of course, also implies the growth of crops, and here we can turn to the evidence from north-west England.

At Barfield Tarn,[52] a kettle hole on the south-western edge of the Lake District, pollen analysis has revealed two episodes of land use in the centuries around the Atlantic/Sub-boreal transition (Fig. 46). Initially there was a slight elm decline marked by the simultaneous introduction of plantain, dock and other weeds. The elm then recovered to its former level of abundance and the weed species died out. Sub-sequently there was a more pronounced elm decline, accompanied by a drop in the abundance of other tree species, notably the oak, and the introduction and rapid increase of cereals. Various weeds became prolific. At the same time there was a change in the lake sediments from an organic mud to a pink clay, the latter deriving from the boulder clay which surrounds the tarn. Here, seemingly, the elm decline was accompanied by forest clearance, the growth of cereals, and tillage of the soil vigorous enough to cause erosion. Regeneration of woodland did not occur.

In southern England there are, similarly, mid-fourth millennium dates for Neolithic settlement and land use. At Shippea Hill in the Cambridgeshire Fens, the elm decline is dated to the mid-fourth millennium bc and is associated with Neolithic occupation debris stratified in peat.[53] Other changes at this site include a slight rise of grass and bracken pollen, a gradual fall in total tree pollen, and the introduction of *Plantago lanceolata*, ribwort plantain, a characteristic pasture plant, all taking place around the level of the elm decline.

But in addition to these peat sites, we are, for the first time, beginning to get the remains of above-surface artificial structures, and the sedi-ments and soils associated with these are equally valuable as sources of environmental data. Relevant sites of fourth millennium age are Broome Heath, Norfolk, an embanked enclosure where there was pollen evidence for forest clearance;[54] Lambourn, Berkshire, a Neolithic long barrow or burial mound;[55] Church Hill, Sussex, a flint mine site (cf. Fig. 54);[56] and Hembury, Devon, a causewayed enclosure[57]—a type of monument in which the enclosing bank and ditch are punctuated by frequent causeways.

By 3000 bc, perhaps 500 years after the initial immigrations, farming communities were firmly established in many areas of the British Isles.

6   Prehistoric and early farmers

Neolithic forest clearance

The elm decline controversy is only one aspect of a recurring theme in the study of ancient human environments, namely the recognition and separation of anthropogenic and natural phenomena, and nowhere is this problem more acute than in the period we are about to study. In his initial investigations of the pollen sequence from south-east England, and in particular from the East Anglian Breckland site of Hockham Mere,[1] Godwin was inclined to see the various vegetational changes of the later pollen zones (VIIb and VIII) as being of climatic origin. These changes include the elm decline, the increase of birch and ash, the opening up of the forest canopy and the spread of grassland and heath (Table 5), and are shown clearly in a more recent diagram from Seathwaite Tarn[2] on the western edge of the Lake District (Fig. 47). A decline of temperature was postulated as the main cause of these changes, and there was convincing evidence in the altered ranges of such creatures as the European pond tortoise that such a decline had taken place. A subsidiary cause of the vegetational changes was thought to be the progressive leaching of nutrients from the soil, brought about in the normal course of soil maturation, and accelerated by the increase of rainfall during the first millennium bc. In effect, zones VIIb and VIII were seen as part of a normal interglacial cycle as exemplified at Marks Tey (Fig. 3) during zone H III of the Hoxnian.

Today, however, it is felt that although such climatic and soil changes have indeed taken place, they were of insufficient magnitude to have brought about the major vegetational changes of the pollen record. These are now thought to be of anthropogenic origin.

The first recognition of the effects of man on the vegetation was made by J. Iversen in 1941 in Denmark.[3] In his classic paper 'Landnam in Denmark's Stone Age' Iversen ascribed fluctuations in the frequencies of various pollen types in Ordrup Bog to a temporary period of forest clearance and cultivation of cereals by Neolithic man. Iversen divided the period into several phases.

1. A *clearance* phase, in which oak declined and herbs became dominant.
2. A phase of *cultivation*, marked by a peak in cereal pollen.
3. A phase of *abandonment* when weeds of cultivation, notably plantain, *Plantago*, became important.
4. *Woodland regeneration*, in which a birch phase preceded the return to oak dominance which characterized the pre-clearance vegetation.

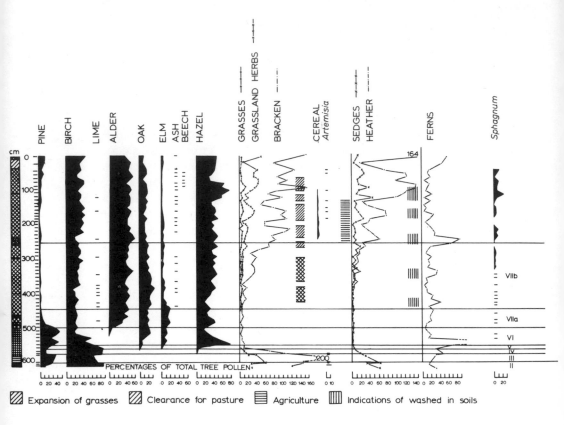

Fig. 47.   Seathwaite Tarn, pollen diagram. (After Pennington, 1970, Fig. 4)

This type of temporary land use was termed a 'landnam'. It is similar in some respects to the early clearance episodes in the British Isles, for example at Fallahogy (Fig. 45), but it differs in one important respect— in the British examples there is almost never any evidence for burning.[4] In the Danish sites, Iversen demonstrated a sharp rise in the frequency of charcoal at the clearance horizon, suggesting the use of fire, a suggestion which was strengthened by the episode of birch forest in the woodland regeneration phase.

We have already shown how Mesolithic communities in Britain made use of fire in clearing woodland, but in the case of Neolithic man in Denmark the use of fire was seen by Iversen as part of the subsequent land-use process and not as the initial mechanism of clearance. This idea was developed by J. G. D. Clark who supported the hypothesis with ethnographic parallels from primitive communities in northern Europe.[5] In essence, it was suggested that the landnam episodes in Denmark were part of a system of shifting agriculture in which successive areas of forest were felled, the timber stacked and burnt, and the fertile wood ash hoed into the soil surface and utilized as a seedbed for cereal crops. Such a process of felling followed by burning has been called variously 'slash-and-burn', 'burn-beating' or 'brandwirtschaft'. Once the fertility of the wood ash was used up (and modern experiments by Axel Steensberg suggest that this could have occurred within a period of two to three years)[6] the clearing was abandoned and a new area of woodland attacked.

In Britain, Godwin was quick to recognize that the opening of the forests of the East Anglian Breckland in early zone VIIb was the work of man.[7] Here, however, clearance was permanent, or so it seemed from the pollen record, there being no subsequent regeneration. This was in the early 1940s. Since then, there has been an increasing trend towards the interpretation of the later Post-glacial pollen record in terms of local vegetational sequences, with particular regard to the various effects of man, and a move away from the establishment of the regional zones once thought to be of climatic origin. As a corollary to these trends, dating by pollen analysis, initially one of the prime attractions of the technique for archaeologists, has become of minimal use, particularly since the development of radiocarbon assay in the mid-1950s. The main reason for abandoning the formerly held ideas was the difficulty of envisaging a climatic change of sufficient severity to cause deforestation while still allowing thermophile trees such as elm and lime to persist, albeit at a reduced level. Moreover, it was difficult to understand the spatial heterogeneity of deforestation over Britain if climate was the causative agent. Add to this the archaeological evidence for the introduction into Britain of farming communities at the very period when widespread deforestation was beginning, and in areas, particularly East Anglia, where clearance was most apparent, and we can readily appreciate the change in emphasis which took place in the field of palynology.

Today there is an overwhelming abundance of pollen diagrams in the literature but we are fortunate in having a number of up to date summaries of the main results. Most useful is *The History of British Vegetation* by Dr Winifred Pennington;[8] this is largely concerned with the Late-glacial and Post-glacial periods, and lays stress on the interaction of vegetation and man. In a recent collection of essays in honour of Harry Godwin, two papers, one by A. G. Smith and the other by Judith Turner,[9] outline the influence of man on the vegetation from the beginning of the Post-glacial to the present day. And the evidence from Ireland has been summarized in a further paper by Smith.[10]

Various types of interference with the vegetation by Neolithic man have been recorded.

1. Elm decline. The selective use of elm (p. 109).
2. Landnam or 'small temporary clearance', as at Fallahogy (Fig. 45).

3. Permanent clearance, as in the Breckland and along the coastal plain of south-west Cumberland.
4. Coppicing of hazel, as in the Somerset Levels. This is a more locally occurring phenomenon than the other types.

One of the determining factors in Neolithic times as to whether an area was permanently cleared or not may have been the type of soil. Although by no means confined to them, Neolithic man shows a definite predilection for lighter well-drained soils such as those on neutral sands and gravels, the Chalk and younger limestones, and it may be that he was present in these areas in such numbers as to prevent woodland regeneration. It is possible too that such soils themselves, being of a generally dry nature, were not conducive to regeneration; but, with the exception of the very light soils of the Breckland which are in one of the most climatically dry regions of the British Isles anyway, this is a less plausible explanation. Nevertheless there certainly appears to be a contrast between man's effect on the forest vegetation in these areas of lighter soil type and in those in the rest of the British Isles.

The Chalk and allied areas: 'large, permanent clearances'

Much of the evidence for the chalklands comes from fossilized molluscan faunas, for pollen is not readily preserved in calcareous and circum-neutral soils.[11] Several sites in north Wiltshire in the rich prehistoric area of Avebury and Windmill Hill show a pattern of woodland followed

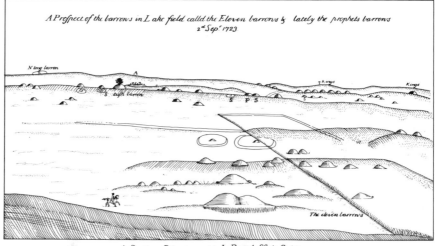

Fig. 48.   Barrows in the vicinity of Stonehenge. (After Stukeley, 1740, Table 31)

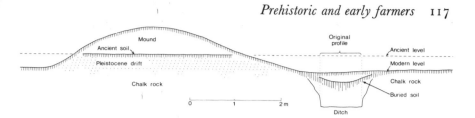

Fig. 49. Diagrammatic cross-section through a bank and ditch.

by clearance in Neolithic times. The sites contain buried soils, and unlike the few we have so far met with such as those preserved under solifluxion debris or tufa these soils occur under man-made structures such as burial mounds and embanked enclosures. For the first time, man was beginning to leave above-ground structural traces of his activities and in so doing sealed small areas of the contemporary land surface together with their soils, fauna, flora and various other clues as to the way in which the land was utilized. Barrows often occur in prodigious numbers as is shown by an early eighteenth-century drawing made by the antiquarian William Stukeley of several barrow cemeteries in the Stonehenge region (Fig. 48); and underneath each is a small area of ancient soil. In addition, the construction of mounds and embankments entailed considerable quarrying operations, in exceptional cases to depths of over seven metres, resulting in the creation of ditches adjacent to the earthworks (Fig. 49). These have frequently become infilled with a variety of lime-rich sediments in which further environmental evidence is preserved. Thus any field monument is a potential source of information which can be divided into that which comes from the buried soil beneath the earthwork and that which comes from the infill of the ditch.

In north Wiltshire, about two kilometres west of the vast stone circle complex of Avebury, is a Neolithic mound known as the South Street Long Barrow.[12] Here, the buried soil has given us a detailed picture of the way in which early farmers utilized the land. Here, too, we have the earliest evidence in the British Isles for the use of the plough.[13] The buried soil shows up in cross-section as a dark zone about 20 centimetres thick (Fig. 50). It is richly calcareous and prolific in the shells of land snails. These can be extracted from soil samples taken at close intervals, identified and classified according to their habitat preferences into categories such as 'shade-loving', 'intermediate' and 'open-country', and then graphed in a manner similar to that used in the presentation of pollen data (Fig. 50). The earliest fauna at South Street comes from pockets, or involutions, of silty wind-deposited material of periglacial origin at the base of the soil, and reflects an open, probably tundra, environment devoid of trees. The fauna is similar to that from the solifluxion deposits at Holborough in Kent (p. 46), and a Late-glacial date is likely. Above this, but penetrating some way into the

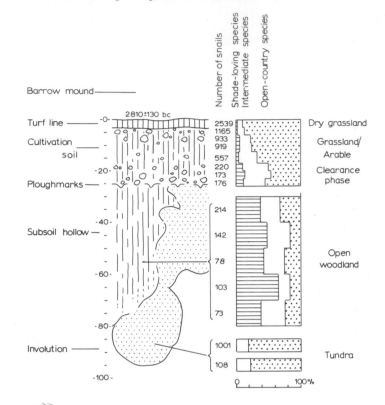

Fig. 50.   South Street Long Barrow, buried soil. Snail diagram.

subsoil, are a series of irregular 'subsoil hollows' filled with earthy material. These are the casts of ancient tree roots which cut through, and are thus later than, the periglacial involutions. Woodland snail species predominate, and fully temperate forms which were unable to tolerate the cold climate of the Late-glacial period now occur. Here we are seeing a reflection of the spread of forest over the Wiltshire Chalk in response to the Post-glacial climatic warming, and the faunal contrast with the underlying periglacial assemblage is marked.

Equally marked, however, is the subsequent return to open-country, a phenomenon ascribed to forest clearance by man. At the base of the soil where the first signs of clearance are to be seen there is evidence of ploughing—criss-cross grooves scored into the subsoil surface (cf. Fig. 64). This process is thought to be a part of the initial breaking up of the soil shortly after the clearance of trees from the site, and not the regular year-in-year-out method of tillage. The latter was probably carried on with spades or hoes, and the stratified character of the soil above the ploughmarks, with alternate stony and stone-free layers, is a likely result of this. In fact the soil has been thrown into a series of irregular hummocks and hollows which overlie the ploughmarks and would have been easily destroyed, along with the stratified character of the soil, by regular cross-ploughing.

At the surface of the buried soil is a thin stone-free horizon or turf line (Fig. 50). This is caused by earthworm sorting, a process, already described (p. 98), in which all large stones are moved down through the soil by the activities of surface-casting worms. This takes place, of course, only in the absence of tillage, and the distinctive molluscan fauna in the surface turf line supports the contention of a grassland, rather than arable, environment at this level. The long barrow was thus built in pasture, and radiocarbon assay of charcoal on the surface of the buried soil dates it to about 2800 bc.

About two kilometres from South Street is a similar, and more or less contemporary structure, the Beckhampton Road Long Barrow.[14] But the buried soil beneath the mound differs from that at South Street in that there is no trace of ploughmarks or of tillage. The molluscan fauna is a woodland one throughout the soil with the exception of the surface turf line where grassland species are present. Here again, as at South Street, we have a reflection of Neolithic woodland clearance; but the subsequent use of the land differed.

These two sites are representative of the main types of soil treatment as yet recognized on chalk and limestone in the Neolithic period, and about ten others fall into one or other category. But we are not yet in a position to relate the environmental evidence to specific economic or agricultural practices until we have more data.

A later group of monuments dating from the late-third/early-second millennium bc takes the environmental history of the chalklands a stage further. These are the ritual monuments known as 'henges'— circular enclosures with a bank and internal ditch, and one or more entrances. Avebury in north Wiltshire is an impressive example, presenting, in its original state, a height difference of eighteen metres from the top of the bank to the bottom of the ditch, and enclosing about twelve hectares. The significant feature of the environmental sequence from the buried soils beneath various Wiltshire henges, after clearance and cultivation had taken place, is the length of time—generally about 500 years—for which an environment of grassland existed.[15] This was maintained, it is assumed, by grazing animals, and it is quite a different situation from the short-term landnam phases recognized in other parts of Britain at this time. Pasture and the grazing of stock were clearly of importance on the Chalk during late Neolithic times.

Two sites close to the Chalk from which pollen data relevant to the period under consideration have been obtained are Wingham and Frogholt in Kent.[16] The sites comprise organic valley deposits which had begun to form by the beginning of the second millennium bc. The pollen spectra from both show that clearance of woodland on the **adjacent** downs had taken place by Early Bronze Age times, and probably before, and that regeneration did not occur. At Julliberries Grave, a Neolithic long barrow in the same area, the land snail fauna from the buried soil indicates an open environment prior to the construction of the mound.[17] Thus a similar pattern to that on the Wiltshire Chalk is implied for Kent.

Another region in which land snails can help is, somewhat unexpectedly, the western coastline of the British Isles. Unexpectedly, because the rocks along this coastline are generally non-calcareous and give rise to neutral or acid soils which are neither conducive to molluscan life nor suitable for the preservation of their shells. However, the coastal belt is characterized by extensive tracts of shell sand blown off the foreshore and driven inland, sometimes for over two kilometres. The deposits are made up of fragments of marine shells and other calcareous matter, and give rise to fertile and well-drained soils. The prevailing vegetation is generally pasture, and the whole complex of underlying sand, calcareous soil and plant cover is known as fixed-dune pasture or, in Scotland and the Western Isles where it is particularly well developed, as 'machair'. Land snails abound on the machair surface and their shells are well preserved within the underlying deposits which have accumulated over the centuries and comprise a series of land surfaces buried by successive layers of blown sand. Often, archaeological material is incorporated into the deposits, and when this is the case the opportunities for obtaining information about the contemporary environment through molluscan analysis are very great.[18]

Detailed work on the molluscan faunas has been done in the Outer Hebrides, the Orkneys and Cornwall. Results show that woodland was once prevalent in these now often wind-swept areas prior to the onset of sand deposition.[19] The age of the deposits is generally Neolithic or later. But it must be pointed out that since they are of littoral origin, earlier deposits may have formed, only to have been destroyed by the rising Post-glacial sea.

Deforestation and the deposition of blown sand in these coastal areas may not be unrelated processes. The spread of sand onto the land will, if accumulated to sufficient depth, destroy the arboreal vegetation. In addition, the very fact of a rising sea will not only submerge lowlying coastal forests but through the harmful effect of salt spray kill off trees in coastal areas not submerged. Factors other than man and his grazing animals may have been responsible for the clearance effects recorded in these deposits. But once created, coastal pastures would have attracted cattle and deer, particularly in the winter when the leafy foliage of the forest trees was sparse. Seaweed no doubt added to their diet and a further attraction would have been the high salt content of the environment. Nor would the potentialities of the habitat have passed unnoticed by Neolithic man who, it is reasonable to assume, exploited them just as farming communities do today. And once

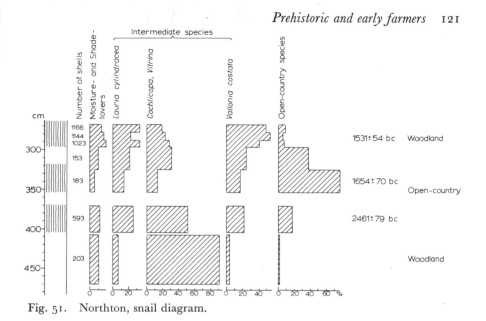

Fig. 51. Northton, snail diagram.

exploitation had begun, whether by wild or domesticated herds, we can imagine that the open nature of the environment was maintained indefinitely, just as it was at Upton Warren (p. 40). Neither at the settlement sites of Gwithian in Cornwall or at Skara Brae in the Orkneys does there seem to have been any regeneration once deforestation had been effected.

We can therefore ally these areas of fixed-dune pasture with the Chalk and younger limestone soils of southern and eastern England, the sands of the Breckland, and, probably, with certain river gravel tracts where heavy concentrations of Neolithic and Bronze Age monuments occur. There is, however, little environmental data, pollen analytical or molluscan, from the latter regions. But it seems likely that areas such as the Boyne Valley in eastern Ireland, Strath Tay in central Perthshire, and various parts of the Thames Valley, in particular around Oxford and Dorchester where ancient monuments of Neolithic date are prolific, that clearance was widespread and more or less permanent. To these we can add the coastal plain of south-west Cumberland, 'a fertile strip of drift-covered lowland' which has been shown by pollen analysis (Fig. 47) to have been permanently deforested by Neolithic man.[20]

In Co. Mayo, extensive systems of stone-walled fields revealed beneath the blanket peat and of probable Neolithic date, attest in a different and archaeologically more satisfying way to widespread clearance.[21] The buried soil beneath the peat shows signs of cultivation in that there are criss-cross ploughmarks at its base, overlain by ridges suggestive of spade cultivation, and in this respect the sequence is similar to that at South Street.

Possible regeneration in later Neolithic times

At several sites in the areas we have been discussing regeneration of scrub or woodland did in fact take place, but not until many centuries after the initial clearance.[22] At Northton, for example, in the Isle of Harris, land-snail analysis has demonstrated an episode of deforestation around 2500 bc followed by a period of woodland regeneration about a millennium later (Fig. 51). This is certainly not a landnam, being of too long duration. Several chalk sites in southern England also seem to have become similarly overgrown some centuries after the initial clearance, although it is difficult to be certain just how widespread this was. Grazing must have been relaxed and cultivation discontinued in these areas.

Interestingly, two changes in the archaeological record may be associated with this episode. One is the increase in the proportion of pig bones on later Neolithic sites, the significant point being that the pig is essentially a forest-dwelling animal. The other change is in arrowhead type (Fig. 52). Earlier Neolithic peoples used pointed 'leaf-shaped' arrowheads, although whether primarily for warfare or hunting is not known. But in later times the 'chisel-ended' arrowhead, similar to, but larger than, those used by Mesolithic man, became fashionable. These were suited to the shooting of small game, in particular birds. The broad cutting edge could slice through a large quantity of muscle thus causing rapid immobilization, essential when hunting in a forested environment if the quarry was not to be lost.

Small temporary clearances

In other parts of the British Isles the land-use pattern of Neolithic times was somewhat different from that just described. Pollen diagrams

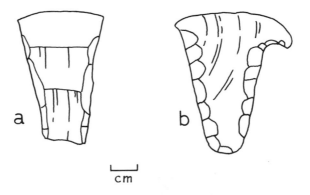

cm

Fig. 52.   Tranchet arrowheads. a, Mesolithic; b, Neolithic.

covering this period do not show consistently high herb frequencies. Instead there are either extremely low values or a series of small peaks suggestive of landnam episodes.[23] In this context too we can usefully begin to consider the Bronze Age, a period which is marked archaeologically by the introduction into the British Isles of the technique of manufacturing tools and weapons of bronze. It began around 1800 bc. Much of the work on the environment of these periods has been done by Judith Turner who has built up a detailed picture of the vegetational changes associated with 'small temporary clearances'. This has been done firstly by taking very close samples through peat deposits, sometimes at 0·5 or even 0·25 centimetre intervals, in order to isolate the pollen rain of only a few years, and secondly by accurate radiocarbon dating.

Bloak Moss in Ayrshire (Fig. 53) is fairly typical. In zone VIIa the high grass peaks suggest sporadic opening up of the forest cover, possibly by hunting communities. Then, towards the end of the zone, there was a more definite clearance episode with grasses, plantain and bracken increasing, and elm declining. This was followed by a pronounced elm decline in which no other species were significantly affected. But from this point until the end of the Neolithic period there is little evidence for any interference with the forest habitat at all. Then, during the Bronze Age and early Iron Age four landnam episodes occurred as indicated by the pronounced peaks of grasses, plantain and bracken. Ash, a light-demanding tree, appeared for the first time as a persistent member of the forest canopy.

A similar pattern is emerging for many other parts of the British Isles, especially in upland regions and areas of impoverished sandy soils. In some cases the Bronze Age clearances appear to have been for pasture, as at Bloak Moss; in others, as in the Cumberland Lowland and the Somerset Levels, they were for cereal cultivation. This is indicated by the absence or presence of cereal pollen and the proportions of weeds of cultivation to plants diagnostic of pasture—the 'arable/pasture ratio'. But neither in these clearances nor in those of earlier Neolithic times is there good evidence for slash-and-burn cultivation. Shifting agriculture involving this technique did not occur. Why then were the clearances temporary? To this question there is as yet no answer. Possibilities such as the over-exploitation of elm fodder, declining soil fertility or the overkill of game can be put forward; but social factors just as much as those of an environmental kind may have contributed to the pattern and method of land use.

Two subsidiary types of forest exploitation which appear to have taken place are the coppicing of hazel in Somerset, possibly to provide long poles for the construction of the bog trackways, and the use of lime—recorded in the pollen record as a 'lime decline'—for fodder or bast.[24]

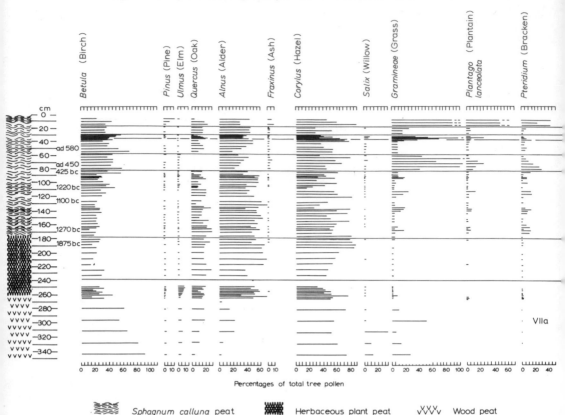

Fig. 53.   Bloak Moss, pollen diagram. (After Turner, J., 1970, Fig. 2)

Stone axes

To effect these clearances and other depradations on the forest
Neolithic and Bronze Age farmers used stone axes made from flint or
particular types of metamorphic or igneous rock (Fig. 54). Occasionally, hard sedimentary rocks known as 'greywackes' were used. We
have already described the utilization of flint by hunting communities
and there is little doubt that the main sources were coastal beaches,
river gravel banks and, perhaps, the seams of flint exposed in chalk
cliffs along the coast. But Neolithic man required flint of superior
quality for his axes, flint which had not been subjected to the battering
action of waves and currents or the stresses of alternating cold and
warm temperatures and which lacked the incipient fracture planes of
surface material. And to obtain such flint he had to mine for it.[25] The
best known flint mine complex is Grimes Graves near Thetford in the
East Anglian Breckland which covers a known area of about 15
hectares (35 acres). Shafts were sunk through the overlying drift into

the chalk. Two layers of nodular flint (known by the Brandon knappers of historical times as 'topstone' and 'wallstone'), weakened by freeze–thaw stresses of former periglacial climates, were ignored, and it was not until a layer of tabular flint, the 'floorstone', was reached at about twelve metres below the surface that exploitation began (Fig. 54). This was done by running lateral galleries out from the base of the shaft, and these often linked up with galleries from adjacent shafts. Other mining complexes of a less sophisticated nature occur in the southern chalklands (Fig. 55). But they have not so far been located in Yorkshire and Lincolnshire. This is curious in view of the heavy concentrations of Neolithic sites in these areas but may be related to the more brittle nature of the flint and tougher quality of the chalk,

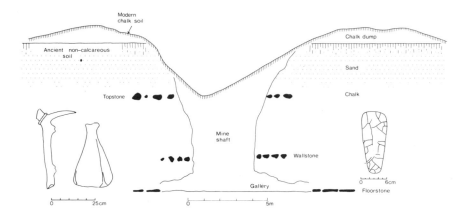

Fig. 54. Section through a flint mine with, on the left, antler pick and scapula used in removing the chalk spoil, and, on the right, a finished chipped axe.

making deep mining a difficult, if not impossible, task.

In other parts of the country away from the Chalk various other types of stone were used for manufacturing axes (Fig. 55). The most suitable were medium- or fine-grained igneous or metamorphic rocks, rocks which could be worked to a sharp edge and at the same time were resilient and tough. Coarse-grained rocks such as granite were unsuitable in that although hard they shattered easily and were difficult to work to a fine edge. Sedimentary rocks such as sandstones were generally too soft or tended to fracture along the bedding planes. In general, where the exact location of factories is known, extraction of stone took place at the surface of outcrops or from scree material, but in two cases, namely the factories on Shetland and at Mynydd Rhiw in the Lleyn Peninsula, underground quarrying took place.[26] The latter site shows clearly the precision with which Neolithic man sought out and utilized particularly suitable rock types. The local sedimentary

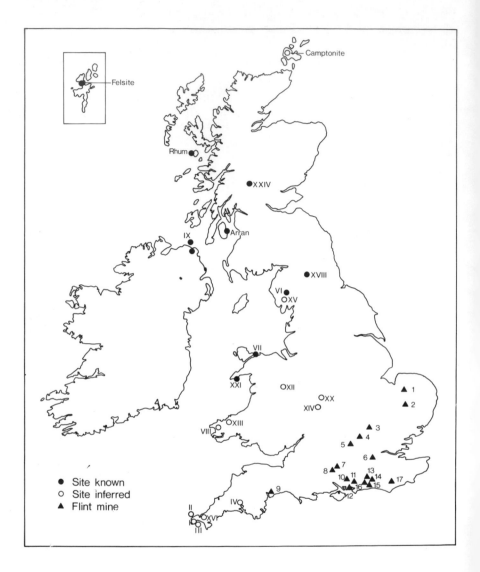

Fig. 55. Distribution of stone (circles) and flint (triangles) axe factories. Roman numerals refer to groups identified petrologically. Flint mines: 1, Massingham; 2, **Grimes Graves**; 3, Pitstone Hill; 4, High Wycombe; 5, Peppard; 6, East Horsley (medieval); 7, Martin's Clump; 8, Easton Down; 9, Beer; 10, Stoke Down; 11, Bowhill; 12, Lavant; 13, Blackpatch; 14, Harrow Hill; 15, Cissbury; 16, Churchill; 17, Windover. Stone axe factories: I and II, unknown; III, Trenow; IV, Balstone Down; VI, Great Langdale; VII, Graig Lwyd; VIII, Ramsey Island?; IX, Rathlin and Tievebulliagh; XII, Cwm Mawr, Corndon; XIII, Prescelly Mountain; XIV, Nuneaton District; XV, unknown; XVI, Camborne area; XVIII, Whin Sill; XX, Charnwood Forest; XXI, Mynydd Rhiw; **XXIV, Killin.**

rock is a shale laid down on an ancient sea bed some 500 million years ago. At a later time during a period of igneous activity, molten matter pushed its way along the bedding planes of the shale and on cooling hardened to an 'igneous intrusion' of a rock type known as dolerite. Such intrusions were often themselves exploited for stone, as in the case of the Cornish greenstones, the felsite dykes of Shetland and the camptonite sills of the Nuneaton district and Orkney. But in the case of Mynydd Rhiw it was the 'contact zone' between dolerite and shale which was important (Fig. 56). The intense heat generated by the igneous intrusion resulted in the alteration of the shale to a metamorphic rock of uniform texture, combining hardness and conchoidal fracture—properties essential for the production of stone axes by flaking. The porcellanite of the factories in north-east Ireland was similarly formed.

The rock sources from which the axes were made have in some cases been identified by petrological examination, under the microscope, of thin sections of the axes.[27] These have been given group numbers (Fig. 55). By plotting the distribution of axes of a particular group in relation to their source we can obtain information about the movements, or perhaps trade routes, of prehistoric man.

The use of stone by early farming communities has two important environmental implications. For ancient man, stone was of great significance in the production of tools and weapons, particularly before the development of copper, bronze and iron working, and we may see the axe factories of the third and fourth millennia bc as the

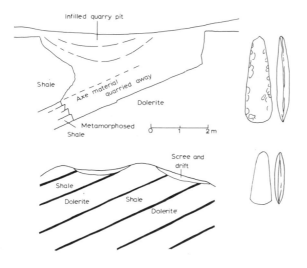

Fig. 56. Mynydd Rhiw, stone axe factory. Upper, detail of one seam; lower, relationship of the three rock types. On the right, two finished products from Nantmor, Caernarvonshire (upper) and Oswestry (lower). (After Houlder, 1961)

highest point of development in prehistoric man's exploitation of stone. So important was the production of efficient stone axes that the distribution of suitable rock types may have controlled the siting of settlements. Raw materials, just as much as factors such as topography, vegetation, soil and animals, may determine site location. Secondly, the axe factories are among the earliest instances of the localized exploitation of mineral resources. Today the waste products of mining— e.g. for coal, iron and china clay—have a considerable impact on the landscape, but as far back as the third millennium bc the complex of Grimes Graves would have constituted a feature of no small magnitude, the chalk waste bringing about the burial of topsoil and the destruction of what may have been valuable pasture or arable land (Fig. 54). However, in the long term, at any rate at Grimes Graves, the result has been one of soil improvement, for whereas the original soil was sandy and susceptible to wind erosion, the soil today, where developed on the chalk upcast, is calcareous and fertile. The side effects of industrial processes are not always detrimental.

Routes to open country

The various ways in which prehistoric farmers exploited the woodland environment, and the routes to the development of open country which stemmed from this exploitation, are not clearly understood. Nor are we in a position to attempt a correlation of the archaeological and economic data with that of the environment. Nevertheless a few observations can be made.

In the English Lake District there is some correspondence between the distribution of isolated axes and local pollen evidence for an elm decline, suggesting that the lopping of leaf fodder took place well beyond the limits of domestic settlement.[28] In addition there is an inverse relationship between the pollen evidence for clearance and domestic settlement on the one hand and the number of axes on the other. This suggests that axes played little part in the clearance of land for settlement and that their prime function was for the collection of fodder. A cattle raising economy is implied and this conclusion is backed up by the skeletal evidence, for cattle generally predominate in the bone assemblages from early Neolithic sites. But cereal cultivation also took place at an early stage as indicated by the pollen record from sites like Barfield Tarn (p. 111) and the impressions of grain in pottery. Moreover, the absence of cereal pollen cannot necessarily be taken as evidence for the absence of crop cultivation since cereals are self-pollinating and the amount of pollen liberated into the atmosphere is slight.

On theoretical grounds, Andrew Fleming[29] has argued that cattle could never have been more than a supplementary source of food at an early stage in the history of forest clearance, for in a totally forested landscape as much as two square kilometres of browsing per year are required for only 20–30 head of cattle. Once concentrations of domestic animals are introduced into an area of course, the destruction of woodland will automatically ensue whether the animals are free ranging or stalled. The establishment of open ground for cereal cultivation will itself lead to more favourable conditions for the intro- duction of stock, for arable land must be left fallow at some stage, and the value of animals in upgrading the soil through their manure was probably appreciated. Scottish crofters, for example, in historical times used stalled cattle solely for providing manure for cereal cultiva- tion. Where forest clearance was widespread, Neolithic communities could have possessed quite large herds of cattle, for grassland pasture can support many times the number of animals that can the same area of forest browsing (p. 86). And the development of grassland would also have enabled the introduction of sheep,[30] for these animals are unable to live at all in woodland. In other words, we are seeing a reversal of those trends which took place at the beginning of the Post- glacial, and a return to the kind of simplified ecosystem with which Upper Palaeolithic man was familiar—open country, a specialized economy and a greater efficiency in utilizing the available energy resources.

Wild animals such as red deer and aurochs continued to be exploited, the former in particular for their antlers which were used in the manu- facture of tools, the latter perhaps for their horn. But such animals may also have been discouraged due to their depradations on cereal crops, their competition with domestic cattle for woodland fodder, and the undesirable possibility of unsolicited crossbreeding with domestic stock, although the latter is arguable. It is from this time too, and for the same reasons—the separation of domestic from wild animals and the protection of cereal crops—that the first enclosures of the landscape began. The evidence has been summarized by Peter Fowler[31] who cites several instances from Ireland and the west of Britain of field walls beneath Neolithic and Bronze Age monuments. Others, as in Co. Mayo, have been revealed beneath blanket peat of Sub-boreal age, and yet others, as in the Isles of Scilly, are now submerged by the sea.

Thus in Neolithic and Bronze Age times there were two main types of forest exploitation and land use. One was the effecting of small temporary clearances sometimes associated with the use of elm for cattle fodder and the growing of cereals. The other was the creation of large areas of open ground with, again, a mixed economy, but one in which sheep perhaps played an increasingly important role. There was perhaps an episode of woodland regeneration in late Neolithic times in these latter areas with an emphasis on pig breeding and a resurgence of small-game hunting but by the Bronze Age, grassland was probably a marked feature of the landscape and the opportunities for an economy based largely on pastoralism manifest. R. J. C. Atkinson has pointed out that the emergence of prehistoric astronomy, as betrayed by the mathematical precision with which stone circles of late Neolithic and Bronze Age date were constructed, could only have taken place in an environment of wide open country across which sitings to the horizon could be made.[32]

But there were, of course, as the pollen record and archaeological distribution maps show, many areas in the British Isles which were neither settled nor exploited by Neolithic man, and which remained virgin forest until the Bronze Age or, as in the case of the heavy clay soils of the English Midlands, right through the prehistoric period. Areas of poor sandy soil which today often support heath or moorland and which are susceptible to rapid erosion and degradation were generally avoided by Neolithic farmers, and this is most strikingly shown in north-east Yorkshire (Fig. 34). Here, Neolithic burial mounds, pits for storing grain, and other evidence for settlement are, with a few exceptions, restricted to the lime-rich soils of the Wolds to the south of the Vale of Pickering and the Tabular Hills to the north. The pattern of settlement by the later, Beaker, peoples was similar. There are extensions of the distribution of these groups in two directions, one into the Vale of Pickering where there are several finds of stone axes, the other onto the generally acidic soils of the moors north of the Tabular Hills where numerous arrowheads have been found suggesting that here were the hunting grounds of these communities.[33] But it was not until the Bronze Age that farming began on the moors.

The North York Moors

The environmental history of the North York Moors has been worked out largely through the pollen analysis of buried soils beneath Bronze Age barrows and beneath the peat cover where this exists.[34] The technique of soil pollen analysis has already been described in dealing with Mesolithic sites (p. 92), and the same principles apply to the study of Bronze Age soils. A useful index in assessing the degree of open country as represented by the pollen record is the non-tree-pollen/tree-pollen percentage (NTP : TP), i.e. the non-tree or herbaceous pollen expressed as a percentage of the tree pollen. A value of less than 100 per cent is equivalent to dense forest; one of 150 to 200 per cent to open country. For example, at the Mesolithic site of White Gill already discussed (Fig. 36) the value below the microlith level is 39 per cent, above this level 104 per cent, suggesting a degree of clearance in Mesolithic times.

The story is continued at two Bronze Age round barrows known as the Burton Howes[35] situated on one of the highest points of the moors and about 2·5 kilometres west of White Gill (Fig. 34). The barrows were built of turf—itself an indication of some grassland in the area. The NTP : TP percentage from the turf core of one of the barrows (4D) was 119 suggesting that the barrow was built in a woodland clearing. Turves from a later addition to the mound gave a value of 150 indicating the enlargement of the clearing. From the second barrow (1A) a value of 168 was obtained. The present-day NTP : TP percentage is 787. The whole sequence can be summarized as follows:

		NTP: TP per cent
Present day		787
Burton Howes	1A	168
	4D, later addition	150
	4D, primary turf mound	119
White Gill	above microliths	104
	below microliths	39

These two sites—White Gill and Burton Howes—show that the moors were once forested. Partial clearance took place in Mesolithic times but the main clearance came in the Bronze Age. The evidence of wood charcoal and the increase of birch in the pollen record after the Mesolithic episode suggests, as already discussed, that fire was the main agency. But in the case of the Bronze Age clearances there was no change in the species composition of the forest and no charcoal. Clearance took place by felling or gradually through the influence of grazing stock. This is not necessarily true of other parts of Britain, for a number of the sites studied by Judith Turner[36] show an increase of birch relative to oak in the regeneration stages of small temporary clearances; but this could just as well be due to soil degradation as to burning, there being no direct evidence for the latter. On the high moors there is, according to Dimbleby, no evidence for the cultivation of crops—cereal pollen, grain impressions in pottery, grain storage pits, querns, sickles and evidence for ploughing being absent; plantain pollen is virtually unrepresented in the pollen record. Clearance is therefore assumed to have been for pasture. Its effect was to cause an increase in hazel around the forest margin and grasses to flourish. This is in contrast to the birch-dominated forest-edge communities of today's woods in heathland areas and the predominance of heather in open country.

The situation on the less elevated Tabular Hills to the south of the high moors is somewhat different,[37] and again the main evidence comes from the pollen analysis of buried soils beneath Bronze Age barrows. Cereal pollen is consistently present in some profiles and in one case the rare occurrence of a cluster of cereal pollen from a fallen anther was recorded. A variety of weeds of cultivation including ribwort plantain, *Plantago lanceolata*, occurs, and saddle querns for grinding grain are recorded from the area.

That cereals could be grown at all on what are now impoverished podsolic soils demonstrates the superior fertility of these areas in the Bronze Age. This is also shown by the presence of base-demanding trees in the pollen record such as alder and lime. It is confirmed too in an interesting manner by the presence of fire-reddened stones in Bronze Age hearth sites in the bleached horizons of podsols. Stones only become reddened by fire if they contain iron and this is not the case with stones bleached by podsolization. Therefore, the presence of these reddened stones implies that at the time of burning, the soil was not podsolized and had a higher iron content than that of today. The fact, too, that the stones are buried implies earthworm activity in the past, for as already discussed (p. 98) these creatures are not found in podsolic soils. Comparison of the present-day podsols, in which the bleached horizon and iron/humus pan are strongly developed, with soils of the Bronze Age where there is only slight iron movement and leaching (Fig. 57) is sufficient evidence in itself to demonstrate the striking changes in soil profile development which have gone on since the Bronze Age.

This work on soil degradation and vegetational history in the North York Moors has been carried out by G. W. Dimbleby.[38] Recently some of his conclusions, particularly those concerning the reasons for clearance of the high moors in Bronze Age times, have been questioned by Andrew Fleming.[39] He has pointed out that three Bronze Age pottery vessels with the impressions of cereal grains are known from the moors. He also states that many of the barrows are

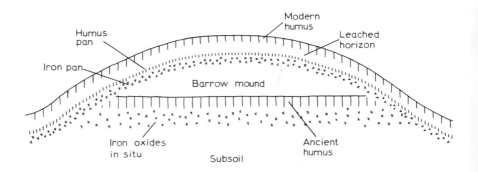

Fig. 57. Section through a Bronze Age barrow showing the ancient brownearth soil and the modern leached podsol.

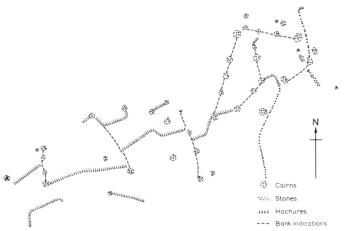

N

Cairns
Stones
Hachures
Bank indications

Fig. 58.   Plan of cairnfields on Kildale Moor in north-east Yorkshire. (After Feachem, 1973, Fig. 3)

made of stone, which, he rightly argues, would have been available only after the original forest soil had been disrupted by agriculture and the surface lowered by deflation (p. 103). On the other hand, the Burton Howes barrows on which Dimbleby's conclusions are partly based are built of turf, not stone. On theoretical grounds, too, Fleming is against the idea of woodland clearance for creating pasture, in that nutritious forest browsing was itself available. But it is not clear whether the destruction of woodland was a deliberate process of felling or one which resulted from browsing. And if, as we have discussed earlier, a purely stock-keeping economy is difficult to support in a forest environment, deliberate clearance would be a natural prerequisite to the exploitation of the area. Unfortunately we do not know to what extent these Bronze Age people were nomadic, or were practising transhumance, or were settled farmers, and until we do, any theoretical grounds for postulating the mechanisms and reasons for clearance must be left aside.

But another of Fleming's arguments warrants more serious consideration, namely the 'cairnfields'. These often constitute a major landscape feature and are to be found in many upland regions of the British Isles from the South-west Peninsula to the Shetlands.[40] They comprise groups of small stone cairns, usually situated (in north-east Yorkshire) between 180 and 300 metres above sea level, and often associated with irregular stone walls or low terraces (Fig. 58) enclosing small plots of land. These are generally considered to represent the surface clearance of fields prior to tillage and the enclosure of areas for growing cereals. Dating is difficult but they are said to begin in some areas in the third millennium and continue into the first half of the first millennium bc. In north-east Yorkshire the majority of cairnfields are on south, south-west or south-east slopes which would ensure better conditions for crop growing. Charcoal and other traces of burning in and under the cairns suggest scrub clearance. The exact function of the cairns in these systems is uncertain owing to the paucity of finds; they may be the result of clearance or they may be ritual or sepulchral, and as Fleming points out there may be no clear distinction between these various possible uses, a burial rite providing a convenient means of, or being adapted to, field clearance.

In north-east Yorkshire it has been suggested that the cairnfields were developed at a late stage in the Bronze Age exploitation of the moors as a response to soil degradation on the high plateaux—people moving to lower, more fertile slopes. But this does not undermine Dimbleby's hypothesis that clearance at Burton Howes was associated with grazing stock since the pollen evidence from that site indicates an early stage in the development of open country. Moreover, Burton Howes lies at about 430 metres, some 120 metres above the upper limit of the cairnfields. On the other hand it is not impossible that at least some of the cairnfields are contemporary with the high moorland clearances and part of one and the same system—the clearances constituting the pastures of a mixed agricultural community, the cairnfields their plots for cereal cultivation.

Soil

In discussing the impact of Mesolithic man, it was shown that in certain areas, forest clearance resulted in podsolization (p. 99). It has also been suggested that soil deterioration may have taken place through natural causes, particularly under the conditions of high rainfall in the Atlantic period. The effects both of climate and man on the soil prior to the Neolithic may have led to vegetational changes— some of our heathlands may have their origin in the Mesolithic, and pollen analysis of degraded Welsh soils suggests associated changes in the forest composition, oak giving way through a pine phase to birch-dominated woodland.[41] Such differences were no doubt recognized by Neolithic man as is suggested by the many of his sites which directly overlie those of Mesolithic age. But excepting the formation of blanket bog on many uplands and in the west during Atlantic times, it is unlikely that either Mesolithic man or climate had much influence on the degradation of soils over wide areas of the country, even although the effect locally may have been pronounced.

The same cannot be said of Neolithic and subsequent farming communities for with the growing of crops and the establishment of grazing land the soil became of fundamental importance and its resources, which had been built up under a cover of mixed deciduous forest in the early Post-glacial, were put under ever increasing strain.

From Neolithic times onwards there is a close relationship between man and the soil. Not only does soil type begin to exert an influence on settlement patterns, but man becomes a predominant factor in soil development, often overriding the effects of climate.

There is no doubt that early farmers knew a good deal about soil structure, drainage and fertility, and the potential of a given soil type to degrade or erode. They avoided areas which are today heath or moor with soils of podsolic type even although, as we have seen (Fig. 57), these same areas in Neolithic times supported base-rich brownearths and a flora of nutrient-demanding trees. At the other extreme is their avoidance of the heavy clay soils of the vales of midland England, an avoidance probably governed by technological factors—the absence of sophisticated ploughs capable of turning a sod and aerating the soil, and the inability to control the frequent flooding which even today, with embanked and controlled river systems, is a problem.

A pioneer in the study of ancient human environments was Sir Cyril Fox, and in two classic works, *The Archaeology of the Cambridge Region* (1923) and *The Personality of Britain* (1932) he presented a masterly integration of the natural sciences and archaeology. One of the main ideas put forward was that soil type was determined by subsoil and that in its turn, both directly and through the forest vegetation to which it gave rise, the soil strongly influenced the distribution of human settlement. Light and pervious soils such as those on chalk, limestone, sand and gravel supported forest with little undergrowth and to which man 'had no difficulty in accommodating himself'. The heavy clay soils supported 'damp' oakwood, 'an unending tree canopy of oak with inter-lacing undergrowth of hazel, thorn, holly and bramble', which was generally shunned by prehistoric man. Fig. 59 shows Fox's map of the distribution of Beaker and Bronze Age finds in the Cambridge region plotted against vegetation as deduced from soil type. There is clear avoidance of 'dense forest' although it is to be noted that the majority of 'finds' (presumably indicative of settlement) occur in the areas designated fen or marsh, not on the open downs; on the latter it is burial mounds which predominate. Fox argued that the siting of these barrows in situations where they were clearly visible from the valleys below was indicative of the open nature of the environment in Bronze Age times—as we now know, through pollen and molluscan analysis, to have been the case. Neolithic monuments on the other hand were often inconspicuously sited as if in a generally wooded landscape; yet the same avoidance of clay soils obtained.

But what is not clear is the relative importance of the two factors—vegetation and soil—in directly influencing settlement. Fox was inclined to see vegetation as the overriding influence, and in particular the presence or absence of undergrowth in the forest, but it is arguable

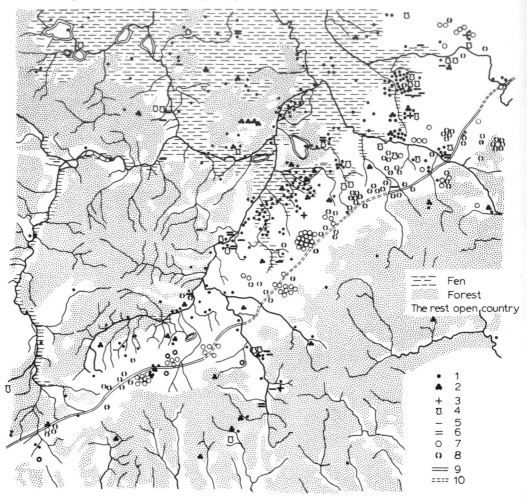

Fig. 59.   Map of Bronze Age sites in the Cambridge region. 1, finds; 2, hoard; 3, settlement; 4, Beaker; 5, 'flat' burial; 6, flat cemetery; 7, round barrow burial; 8, round barrow not examined; 9, trackway, known; 10, trackway, inferred. (After Fox, C., 1932, Fig. 23)

that such a distinction ever existed. Fox does not quote his source for defining the shrub layer of his two types of forest. Dense canopy woodland, as in many beechwoods today, may be inimical to shrub growth; it is in fact more reasonable to suppose a thick growth of scrub and bramble in open canopy woodland. Conditions in present-day forests may be a poor guide due to variation in management and history, but there is certainly not the clear distinction which Fox envisaged.

Furthermore, under woodland, given relatively uniform climatic conditions, soils in north-west Europe tend towards the brownearth type irrespective of subsoil. As already explained (p. 95) a cover of woodland accelerates drainage and maintains the base content of the soil, and thus its structure and fertility. Our present-day heavy clay soils 'unbelievably sticky, caking into ironhard clods in summer' and 'very retentive of water'[42] are a legacy of at least 2000 years of human exploitation. They are not representative of the soils in the same area under conditions of natural woodland; these would have had an upper humus horizon fully friable and well-drained, with a high base content. Neolithic man could certainly have cultivated such soils successfully for a few years, but cropping or grazing and the absence of liming and manuring would have led rapidly to a loss of nutrients, a loss of structure and to waterlogging. Likewise with the acidic soils of moors and heathlands. These too were once brownearths (Fig. 57) and were indeed cultivated in later prehistoric times, but with results which are only too apparent today. It is largely through agriculture that the diversity of soil types with which we are familiar has come about.

Thus it seems that it was the potential of a soil to withstand agricultural processes, and not simply the contemporary soil type or vegetation, which was important in determining settlement areas in Neolithic and Bronze Age times. This is very remarkable and implies a sophistication in man's knowledge of the environment which it is hard for us to appreciate but which stresses the importance of soil to these early farmers.

In 1933, directly after and consequent upon the appearance of *The Personality of Britain*, Wooldridge and Linton[43] published their paper on the loam terrains of south-east England (p. 63) in which they recognized a group of soils with properties intermediate between those on heavy clays and those on light porous subsoils, and which presented optimum conditions for cultivation. These include a wide variety of solid and drift geological deposits—brickearths, terrace gravels, calcareous boulder clays, marls and Lower Chalk—but whose properties are essentially similar—high fertility, good (but not excessive) drainage and a strong ability to withstand grazing and cultivation. Part of the uniformity of these soils is due to their loess content (p. 63), material which contributes a silt-size grain and a variety of minerals, thus enhancing both the structural and chemical fertility of the soil. The loam terrains stand out as areas of early prehistoric settlement. It can be argued, for example, that the importance of the chalklands to prehistoric man lay as much in the ambient areas of low-lying Lower Chalk as in the main masses of the Middle and Upper Chalk plateaux. There is certainly a strong contrast today in north Wiltshire between the grassland cover of the downs and the predominantly cereal-growing areas of the vales and plains.

On several accounts, therefore, we must be cautious in generalizing about soil type on the basis of geological maps. The Chalk, for example, is not everywhere free of drift. In the Chilterns there is a thick cover of Clay-with-flints which in places is as tenacious and intractible for cultivators as are the heavy clay soils of the lowland plains; the paucity of Neolithic and Bronze Age settlement in these hills is almost certainly due to this factor.[44] But the drift maps, too, may be misleading. In Ireland, although six per cent of the surface is covered with peat this was not always present, having formed at various times in the past; it often overlies formerly fertile soils, which may bear the traces of prehistoric cultivation (p. 121). W. F. Grimeswas one of the first archaeologists to appreciate the importance of detailed soil maps in studying the settlement distribution of early man.[45] He pointed out, in 1945, that in Anglesey the boulder clay was a very variable deposit and that it was not sufficient to consider settlement simply in terms of the drift map. If one did this, there appeared to be a preference for boulder clay areas, 87 per cent of Neolithic, 55 per cent of Bronze Age and 69 per cent of Iron Age sites being on this deposit. If on the other hand settlement was considered in relation to the soil map, the true picture emerged, for much of the boulder clay supported light or well-drained soils, on which the majority of sites were to be found.

In upland Britain, coasts and river valleys were favoured areas of settlement, and no doubt the fertile soils of the alluvial flood plains and raised beaches '. . . in a landscape not otherwise responsive to primitive methods of tillage . . .' were a factor in this preference.[46] In some cases, however, as Audrey Henshall has shown for north-east Scotland,[47] raised beaches were often avoided when more fertile but equally light soils were available. Outside the zone of isostatic recovery where raised beaches and, often, broad alluvial flood plains are absent, soils may be equally fertile, as with the machair of the Western Isles, one of the main factors responsible for the concentration of prehistoric settlement there. But even where none of these desirable drifts is present, many enclaves of highly fertile bedrock are to be found within the upland regions of Britain, as in Orkney where the rolling landscape with its fields of oats and barley is astonishingly similar to that of Wessex, its Highland origin betrayed only by the numerous lakes and heather clad hills. There is no doubt, too, that settlement was not entirely restricted to light soils, and this is particularly the case in Ireland where many prehistoric sites are on the calcareous boulder clay. We can usefully draw a parallel from east Jutland where the discovery of ploughmarks beneath Neolithic tombs on clay soils shows that even these were not beyond the capacity of primitive ploughs.[48] But light soils were evidently favoured.

Changes of soil type

Since the introduction of agriculture into the British Isles sometime in the fourth millennium bc there have been several changes of soil type caused by man. Some may be of even greater antiquity, brought about by the activites of Mesolithic communities. Yet others may be due to natural phenomena. One of the most disastrous results of forest clearance and subsequent land exploitation—whether for pasture or arable—has been soil erosion. Not only are the calcium and water cycles broken by removing the tree cover, but the uprooting of trees breaks the soil surface creating small nuclei of erosion. We have already described the consequences of forest clearance in a Mesolithic site at Iping (p. 98) where the products of erosion buried the prehistoric land surface. In the Lake District, several of the lake basin sites studied by Winifred Pennington show a band of silt just above the level of the elm decline.[49] This reflects an increase in the rate of deposition and suggests that the elm decline involved sufficient interference with the forest on the slopes surrounding the lakes to initiate soil erosion (Fig. 46). Grazing has a similar effect if carried on for long enough. Grazing animals take away calcium, phosphate and nitrogenous substances from the soil, substances which are essential for plant growth. This effect is particularly marked if animals are brought in from the pastures at night and their manure subsequently mucked out onto arable plots. Grassland fertility is reduced. The effects are similar to leaching by rain—loss of nutrients and soil degradation. The breakdown of soil structure ensues, surface vegetation is broken and soil erosion by wind or water action quickly follows. This has happened in the Hebrides where hillslopes above the machair are often totally bare of soil. But it is important to remember that stripping of the surface vegetation alone does not necessarily lead to erosion; the soil must be in a degraded and structureless state before this can take place (p. 95).

The intensity of grazing is naturally important,[50] and in upland areas the trampling effect of sheep may, initially, favour the development of grassland from less desirable vegetation such as bracken and heather. Grasses grow by 'tillering', a process in which the stems when laid flat on the ground become rooted at the nodes, giving rise to new plants; and if trampling is not too intense a dense mat is eventually formed. If, subsequently, upland grassland is abandoned, leaching ensues and the loss of nutrients results in the spread of first the unpalatable and fibrous mat grass (*Nardus stricta*) and various species of rush and later of heather and bracken. These are less nutrient-demanding plants, and as such lead to increasing impoverishment of the soil. Manuring is important in the maintenance of hill pasture, and the folding of sheep on the land may add to its fertility. This can be seen in many parts of Britain today where field boundaries separate land

Plate 9. The Burren, Co. Clare. Carboniferous Limestone pavement exposed by soil erosion.

which has been maintained as pasture from land which has been abandoned. That such differences are due to land use and not to altitude or soil type is demonstrated clearly where the relevant field boundaries run at right angles to the contour.

One of the most dramatic areas of soil degradation and erosion in the British Isles is the Burren in Co. Clare. Here the surface strata of the Carboniferous Limestone are totally exposed (Plate 9).

If they were ever covered with Glacial Drift, it is vanished. If they had a friendly covering of peat—and the flora suggests that they had—it is gone likewise, and for miles the bare grey rock lies open to the sky, its surface a network of deep fissures and little drainage channels, all strewn with angular blocks large and small . . . The hills are soil-less, treeless, waterless . . . The strangeness of this grey limestone country must be seen to be realized . . .

A vivid description by R. Lloyd Praeger.[51]

Adjacent to the limestone of the Burren is the Millstone Grit—an acidic rock. And here, degradation has led to a different landscape. Peat now covers these hills, but, like the limestone rocks, they too were once forested as is shown by the presence of tree stools at the base of the peat (Plate 8). Indeed in Boreal and Atlantic times we may envisage a uniform soil and vegetation cover over these hills. Nowhere have the processes of soil degradation brought out differences in geology more strongly than are to be seen at the junction of the Carboniferous Limestone and the Millstone Grit.

On the Chalk, the study of ancient soils beneath prehistoric monuments has shown differences from those of today. In general these ancient soils were, as now, highly calcareous and with no marked zone of decalcification—a soil type known as a 'rendsina'. But in some cases, as in parts of the Yorkshire Wolds, the Neolithic soil was a non-calcareous brown earth where now there is a rendsina.[52] Such a change was probably brought about by tillage, the plough biting into the subsoil and bringing up chalk lumps into the body of the soil thus upgrading its lime content. A similar process has taken place in certain limestone areas, for example the Cotswolds.

Another process which has occurred on calcareous rocks is dissolution by rain water charged with carbon dioxide—in effect a dilute solution of carbonic acid. This has resulted in the loss of about 30 centimetres on parts of the Chalk in 4000 years.[53] The process has been detected where an ancient monument has protected the surface of the bedrock and thus preserved it at a higher level than the surrounding land—a phenomenon known as 'differential weathering' (Fig. 49). Ploughing around a monument, as often happens, may have accelerated the process by making the soil susceptible to erosion by rainwashing or wind. The study of buried soils preserved under field monuments is thus important not only for the information they can give about the land use and environmental history of an area, but also in indicating the type of drift on which the soil developed and which elsewhere may have been destroyed by these weathering processes. This is shown in the case of the South Street Long Barrow where the present-day subsoil is bedrock chalk but the parent material of the early Post-glacial and Neolithic soil a complex of periglacial drift. The latter is of interest to the geologist as evidence of processes which obtained under sub-arctic conditions, and to the biologist as yielding a fossil land-snail fauna of a type now foreign to the present climatic regime of the British Isles. The preservation of ancient soils by archaeological structures has implications which go far beyond their immediate environmental significance to the prehistorian.[54]

Forest clearance and tillage on the slopes of river valleys leads to downslope movement of soil by rainwashing and its accumulation in the valley floor. Some of this material is carried downstream by river action and eventually becomes deposited at the mouth of the river where it may build up as a delta fan. Thus one of the indirect effects of forest clearance is to choke the mouths of rivers with debris, render harbours useless and push out to sea the margin of the land. It is not known how serious a process this was in prehistoric Britain but it is possible that the coastline of parts of south-east England, where depositional processes are at a maximum, was affected to some extent.

More certain is that river flood plains have been built up by hillwash material which has not found its way to the sea. Many accumulations of 'flood loam' are little more than hillwash deposits; they are often indistinctly bedded, contain a terrestrial (or at most a marsh) snail fauna, and often include archaeological material such as potsherds. In prehistoric times, prior to widespread cultivation, lowland rivers probably presented an appearance more like those of the highlands today—a braided course with a wide flood plain consisting of low gravel banks in varying states of vegetation (Plate 1). Deliberate embanking with artificial levées and alder-wood revetments has, of course, contributed to the present canalized appearance of many of our rivers which under normal conditions now run at a level many feet below the surface of the ambient flood plain. But accumulation from the valley sides has undoubtedly played its part.

The changing form of river courses has several implications for the prehistorian. In the first place, once a river was restricted to a single, narrow channel, more land would become available for cultivation, pasture or settlement, particularly as it was formed by terrestrial rather than fluviatile processes and was thus often out of reach of flooding (compare the formation of solifluxion gravel, p. 60). Secondly, prehistoric material on the gravel banks of the earlier flood plain would be buried. At Llancarfan in Glamorgan there is about three metres of Roman and later 'flood loam' overlying the pre-historic valley surface. And thirdly, the present-day depth of the river would be greater than that in prehistoric times. River transport would have been less easy than in the same rivers today, and one wonders in this context about the transport of the bluestones up the Wiltshire Avon to Stonehenge—a practical feat today, but would there have been sufficient depth of water for the operation in Bronze Age times?[55]

Climate

Another group of factors which may have contributed to the changes we have been discussing are those of climatic origin. The Neolithic and Bronze Age periods fall within the later part of the Climatic Optimum, and although there is no good evidence to indicate exactly when this came to an end it seems likely that by the end of the second millennium bc temperatures had assumed their present-day range.

An as yet unresolved problem is the status of Bronze Age climate in the British Isles. It will be remembered that certain vegetational sequences in Scottish peat bogs showed two horizons of tree stumps reflecting episodes of relatively dry climate when the bog surface dried out. These were termed the Lower and Upper Forestian and equated with the Boreal and Sub-boreal periods respectively (p. 79).

However, as Winifred Pennington has pointed out,[56] neither peat nor lake sediments show a lower boundary to the Sub-boreal at the zone VIIa/b transition as defined by pollen analysis, and it is only later on during the second millennium as the Sub-boreal was reaching its close that a period of slowing bog growth and the formation of humified peat attest to a shift towards drying climatic conditions. Similarly, evidence from the Somerset Levels indicates the absence of flooding or peat growth during the second millennium, during which time no trackways were built and a zone of highly humified peat formed (but see below, p. 146).[57]

Another line of evidence which has been used to suggest a period of dry climate during the Sub-boreal is the plant record, and in particular the evidence for deforestation. This is of relevance to prehistorians since the suggestion has been made that the dry climatic conditions prevented tree growth on the Chalk and lighter soils and that in consequence these were the first to be settled by immigrant farmers. However, ecologists now feel that the British climate was never sufficiently dry during the Post-glacial to inhibit woodland, and as we have seen from the record of peat stratigraphy, it was the later part of the Sub-boreal which showed a trend towards dryness. Deforestation on the Chalk took place as early as the middle of the fourth millennium bc, and is now confidently ascribed to the activities of man and his animals.

Evidence from Bronze Age soils for contemporary climatic dryness has been championed by I. W. Cornwall.[58] His main approach to the problem was 'particle-size analysis' in which the relative proportions of gravel, sand, silt and clay in a soil were measured, and from the results of which various conclusions reached about the environmental conditions under which the soil formed. The results of this method are plotted as a cumulative percentage graph in which the horizontal axis represents particle size and the vertical axis the percentage (Fig. 60). Flat or gently sloping sections of a curve indicate low quantities of a particular size grade, steep sections high quantities. In a normal soil which has formed by *in situ* weathering there are approximately equal proportions of sand, silt and clay, with a few stones; such a mixture is called a loam (Fig. 60). But where some form of rapid transportation is involved—for example by wind or fluviatile action—a soil becomes sorted for a particular size grade. We have already seen the effects of this in the river terrace deposits at Swanscombe where fine and coarse layers reflect different rates of transport. Wind, however, has much greater sorting powers and favours the transportation of silt; sand is too heavy to be carried far—hence the general restriction of marine-derived sand to coastal regions—while clay particles tend to remain suspended indefinitely. High silt concentration can thus be taken to indicate wind transport, and in the case of several Bronze Age

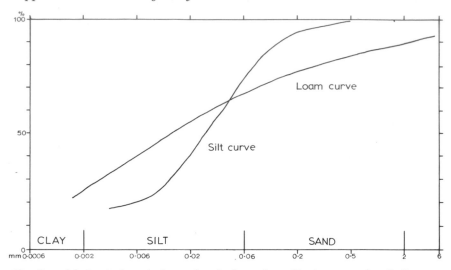

Fig. 60.   Mechanical analysis graphs of a loam from Cassington and a silt from a buried soil beneath a Bronze Age barrow at Stanton Harcourt, both in Oxfordshire. (After Cornwall, 1953, Figs. 5 and 6)

soils and ditch deposits, Ian Cornwall has indeed shown that this has taken place.

Fig. 60 shows a typical sigmoid curve with a noticeably steep portion in the silt grade. This is from a buried soil beneath an Early Bronze Age barrow at Stanton Harcourt in Oxfordshire. A similar curve has been obtained from the fill of one of the Y-holes at Stonehenge, also of Early Bronze Age date. Both indicate wind transport. And these are only two of several sites in Oxfordshire, Wiltshire, Dorset and Derbyshire, clearly indicating the widespread occurrence of wind transport during Bronze Age times.

On the basis of these deposits and soils it has been argued that the Bronze Age climate was drier than that of today.

For wind to be an important agency in filling artificial pits and ditches requires a climate at least seasonally dry and a cover of only sparse vegetation, so that bare soil is exposed to wind erosion. These conditions do not ever obtain at the present day, but it appears as if they did so during at least part of the Bronze Age.[59]

However, the destruction of ground-layer vegetation is unlikely to have been caused by climatic dryness alone; overgrazing and cultivation are more likely causes. And it is incorrect that conditions leading to wind erosion do not obtain today. Thus J. Radley and C. Simms[60] commenting on the wind erosion of agricultural land in east Yorkshire in February and March of 1967 linked it to the removal of hedges and the introduction of mechanized arable farming in the area. But they pointed out too that wind erosion was associated with freak weather conditions—below average rainfall, above average temperatures (both factors leading to a lowering of the water table and drying of the top-soil) and a very high frequency of gale-force winds. The recent dust storms in East Anglia are probably of similar origin.

It is to be pointed out that these two areas in which modern wind erosion has taken place are in that part of the British Isles which today suffers the most continental climate. As far as I know such dust storms are not recorded from present-day Derbyshire, Oxfordshire, Wiltshire or Dorset, but there is clear evidence that they occurred there in the past. This certainly seems to imply the existence of a drier climate in those parts as evidenced by the transportation and deposition of silt during the Bronze Age, whatever the origin of the bare ground surfaces from which the material derived.

Much of the evidence for the alternations of rainfall and dry periods in the Post-glacial comes from raised bogs where standstill phases in peat growth indicating a drying out of the bog surface alternate with periods of renewed growth known as 'recurrence surfaces' (*rekurrensytor*, or RYs, in the Swedish terminology).[61] The fluctuating halogen content of lake sediments in the Lake District has already been referred to (p. 77) as an index of alternations in precipitation, and these continue into the later part of the Post-glacial. A cycle of 500 to 1000 years has been inferred,[62] and a link with the recurrence surfaces in peat bogs seems reasonable. Some of the more important wet-climate periods are listed below with their equivalent recurrence surfaces where applicable.

Calendar years	Radiocarbon years	Recurrence surfaces	Archaeology
AD 1900–40			
AD 1200		RY I	Late medieval
AD 400		RY II	Late Roman
AD 1			Late Iron Age
600 BC	550 bc	RY III	Late Bronze/Early Iron Age
1400 BC	1200 bc	RY IV	Early/Middle Bronze Age
2900 BC	2300 bc	RY V	Neolithic
4000 BC	3300 bc		Early Neolithic

In the Somerset Levels, wooden trackways were built by prehistoric man across the bog surface to link islands of higher ground. These fall into two groups as dated by radiocarbon, one group being Neolithic (2800–2000 bc), the other Late Bronze Age to Early Iron Age (900–450 bc).[63] They were built as a response either to the formation of

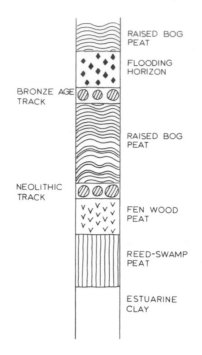

Fig. 61.   Schematic section through the Somerset Levels. (After Godwin, 1960, Fig. 15)

raised bog or to the flooding of the Levels and their conversion to wet sedge fen during periods of deteriorating climate in an attempt to keep communications open (Fig. 61). But a measure of the complexity of using these trackways as indices of deteriorating climate is an alternative hypothesis put forward by John Coles and Alan Hibbert[64] to explain the construction of the earlier group. The general sequence in the Levels comprises marine clay overlain by reed-swamp peat followed by fen wood, or carr, peat and raised bog (Fig. 61). Transportation in the reed-swamp stage would have been by boat; the building of trackways in the fen wood stage (and almost all occur at this, and not the later raised bog, stage) may thus be seen as a response to a drying environment. This does not, however, invalidate the hypothesis of a dry, followed by a wetter, period in the second millennium bc.

The period of climatic dryness in the later part of the Sub-boreal is emphasized all the more in the peat bog record by the subsequent climatic deterioration—the Sub-atlantic or Upper Turbarian—which resulted either in flooding or in the renewed growth of *Sphagnum* moss (Table 5). This material is weakly humified and contains visible plant remains; it is sometimes referred to as the 'upper *Sphagnum* peat' to distinguish it from the strongly humified and often amorphous 'lower *Sphagnum* peat' beneath. In the Somerset Levels (Fig. 61) both *Sphagnum* peat and flooding horizons are present, overlying trackways of Late Bronze Age date. Radiocarbon dates from several of these and the peat above and below a recurrence surface ascribed to the beginning of the Sub-atlantic (both in the Somerset Levels and elsewhere) have been listed by H. Godwin.[65] They average out as follows:

	Average	*Range*
Peat above recurrence surface	625 bc	247–1280 bc
Trackway	654 bc	350–902 bc
Peat below recurrence surface	1009 bc	532–1260 bc

We must therefore see the climatic deterioration as a gradual process covering the first half of the first millennium bc, and in terms of calendar years, extending well into the second millennium. It may include not only RY III, the classic boundary of the Sub-boreal and Sub-atlantic periods, but RY IV as well. The archaeological significance of this to the dating of several later Bronze Age objects recovered from peat bogs has recently been discussed by Stuart Piggott.[66]

The Highland Zone/Lowland Zone division

It is from this time onwards that the division of the British Isles into Highland and Lowland Zones becomes relevant. The division has been used by geographers to explain differences in settlement patterns, farming practices and the quality of material culture between the two zones, and Cyril Fox exploited it to a considerable extent in *The Personality of Britain*.

In brief, the Highland Zone (Fig. 62) is that part of the British Isles which is made up of the most ancient group of rocks, those formed in the Palaeozoic Era. They lie in the north and west and the division with the later Mesozoic and Tertiary rocks of the Lowland Zone falls roughly on a line from the mouth of the Tees to the mouth of the Exe. The Palaeozoic rocks are generally hard, forming mountainous regions, with continuous stretches over 300 metres above sea level. Plains and vales are not extensive. There are steep slopes and crags making cultivation difficult or impossible, and soils are often thin, stony and impoverished. Rainfall is high and there is a strong correspondence between the chief moorland areas and mean annual rainfall.[67]

Lowland Britain, on the other hand, is made up of geologically younger rocks which are softer, and which have given rise to a series of low-lying, rolling hills and intervening extensive vales and plains. Slopes are gentle, crags few and almost all the land is available for tillage, pasture or settlement. Soils are generally fertile and there is

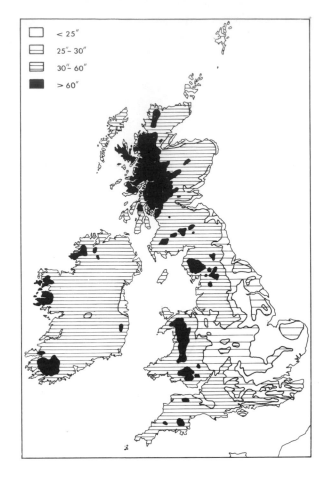

Fig. 62.   Annual rainfall map.

little evidence of erosion. Rainfall is light and there is little waste ground.

But there are many topographical exceptions, in particular various lowland areas within the Highland Zone. Some of these are relatively small—the Vale of Glamorgan, the Hebridean machair and certain fertile river valleys such as Strath Tay. Others are of much greater extent, including the Central Scottish Lowlands, East Banff and Aberdeen, and the Orkney Islands. Ireland can be divided topographically into its own Highland and Lowland Zones, and presents an anomaly in that approximately half the country is essentially lowland but situated in a high rainfall area. Estyn Evans sees Ireland as a separate Pluvial Zone.[68]

Indeed, the key distinction between the Highland and Lowland Zones is not so much elevation and topography as rainfall which is greatest in the west (Fig. 62) since this is the direction from which the main rain-bearing winds blow.[69] And prior to the climatic deterioration it is arguable whether the distinction is justifiable at all. For example there is plenty of evidence for the growing of crops prior to the Iron Age in the Highland Zone proper at heights of over 300 metres. The evidence for ancient fields has been summarized by R. W. Feachem.[70] They occur in the West Country, Wales, various parts of northern England, Scotland, Ireland and the Shetlands. They comprise groups of fields defined by irregular stone walls, earth banks or terraces, and are often associated with clearance cairns. Sometimes there are the remains of a circular hut, or huts, associated with each group. In Yorkshire we have already drawn attention to such systems (Fig. 58) where a date in the later Bronze Age was suggested. The fields are considered to have been for the growing of cereals and it seems clear that this would have been difficult under present climatic conditions or indeed at any time since the onset of the Sub-atlantic. There would have been insufficient summer warmth to ripen the grain, while the excessive rainfall in leading to over-development and weakening of the straw, would have made harvesting difficult.

Abandonment of these fields may thus have been for climatic reasons, although since their dating is often inferential we must beware of circular argument. But Feachem points out that there is a total lack of evidence for field systems associated with monuments of known Iron Age date, and in some cases fields have been exhumed from beneath a covering of Sub-atlantic peat. In Yorkshire, progressive podsolization of the soil as a result of overcropping and insufficient manuring has been suggested as a possible cause for abandoning the cairnfields.[71] Soil podsolization has been linked in the past with the Sub-atlantic rainfall increase, but Dimbleby has show, in his study of heathland soils, that this process is quite clearly linked to human interference with the soil and vegetation, and has taken place at various times since the Atlantic period.[72] Podsolization and peat growth may thus be the result of abandonment, not the cause.

In a few parts of the Lowland Zone, notably southern Wessex, field systems of Early Bronze Age date occur. These were deliberately slighted in later Bronze Age times by 'ranch boundaries', linear earthworks of bank-and-ditch type demarcating much larger areas of land and probably part of a trend to pastoralism.[73] Can this too be linked with the climatic deterioration?

A further possible reason for playing down the distinction between the Highland and Lowland Zones until the beginning of the Iron Age is related to a different factor—mineral resources. The importance of igneous and metamorphic rocks to Neolithic and Bronze Age man has already been stressed, and the ores of gold, copper and tin were equally desirable to the Bronze Age people. Fox discusses this aspect and shows how objects of Irish copper and gold were traded all over the British Isles and even onto the Continent.[74] It is interesting that while deposits of tin, gold and copper are to be found exclusively in the Highland Zone, iron ores are virtually restricted to Lowland Britain, that is, with the exception of extensive bog iron deposits in the west. This is largely a function of their mode of formation. Iron ores occur in association with sedimentary rocks, generally of Liassic and Jurassic age. Tin, gold and copper, however, are generally formed during periods of igneous activity and often occur in zones around an igneous intrusion, the 'metamorphic aureole', as is the case with many metalliferous deposits in Cornwall.

Thus for a variety of economic and environmental reasons, the first millennium bc represents a period of significant change in the Highland Zone. Fields were abandoned and either reverted to pasture or waste ground, or became covered by peat. In low-lying areas communications became difficult because of mire formation or flooding. The importance of stone and Highland Zone metal deposits dwindled. And there was no great exploitation of timber for iron smelting as occurred in the Lowland Zone. Indeed, it is from the beginning of the Iron Age that the Highland Zone as a whole assumes the pastoral character which it has retained ever since.

It is generally understood that . . . the remains of the monuments and material constructed or used throughout Britain reveal no noticeable differences in quality between the lowland and highland areas until well into the first millennium bc, but that thereafter a contrast developed between the two areas, comprising a falling-off of the material culture of the highland in comparison with that of the lowland—a contrast which has lasted to the present day.[75]

Of course, we must beware of over-generalization. Cereals are grown today in many areas of Wales to over 300 metres, for example on the Black Mountains, and even in this century crops were harvested in Perthshire on the slopes of Schiechallion at heights, again, of 300 metres above sea level.[76] Certain pollen diagrams too suggest episodes of cereal cultivation well into the opening of the Iron Age in highland regions. And in Cornwall, in contrast to other highland areas, agriculture occupied an important place right through to Roman times. But mostly, it needs zeal and a considerable degree of agricultural skill to push upwards the boundary between arable and pasture beyond the 300 metre level today (see also p. 175).

Iron Age and Roman times

The Iron Age, which began in Britain during the first half of the first millennium bc, saw the introduction of iron tools which were not only more efficient in clearing woodland and breaking up the soil than their predecessors, but which necessitated the use of considerable quantities of timber in extracting the metal for their manufacture. The beginning of the Iron Age is clearly marked in the environmental record.

After the period of small temporary clearances witnessed in the Bronze Age, certain areas of the Highland Zone were extensively cleared of forest—e.g. west Wales around Tregaron Bog (400 bc) (Fig. 63), the Somerset Levels (300 bc) and an area around Malham Tarn in the Yorkshire Pennines (early zone VIII).[77] In many of these the high grass pollen count indicates that clearance was for or associated with pasture. Other areas more securely situated in the Highland Zone retained the pattern of small clearances until much later. Thus at Bloak Moss (Fig. 53) widespread clearance did not take place until around ad 450, and the same appears to be true for much of north-west Britain as a whole. Judith Turner points out that these areas where large-scale clearance was late are notable for their paucity of Iron Age finds. Certainly the mighty hillforts which are such a characteristic feature of Wales and eastern Scotland are unrepresented in the north-west; in the latter area the characteristic homestead is the stone-built 'broch' which in general belongs to the beginning of the Christian era.

A development which is being applied to the problem of locating the areas of forest clearance, and estimating their size and subsequent land use can be usefully mentioned at this point. This is the use of 'three-dimensional pollen diagrams', and the technique has been developed by Judith Turner.[78] A simple example from Tregaron Bog is illustrated in Fig. 63. The grass pollen frequency has been used as an index of open country, and the position of the three separate diagrams from the bog in relation to the surrounding hillslopes is indicated. The diagrams are broadly comparable, with the important exception that the arable phase between the twelfth and nineteenth centuries ad is not

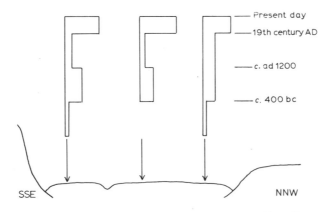

Fig. 63. Three-dimensional pollen diagram from Tregaron Bog. Grass curves. (After Turner, J., 1965, Fig. 27)

represented in the north-north-west diagram and was therefore confined to the slopes on the south-south-east side of the bog.

In the Lowland Zone, there is abundant evidence that the Iron Age economy was based on a vigorous corn-growing policy. Here we have the plough shares, the sickles, the pits for storing grain, the querns for grinding it, numerous examples of grain impressions in pottery, and often the charred grain itself. We also have the fields—the so-called 'Celtic' fields—in which the crops were grown. These are small rectangular or oblong plots defined by low banks or lynchets, groups often covering several acres of land. Generally they are preserved on areas of chalk downland which have been pasture since their abandonment, and they constitute one of the finest examples of a fossilized arable landscape from the prehistoric past.[79] It is thus unfortunate that many of these systems of ancient fields have been destroyed as, for example, by the expansion of arable acreage which took place during the Napoleonic Wars, and indeed are continuing to be destroyed in the present downland 'plough-up' policy. In some of the fields recently excavated by Peter Fowler on Overton Down, north Wiltshire, the marks of prehistoric ploughing scored into the subsoil chalk are preserved.[80] These are similar in their spacing and criss-cross pattern to ploughmarks of earlier periods at Gwithian in Cornwall,[81] where Bronze Age ploughmarks, also in fields, were dis-covered, and South Street already described. There is evidence, as mentioned above (p. 149), from a few are asof southern Wessex that the parcelling up of land for growing cereals was taking place in the Bronze Age, and in view of the frequency of field systems of second and third millennium date in the Highland Zone, their occurrence in the lowlands should not be surprising. There has simply been more destruction due to the continued use of the land for arable. The development of field systems in the Iron Age can therefore be seen as the culmination of a tradition which had its origins in Neolithic times.

The formation of field banks, or lynchets, is part natural, part artificial (Fig. 64). A variety of boundary types was used—stone walls, fences, ditches and hedges—and when ploughing began, downslope movement of soil caused a build up against the field boundary. This is known as a positive lynchet. On the downslope side of the boundary, removal of soil creates a negative lynchet, and most of the grassed-over lynchets we see today are made up of these two elements. Often a buried soil is preserved beneath the positive lynchet, particularly if the original boundary was a wall, and from this and the subsequent lynchet deposits, land snails and pollen can give information about the environment prior to cultivation of the area, and about the changes which ensued as cultivation took place.[82]

Similarly in western Britain on areas of shell sand, as at Gwithian, molluscan analysis is an important source of environmental data. The

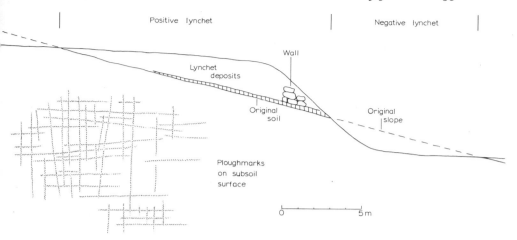

Fig. 64. Section through a lynchet, and plan of cross-ploughmarks on the pre-lynchet surface.

deposition of sand onto the surface of the fields may lead to their preservation; sometimes a whole succession of field surfaces each with their marks of tillage may be separated out.[83]

It has often been suggested that the abandonment of the downs and the trend towards farming the soils of the vales was due to exhaustion and erosion of the thin chalk soils.[84] There is indeed plenty of evidence that erosion took place. Lynchets themselves are sometimes built up to two metres with material which is poorly humic, and numerous valleys cut into the Chalk escarpments are choked with hillwash deposits containing Iron Age and Roman pottery and whose origin can be ascribed to the intensification of downland tillage which these periods saw.[85] But due to the high calcium content of chalk soils and their earthworm faunas, and to the high nutrient-demanding nature of the recolonizing vegetation, the status of a degraded chalk soil is rapidly returned to its former level. The situation is quite different from that on acidic, sandy soils. For this reason, it is unlikely that abandonment of downland for cultivation took place because of soil degradation. Moreover, the Iron Age farmers knew about manuring for we often find domestic refuse—mainly potsherds and animal bones—which was scattered on the fields; equally they would have been aware of the value of letting fields lie fallow, and of folding stock on them. The shift to the heavier soils of the vales was probably brought about by economic or technological factors—for example, the introduction of more sophisticated ploughs fitted with a mould board (p. 166) and capable of turning the earth.

As in the Highland Zone, the effect of Iron Age farming on the vegetation shows up in the pollen record as a massive and sustained rise of grasses, and contrasts markedly with the impact of Bronze Age peoples.[86]

Rather surprisingly, the Roman occupation of Britain appears to have had little impact on the rural economy, the pattern established during the Iron Age continuing right through. This, at any rate, is the picture presented by the pollen evidence (Fig. 53).[87] The main impact of Rome was in the military sphere—the construction of roads and various types of fortification. The Romans brought with them no innovations in agricultural technology. On the contrary, they exploited Britain to the extent of exporting her cereal crops to the Continent.

Such improvements as accrued to British agriculture from the Roman occupation were incidental . . . Rome did not increase the fertility of the land, but by her system of roads and the enforcement of peace she made more of it accessible and allowed it to be more intensively worked; similarly she did not improve on the . . . plough, but by organized production and marketing she made it more widely available.[88]

When we turn to the post-Roman period much of our evidence for ancient environments is derived from documents. There are, however, two forms of evidence which fall on the border line between the documentary and the standard techniques of environmental archaeology, and which are applicable to prehistoric times. These are rock art and models. We have already met with both groups in discussing Upper Palaeolithic environments—the cave paintings and mobile art objects which so vividly depict the animals of the Ice Age. For the

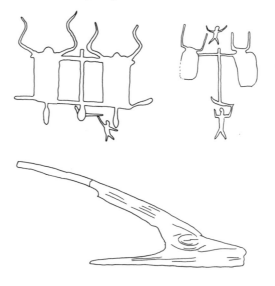

Fig. 65.   Rock carvings of Iron Age plough teams from Monte Bego in the Italian Maritime Alps. (After Bicknell, 1902.) Below, an Iron Age ard from Horslev, Denmark. (After Glob, 1951, Fig. 6)

Plate 10. Bronze model of a Roman plough team from Piercebridge, Co. Durham.

period of prehistoric agriculture there are in Europe, although not in Britain, numerous rock carvings of Bronze Age and later date which, equally vividly, illustrate various aspects of farming—notably plough teams and scenes of ploughing.[89] In one example from Bedolina in the Val Camonica, north Italy, the layout of houses, fields and irrigation channels is shown—a map, in fact, of the type of enclosed agricultural landscape which was such a feature of later prehistoric Britain. The ploughs, drawn by oxen (Fig. 65), are of simple type, sometimes known as ards; they lack mould board and coulter. Actual examples preserved in Danish peat bogs (Fig. 65) confirm the accuracy of the carvings.[90] Wooden shares have occasionally been found in Britain—as from Milton Loch, Kirkcudbright and Usk, Monmouthshire[91]—but iron shares are more commonly preserved.

In Britain we have two bronze models of Roman ploughs, one from Sussex, the other from Piercebridge, Durham (Plate 10).[92] They are of simple type having neither wheels nor mould board, thus supporting the archaeological evidence that neither element was a normal feature of the Roman or pre-Roman plough. The Sussex model has lateral wings, or 'ground wrests', whose function was to ridge the soil over the broadcast seed and create channels for drainage. But it is uncertain whether these would have been capable of turning the earth right over in the manner of a true mould-board plough. There is only scant field

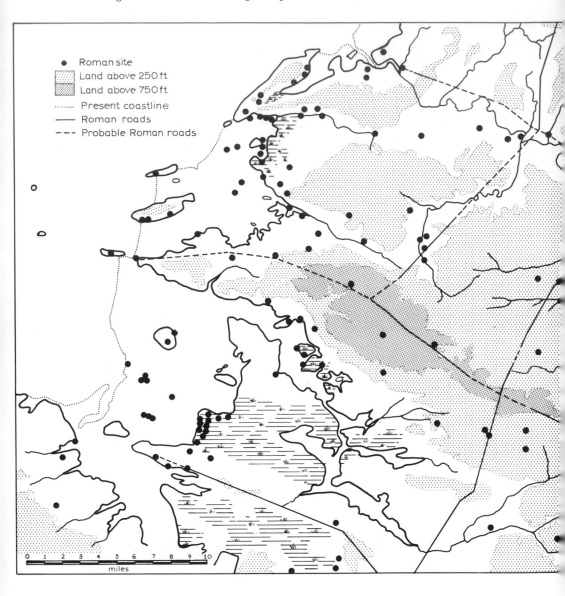

Fig. 66.   Map of the Somerset Levels in Romano-British times. (After Cunliffe, 1966, Fig. 1)

evidence of ridge cultivation in Roman times, and some of this could be the result of spade dug 'lazy beds' (see p. 173) rather than ploughing.

Coulters, however, are known, several having been found in metal-work hoards of the fourth century AD together with shares. The coulter is an iron knife fitted vertically to the beam of the plough. Its function is to cut through the sod and facilitate the breaking up of land which has long been under grass. It is unlikely that the normal form of ard in use in prehistoric times would have been capable of ploughing up pasture or downland without prior treatment of the ground, for example with spades or mattocks. The introduction of the coulter removed the need for this operation. Belgic coulters have been claimed from time to time but these are either not coulters or they are of Roman date. There is no evidence for any change in plough technology in Belgic from that of prehistoric times, or indeed in the Roman period until the fourth century. 'We may, therefore . . . consign the heavy Belgic plough with its coulter and wheels to the mythology of archaeology.'[93] The fact that some late-Roman coulters are asymmetrical indicates their probable use with a mould board, but no actual examples of this contentious artefact have yet come to light in a Roman or pre-Roman context.

There is thus good agreement between the technological and environmental evidence for land exploitation in the later Iron Age and Roman periods, both forms indicating that no significant changes took place. Major changes came early on in the Iron Age with the introduction of iron axes, iron shares and the use of timber on a larger scale than previously for smelting ores, and it is not then until Anglo-Saxon times that further technological developments bring about a shift in the pattern of land use. This is a point of some importance since it has often been suggested that the Belgae in southern England were the first to exploit the heavy clay soils. Certainly there was some colonization by the Belgae and Romano-British people of areas not previously taken up, as Fox has shown for the Cambridge region,[94] but Wooldridge and Linton point out that although many of these areas are formally boulder clay, the soils belong to their category of intermediate loams.[95] The spread onto these lands may simply have been an expansion of people, or a different land tenure system demanding more space.

There is some evidence for flooding in Roman times, for example in the Somerset Levels[96] where the conjectured coastline is shown in Fig. 66. Local shifts in population would obviously have been caused by this sort of event. But the climate was little different from that of today. On the one hand, contemporary writers such as Tacitus make no mention of frozen rivers or harbours whilst, on the other, attempts to cultivate the vine met with little success.[97] There is the possibility of a minor oscillation to drier conditions followed by a return to wetter climate about ad 200 and recurrence surface, RY II, recognized in continental bogs, and possibly too at Bloak Moss (Fig. 53), falls around ad 400.[98]

7 The historical period

Eleven kilometres from Salisbury in south-east Wiltshire, close to the Hampshire border, lies the small village of Whiteparish. Undistinctive, and consisting largely of a single street of brick cottages, an architecturally uninspiring church and a nucleus of very new houses on the original Saxon green, there is little here for the rambler in search of rustic charm or the magic of the English countryside. In the parish as a whole there are several scattered farms and cottages set in a rural landscape of fields and extensive areas of woodland. But like so many parishes there lies behind this plain façade a long, complex and fascinating history of landscape change and settlement, and it is the special fortune of Whiteparish to have had these changes worked out.[1] This has been done by C. C. Taylor, and as an introduction to some of the broader aspects of environmental evolution over the past 1500 years it is proposed to summarize the history of this forest edge parish.

The bounds enclose an area of 2430 hectares (c. 6000 acres) and include a variety of soil types (Fig. 67). Belts of chalk, sand and clay traverse the parish, and a small detached portion of the parish to the south may be related to an isolated patch of sand in a generally clay

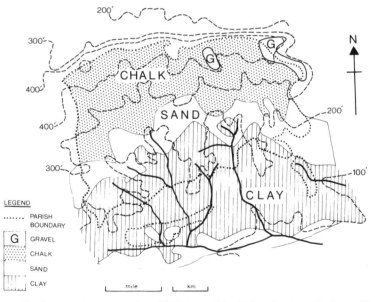

Fig. 67. Geology and topography of Whiteparish. (After Taylor, C. C., 1968, Fig. 1)

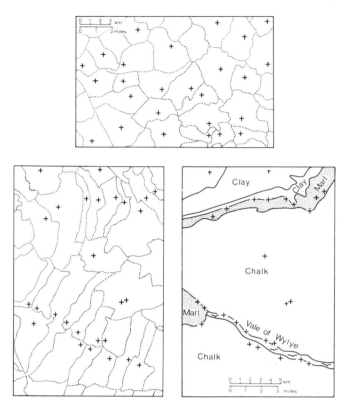

Fig. 68. Parish boundaries and settlement distribution of medieval villages as controlled by the environment. Top, clay area with few topographical contrasts; bottom right, chalk area with strong topographical contrasts; bottom left, same area showing parish boundaries. (After Stamp, 1969, Figs. 15 and 16)

area. Topographically the land slopes from 120 metres in the north to less than 60 metres in the south. Small streams flow south on the impervious clay, eventually to link up and join the River Test. In general terms, Whiteparish lies at the junction of Salisbury Plain to the north and the New Forest to the south. The siting is typical of many parishes on the edge of the Chalk in which several different environments are exploited—various soil types, plant communities (woodland and downland) and aquatic habitats (streams and watermeadow). Indeed, so strong are these environmental controls that the shape of parishes and their distribution is often determined by them. For example, the Chalk escarpments have often brought about extreme elongation of the parishes traversing them, in contrast to the irregular shape of those in land of less regimented topography. Stream courses have a similar effect (Fig. 68), and the well known phenomenon of 'spring-line settlement' is an extreme example of this form of geographical determinism.

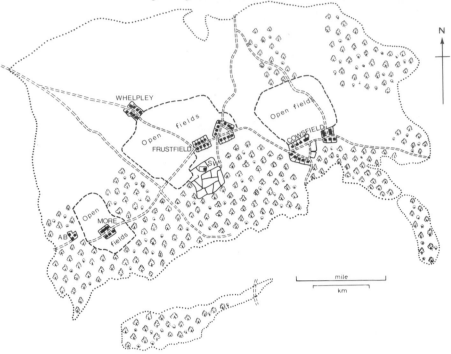

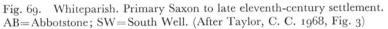

Fig. 69.   Whiteparish. Primary Saxon to late eleventh-century settlement.
AB=Abbotstone; SW=South Well. (After Taylor, C. C. 1968, Fig. 3)

The prehistoric and Roman history of Whiteparish is largely
unknown, but Celtic fields can be traced over much of the northern
third of the parish on the Chalk. Taylor points out that 'it is significant
that all the remains lie beyond what is known to be the furthest extent
of medieval cultivation', and we are probably seeing here the differential preservation of prehistoric remains through later land-use patterns
(see p. 169).

The distribution of forest and downland at the time of the earliest
Anglo-Saxon settlement is shown in Fig. 69. This reconstruction is
based on the known areas of prehistoric and Roman cultivation which
were probably still more or less open in Anglo-Saxon times, the present-
day distribution of woodland in which no former field boundaries occur,
and the distribution of various soil types. The details may be inaccurate
but the general picture is probably correct. The two earliest settlements
were Frustfield (later to become Whiteparish) and Cowsfield which
were sited on the edge of the forest, each with their own area of arable
land to the north, cultivated in the medieval open-field system.
Beyond lay the open downland on which sheep were grazed, and to the
south lay woodland which was exploited for timber for building, for
agricultural and domestic implements, and for firewood. The forest
too provided pannage for swine.

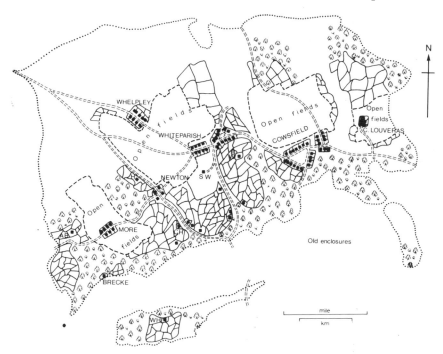

Fig. 70. Whiteparish. Mid fourteenth-century settlement. AB=Abbotstone; CH=Chadwell; BW=Blackswell; SW=South Well; WH=Witterns Hill. (After Taylor, C. C., 1968, Fig. 4)

But even by the Domesday Survey in 1086 the parish had elements of two features later to become more prominent. These were the creation of daughter settlements and the enclosure of small fields for stock (Fig. 69). The two main daughter settlements were Whelpley— 'clearing of the cubs or whelps'—and More, both now deserted.[2] Inhabitants of the former worked the same open fields as those of Frustfield, but in the case of More a portion of woodland was cleared to create at least part of a new open-field system, thus representing the first major inroad of the colonizers into the forest. Two other settlements, Abbotstone and South Well, were simply small farmsteads situated on the edge of the forest; there is no documentary or other evidence that these worked open fields, and it seems that they had enclosed fields from the first.

The next major episode was the medieval expansion of population which took place from the eleventh to the mid-fourteenth century and was reflected in an extension of arable land. The establishment of new settlements, the clearance of forest and the creation of new open fields all took place. On the periphery of the open fields, enclosure of downland began (Fig. 70).

The clearing of forest was known in medieval times as 'assarting'.

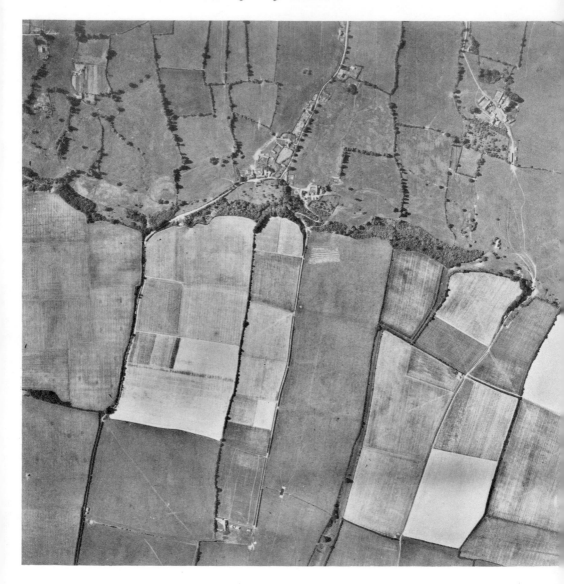

Plate 11.   Land-use differences on two types of geological solid, Oxfordshire. Upper, Oxford Clay: small irregular fields under pasture. Lower, Corallian Limestone: large regular fields, mostly cultivated.

At Whiteparish, assarts were made along the valley bottoms, leaving forested strips (still preserved today) between them on the ridges, along which ran tracks. Small settlements, generally single homesteads, grew up along these tracks. The process of assarting was frustrated by the fact that most of the woodland was part of the royal Forest of Melchet in which the felling of trees and the enclosure of land were forbidden. But because of this we have a detailed record of the several assarts from the Forest Eyres—the records of court proceedings—which list the fines for the intake of forest land. Individual assarts were small—between one-fifth and one hectare (about a half and two-and-a-half acres)—and were enclosed by an earth bank and hedge. Today these areas are still characterized by small irregularly shaped fields which contrast markedly with the larger more regular enclosures of the same age on the chalklands to the north (Fig. 70).

A similar contrast in field types can be seen in lowland England as a whole between areas of heavy clay—the Chiltern Hills and parts of Essex for example—with their dispersed farms, narrow winding lanes, irregular fields and frequent remnants of woodland, and areas of better drained soils in which nucleated villages and larger more regular fields are typical (Plate 11).[3]

The main period of land intake by assarting in Whiteparish took place during medieval times, and since then there has been little further encroachment upon the forest. The present-day distribution of woodland is thus essentially of medieval origin.

In addition to the need for arable, pasture and woodland a settlement required meadowland for the production of hay (p. 180). Most suitable for this purpose is land which is lowlying, frequently flooded and generally adjacent to a river. It is often the case, for example, that medieval parish boundaries in a large river valley run at right angles to the valley axis so that each parish might get a quota of the available meadowland (Fig. 68). The daughter settlement of Cowsfield Louveras did not have adequate meadowland due to the fact that Sherfield, an adjacent settlement in the next parish, had already acquired rights over the most suitable area. In consequence, the people of Cowsfield Louveras had to clear land beyond Sherfield, thus creating the small detached part of Whiteparish to the south east (Fig. 70).

From the fifteenth to the seventeenth centuries desertion of several daughter settlements and the partial desertion of Cowsfield took place, and more land was enclosed, including some of the original open fields. The reasons for desertion are unknown, but the Black Death does not appear to have been directly responsible.[4] Desertion may have been part of a trend, beginning in some parts of England in the thirteenth century, which saw the breakdown of the manorial system thus making movement of people more flexible. In Wiltshire the growth in the prosperity of the wool trade during the fourteenth and fifteenth centuries led to greater wealth and larger farms. It was possibly as a consequence of these factors that the move to the main focus of the area, Frustfield, or, as it had become by this time, Whiteparish, took place.

Enclosure continued in the sixteenth and seventeenth centuries, partly as a result of the influx of 'a new landowning class, who had often made their fortunes in commerce and industry as well as agriculture'.[5] New farms were built in the parish, and there was a tendency towards the earlier form of dispersed settlement. Enclosure of the remaining downland in the north took place in the eighteenth century and of a remaining nucleus of open fields in 1804 by Act of Parliament, thus completing a process which had been initiated in Anglo-Saxon times.

But the history of the fields was not yet at an end. Two groups were enlarged by the removal of some of the original hedges—the small fields which had been assarted from the forest by direct enclosure and the fields created by parliamentary enclosure. In both cases the original area enclosed was found to be uneconomical by later people. Today, the introduction of massive agricultural machinery has led to the further removal of hedges and the creation of yet larger fields—a trend back to the landscape, although not the land-use system, of the open fields.

After about AD 500 we are more dependent on documentary evidence. The methods which are applied to the study of prehistoric environments have not in general been used for the historical period, and this for a number of reasons. In the first place, the written record is often more precise both in describing environments and in dating them. Secondly, the upper part of peat deposits has often been destroyed by peat cutting so that there may be no pollen data relevant to the period. And thirdly, historians often have no need to excavate to obtain their data and thus may not be aware of potential environmental material as it comes out of the ground.

There is however plenty of data available. Various pollen diagrams such as those from Tregaron Bog (Fig. 63), Bloak Moss (Fig. 53) and several from Ireland,[6] cover the medieval and later periods, demonstrating that not everywhere have the relevant peat deposits been destroyed. In some cases, as on parts of the Pennines, blanket bog formation may not have begun until medieval times.[7] At Dinas Emrys, a Dark Age site in Caernarvonshire,[8] the organic sediments of a pool or cistern yielded a pollen diagram whose several phases could be closely linked to episodes of human activity on the site and in the adjacent valley. Earthworks such as motte-and-bailey castles and ring-works preserve a buried soil and ditch sequence which can be used to extract environmental evidence in the same way as from prehistoric sites.[9] The upper levels of the infill of prehistoric ditches are often of medieval origin, although accurate dating of these is sometimes difficult. Medieval sites such as moats are often situated in low-lying places (Fig. 71) and as a result the deposits are frequently waterlogged, providing ideal conditions for the preservation of organic remains such as seeds, wood and insects. Current excavations in the cities of Dublin and York are yielding organic material in vast quantity. At Winchester, the eggs of parasitic worms were preserved in the fill of medieval cess pits, so perfect were the conditions of preservation.[10] In Dublin the preserved stomach contents of a female Viking burial contained twenty-five species of plant coarsely ground to form a 'poor man's porridge'. And another corpse, of fifteenth/sixteenth century age discovered ten feet down in an Irish peat bog at Castleblakeney, Co. Galway, was intact, complete with clothing and stomach contents, like the better known series of prehistoric burials in Denmark.[11]

Indeed, the amount of evidence for land use, landscape change and other aspects of the environment is so prodigious that it would be fruitless to attempt a comprehensive survey in the final chapter of a book devoted mainly to the prehistoric period. We may, instead, discuss some of the more important and widespread aspects of environmental change, and draw attention to differences—and in some cases similarities—between the historic and prehistoric environments.

The historical period, for example, provides us with an insight into various aspects of the life of prehistoric communities. We may cite the creation of royal hunting forests by the Norman kings. As Dudley Stamp[12] has pointed out, many lay on areas of poor, light sandy soil generally avoided by Anglo-Saxon farmers as being unsuitable for cultivation. Few lay on that other zone of marginal land, the very heavy clays. A good hunting forest needs areas of open ground, not only for the successful use of the bow but also for the creation of grazing lands, particularly necessary for maintaining deer through the winter. '. . . a Forest must be stored with great woods . . . and also with fruitful pastures . . . if the wild beastes have not these fruitful pastures within the Forest for their feed, then they pine away and starve . . .'[13] Of the marginal soils, the lighter ones are the more suitable. Heavy clay soils become baked hard in summer, while in winter they revert to deep sticky mire, especially if subjected to continuous trampling by deer and cattle. Similar factors may have governed the location of the hunting grounds of that more ancient adept of the chase, Mesolithic man, for his pursuit of game often took him to areas of light sandy soils, and where, too, the pollen record suggests there were tracts of open ground (p. 103).

Much of the evidence for the sequence of Anglo-Saxon and later medieval settlement in lowland England is derived from place names. The distribution of pagan burials also gives an indication of the areas early colonized by the new immigrants. In Buckinghamshire, for example, the earliest settlements are to be found on the lighter soils— at the foot of the Chiltern escarpment, on the Thames gravels in the south of the county, and in the north on isolated patches of limestone, areas which had perhaps been opened up by Romano-British times.[14]

Later on, the claylands of the Vale of Aylesbury and various parts of the county further north were taken in, and it is here that the best areas of ridge and furrow cultivation are preserved.[15] The great forte of the Anglo-Saxons was the intake of claylands not previously cultivated. But the area of Clay-with-flints on the Chiltern plateau was deemed too intr actable for even the Anglo-Saxon farmers. Here there were no open fields or early settlements. The establishment of isolated hamlets and piecemeal enclosure from woodland took place at a late stage in the historical period in connection with the woodworking industry of the area, and the settlement pattern has many of the characteristics of the Highland Zone—small irregular fields, non-nucleated settlements and narrow lanes.

The typical form of land use in lowland Britain was ridge and furrow cultivation in open fields. This was brought about by the use of a plough with a mouldboard fitted to one side of the share, an innovation which may go back to late Roman times (p. 157). The mouldboard turned the soil over, thus affording maximum aeration and drainage— very necessary in the cultivation of the heavier soils. The soil was always turned in the same direction, so that ploughing in strips of land resulted in the formation of ridges. These, however, could be destroyed either by cross ploughing or by ploughing furrows down the ridges in a subsequent year, as is done today in the open fields at Laxton in Nottinghamshire.[16] So, the creation of ridge and furrow was a deliberate process, either for cultural or environmental reasons. For example, in certain cases the ridges constituted units of land tenure, adjacent ridges belonging to different farmers. On the other hand, drainage was sometimes an important consideration, only the ridges being cultivated while the furrows acted as drains. This is substantiated in many instances where today there is a strong vegetational contrast between grass grown ridges, and furrows in which rushes and other marsh plants abound, or in which standing water may be present for part of the year. Also, where detailed maps show individual strips, it is often not possible to equate these with the actual ridges on the ground.

Among the earliest records of ridge and furrow are the groups from Hen Domen in the Welsh Marches and Gwithian in west Cornwall, and in both cases the evidence is of an archaeological kind.[17] At Hen Domen, ploughmarks suggesting this form of cultivation, with a ridge width of about four metres, occurred beneath a castle motte, but overlay an immediately post-Roman building. At Gwithian, the ploughmarks were preserved beneath a deposit of wind-lain sand. Both groups are of pre-Norman date. Most of the ridge and furrow which is preserved today, however, seems likely to have been formed between the eleventh and fourteenth centuries; this applies particularly to the 'broad rig' which has a ridge width of five metres or more. 'Narrow rig', with a ridge width of substantially less, is probably of

Plate 12. Nether Chalford, Enstone, Oxfordshire. Deserted medieval village with adjacent strip lynchets.

later origin and was being formed up to the eighteenth and nineteenth centuries.[18] The reasons, whether technological, cultural or environmental, for the change from broad to narrow rig are not clear, but the trend to root-crop agriculture which took place in the post-medieval period may have been an associated factor. The narrow spade-dug ridges known as 'lazy beds' which are to be seen in many parts of the Highland Zone are largely used for root-crop cultivation, although this may be a recent innovation.

Ridge and furrow occurred in irregularly grouped blocks or furlongs (i.e. furrow lengths) set around the medieval village. There were no fences or hedges between the strips or the furlongs, and stock was prevented from straying onto the fields by means of hurdles. On steep slopes, cultivation took the form of terraces known as 'strip lynchets'. These characteristic open fields were in marked contrast to the enclosed landscape of much of Britain during the period of prehistoric agriculture with its small fields each demarcated by hedges, walls or lynchets of various kinds. Today, where ridge and furrow and strip lynchets are preserved they are generally under permanent pasture, for modern ploughing destroys the ridges in a few seasons. The grassed-over medieval fields, together with the villages, many now deserted but with their house platforms and streets all clearly showing, are a characteristic feature of many parts of England. Viewed from the air they constitute a classic fossilized rural landscape (Plate 12).

The preservation of ridge and furrow and deserted village sites is due to their having been maintained under permanent pasture, and is not a true reflection of the original distribution of the open-field system. In many areas, much has been destroyed by later ploughing and in particular by market gardening. In Buckinghamshire we find that while place-name evidence suggests medieval settlement in the Thames Valley, field evidence indicates only one or two deserted villages and no ridge and furrow (p. 165). This must be because the area has continued as an important corn-growing region to the present day whereas the heavier soils in the north of the county, where some of the best ridge and furrow is to be seen, have been given over to pasture. Ploughed-out ridge and furrow can still be preserved as plough traces but we are unlikely to fill in gaps in the distribution maps with this kind of evidence for a very long time.

This raises the interesting question of the preservation of archaeological sites as related to later land-use patterns. A classic example is the distribution of Bronze Age barrows. On chalk and limestone uplands these have been preserved due to the widespread abandonment of these territories for arable in medieval and later times. Iron Age and Roman cultivation may have destroyed some, but as a rule barrows were incorporated into the boundaries of these earlier field systems rather than levelled. It is also to be noted that there was some medieval cultivation on the Chalk as shown by the preservation of patches of ridge and furrow, but this was not a widespread practice. On the Thames gravels, however, and particularly upstream from the Goring Gap, although barrows were once prolific, most have long since been levelled by ploughing. Early antiquarians were not aware of this and a totally erroneous view of the distribution of these barrows grew up. But with the advent of air photography the ditches and central grave pits of the barrows were clearly recognized as crop marks, and the area is now seen to have been almost as important as that of the Chalk in Bronze Age times. The situation is shown diagrammatically below:

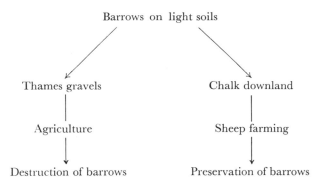

Some of the problems attendant upon attempts to integrate various kinds of evidence for past environments and the reasons for particular settlement patterns are well illustrated by C. C. Taylor's study of Cambridgeshire moats.[19] Moated sites are small, generally square or rectangular enclosures of single farmstead status with a surrounding water-filled ditch. They are widespread in lowland areas, as shown by their distribution in Yorkshire (Fig. 71). Their construction took

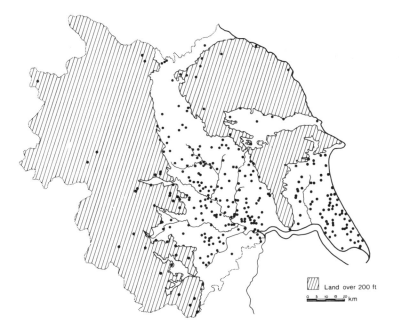

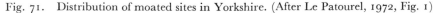

Fig. 71. Distribution of moated sites in Yorkshire. (After Le Patourel, 1972, Fig. 1)

Fig. 72.   Distribution of all types of moated sites in Cambridgeshire. (After Taylor, C. C., 1972, Fig. 34)

place in England mainly between 1250 and 1320, and in Ireland slightly later. It has been suggested that in England the climatic deterioration (p. 175) encouraged moat building, but there is no support for this attractive hypothesis in Ireland where moats were primarily defensive, being constructed as a response to increasing pressure on the Normans from the native population.[20]

The situation in Cambridgeshire is complicated. The distribution of moated sites as a whole shows an avoidance of the Fens and the light soils of the Chalk, but otherwise there is no special affinity with the heavy boulder clay areas (Fig. 72). If, however, one considers only the isolated sites, i.e. those away from the villages or hamlets, a definite relationship with the boulder clay emerges (Fig. 73). Certain evidence—the absence of pagan Saxon burials and the prevalence of *weald* and *ley* elements in the place names, elements unknown outside the boulder clay zones—suggests that these areas were well wooded long after the primary settlement of the county as a whole. It seemed possible that the isolated moated sites were associated with the late intake of woodland and were perhaps built for the purpose of defence against forest animals and brigands. This theory gains support from other counties such as Essex and Warwickshire where, too, moats appear to have been built in forested regions. But closer examinations of the documentary evidence for Cambridgeshire suggests that woodland had already been cleared from the boulder clay lands before the main moat-building period. Factors other than vegetation must, therefore, be sought to explain the distribution of these isolated moats. One possibility is soil type, the boulder clay areas being taken up at a late stage in the moat-building period by farmers hiving off from the

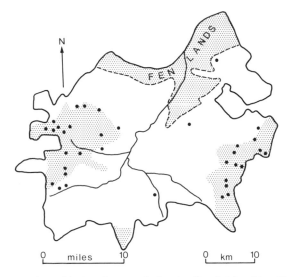

Fig. 73. Distribution of isolated moated sites in Cambridgeshire. Boulder clay areas stippled. (After Taylor, C. C., 1972, Figs. 33 and 35)

main village settlements. But until more is known of the exact purpose of these sites, the reasons for the details of their distribution are likely to remain obscure.

At this point we may turn our attention to Ireland. Here, the typical settlement unit of the first millennium was the single farmstead, known as the 'rath', the origin of which may lie in the later prehistoric period.[21] This type of settlement is said to be in marked contrast to the small farm communities or nucleated settlements of Neolithic and Bronze Age times, although only one or two examples of the latter, such as Lough Gur, Co. Limerick, are known. Raths are most abundant in lowland areas and proportionately fewer in areas of light soils where, possibly, the loose farm clusters, or 'clachans', of earlier times survived. There is evidence too from place names to suggest the co-existence of two types of settlement in late Celtic and Early Christian times, the *baile* (anglicized *bally*) element, which is possibly of pre-Celtic origin, predominating in areas where raths are least common. In certain cases, raths are set in areas of small squarish fields which may be contemporary.[22] V. Proudfoot's key synthesis of the economic basis of the rath dwellers[23] concludes that their farming economy was essentially a mixed one, complete specialization on crop or livestock production being rare.

The early monastic system in Ireland gave an impetus to the rural economy of the first millennium, as suggested by the pollen record, and encouraged the expansion of arable farming.[24] Lowland forests shunned by earlier farmers began to be exploited from the seventh century onwards,[25] and monasteries like that at Glendalough in the Wicklow Mountains were often sited in remote situations, bringing about the intake of land which might otherwise have remained virgin forest.

The Celtic traditions were, however, generally absorbed into Irish Christianity, not replaced, and it was not until the Anglo-Norman immigrations of the later twelfth century that further changes in land-use patterns occurred. By the mid-thirteenth century, Anglo-Norman barons had control of about two-thirds of the country, the area colonized corresponding to the main lowlands of Ireland;[26] the mountainous regions of the west and much of the north were not settled. Geologically the area in question is largely (although by no means entirely) of Carboniferous Limestone. It is, too, a region of level boulder clay plains with spreads of glacial sands and gravels, in contrast to the highland rocks of the north and west which are acidic, and which give rise to soils unsuitable for cultivation. Geology, soils and relief thus all contribute, as in the rest of Britain, to a division of the country into highland and lowland zones. But unlike the situation in the true Lowland Zone, most of Ireland has a high rainfall, in excess of 75 centimetres, which, together with poor drainage and low evaporation even on the lowlands, makes the growing of crops difficult. Estyn Evans sees Ireland as a Pluvial Zone,[27] distinct from both the Highland and Lowland Zones of the rest of Britain. We find, perhaps as a result of this, that the establishment of the feudal system with its open-field agriculture was only successful in a small area of low rainfall in the east around Dublin known as the English Pale. Thus while deserted Anglo-Norman settlements and the small rectangular earthworks of the same age are a common feature of the lowland Irish landscape, grassed-over ridge and furrow cultivation is not.

During the medieval period the land was farmed in the Rundale or 'run-rig' system, a system also to be found in much of Scotland at this time. Its origin is unknown but it was possibly introduced by the Vikings. The system comprised a farmstead or farm cluster and land divided into 'infield' and 'outfield'. The infield was an unenclosed area close to the settlement and in continuous cultivation; it was manured with dung from stalled cattle kept in byres through the winter. Beyond lay the outfield, only a small part of which was in cultivation at any one time, the rest being fallow. Still further from the settlement were areas of moorland and rough pasture on which cattle were grazed during the warmer months of the year. The movement of cattle to distant summer grazings—a phenomenon known as 'booleying'—still takes place in parts of Ireland, and we may see in this a direct comparison with, although on a smaller scale, the seasonal migrations of the reindeer herds of Europe in Upper Palaeolithic times.

Thus as in England, arable farming was important in the medieval period. The Irish landscape was largely unenclosed and superficially similar to that of southern England but without the rigid organization of furlongs and strips. Early enclosure, at least on a large scale, was not characteristic, and as in the period of the raths, cattle raising had not yet assumed its present-day legionary proportions. This is in contrast to parts of western England and Wales where the enclosed fields are often of very ancient, perhaps even prehistoric, origin (p. 177). Even in these areas, however, we must not overstate the ancient dominance of cattle raising. This point has been made by Leslie Alcock[28] in a discussion in which the archaeological and documentary evidence for the economy of Dark Age Wales are compared. The archaeological evidence—bones of pig, cattle and sheep, and various artefacts relating to domestic crafts dependent on animals for their raw material such as skinning knives, iron awls for piercing leather, loom weights and spindle whorls—supports the traditional picture of a Welsh economy based on pastoralism. Literary sources, however, demonstrate the place of arable husbandry, and it is concluded that unspecialized mixed farming was the normal practice.

In the 'harsh Atlantic world of stone, moorland and bog' Celtic culture maintained its dominance, and here, names descriptive of topographical features are characteristic. The best example is that of the element *druim* meaning a ridge, the distribution of which coincides remarkably with that of the drumlins (Fig. 25).[29] It is not known what type of field system prevailed in these areas prior to Anglo-Norman times, but the Rundale system was used subsequently, and by the eighteenth century its distribution was even increasing due to the rising population. Spade-dug ridges known as 'lazy beds', initially for the cultivation of cereals but later adapted to the growing of root crops, are characteristic, and often to be seen, generally in a fossilized state, in the transition zone between the areas of arable and rough grazing land.

In lowland Ireland, however, a new wave of English immigrants in the sixteenth and seventeenth centuries initiated the process of land enclosure and the break up of the Rundale system. The loose farm clusters were consolidated, farmers evicted and a shift from small-scale mixed farming to commercial stock-raising took place. We see a similar process in western Scotland with the Highland Clearances although sheep, not cattle, were the main animal there. Only in areas such as the glens and upland fringes of the Wicklow Mountains was the Rundale system maintained. Enclosure took place too from primeval forest, moor and bog. Various patterns can be recognized. For example, in eastern Ireland[30] the amalgamation of Rundale strips led to larger but still elongated units, while the enclosure of common grazing land gave rise to large square fields (Fig. 74). On the other hand, the en-

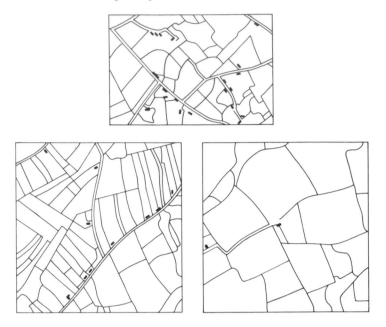

Fig. 74.   Field types in eastern Ireland. Top, irregular enclosures associated with nineteenth-century squatter encroachments; bottom left, fields resulting largely from the enclosing of old open-field strips; bottom right, typical field pattern resulting from parliamentary enclosure. (After Aalen, 1970, Figs. 13.1 and 13.2)

closure of common land by illegal squatter communities on a piecemeal basis produced small, irregular units (Fig. 74), rather similar to those at Whiteparish taken in, again illegally, from Royal Forest.

Thus from a situation down to the end of the seventeenth century with relatively few enclosures, crops being protected by temporary hurdles, we find a marked and widespread change to the modern enclosed fields and predominantly pastoral landscape. One result of this has been the better overall preservation of archaeological field monuments than obtains in southern Britain.

Climatic factors—rainfall, temperature and sunshine—are the key to the distinction between the Highland and Lowland Zones, but it was probably not until the deterioration of the late second millennium bc that such a distinction became relevant to the type of farming adopted in a given area. The climate of Roman Britain was indeed little different from that of today, but Anglo-Saxon times saw a trend to drier and less stormy conditions, a trend which was to culminate in the 'Little Climatic Optimum' of the medieval period.[31]

Amelioration began in the sixth or seventh centuries, the evidence coming largely from Scandinavian documents which describe a period of successful harvests and voyaging overseas. It is indeed possible that this lay behind the whole Viking expansion of the later part of the first millennium. The peat stratigraphy does not altogether support the documentary evidence, there being a marked recurrence surface (RY II) in some European bogs dated to between ad 400 and 700; but at Tregaron ad 473 marks the beginning of a standstill phase which persisted until 1182.

During the Little Climatic Optimum of the eleventh and twelfth centuries, Britain experienced summer temperatures of perhaps 1 °C higher than those of today. Historical records comment on the freedom from ice of the seas in the Iceland–Greenland region, and the spread of vine cultivation as far north as Hereford and the Wash.[32] In the north of England, for example at West Whelpington in Northumberland, the remains of medieval ridge and furrow extend well above the present limit of cultivation into an area which is now moorland. This suggests more favourable climatic conditions, although the possibility should not be overlooked that economic factors were responsible for this temporary expansion of arable.[33] The continuation of this episode of warm climate into the thirteenth century is suggested by the setting up of fire-prevention plans for London in 1237 and 1248, by bumper acorn years and by wide tree rings in timbers dated to the early years of the century.[34]

But in general the thirteenth century saw the beginnings of climatic deterioration. There is a marked recurrence surface at about ad 1200 (RY I) in the Scandinavian raised bog sequence, and similarly in Britain at Tregaron. Documentary evidence indicates a period of increased storminess and episodes of flooding in the fourteenth and early fifteenth centuries, as well as an increase of ice around the coasts of Iceland.[35] Many coastal villages, particularly in western regions of the British Isles, were overwhelmed by wind-blown sand, and the inhabitants forced to leave their homes. It was at this time too that cloister walks in monasteries, previously open, were glazed. Later on, the recorded behaviour of glaciers and the direct evidence of the instrumental record can be brought in, and these point to a deteriorating climate which became marked between 1560 and 1590 and lasted until the middle of the nineteenth century. Some have referred to this as 'The Little Ice Age'. The episode saw the greatest advance of Icelandic and Scandinavian glaciers in the Christian era, maxima occurring in 1745–50 and 1850. Since then, retreat has been predominant.[36]

The use of instrumental and various other kinds of data in estimating past climatic conditions has been critically discussed by Gordon Manley.[37] The full impact of man on the environment which becomes increasingly felt from Neolithic times onwards makes the interpretation of any environmental, economic and social change in terms of climate hazardous, and this is especially so for the historical period when man's technology enabled him to become ever more divorced from climatic control. For example, the growth of vines northward to the Wash during the Little Climatic Optimum took place 'at a time of ecclesiastical enthusiasm'; 'we know little about the quality of the wine' and 'under monastic conditions we can presume the shelter of well-walled gardens which, by analogy with city squares, might easily have allowed mean summer temperatures fully 1°C above that of the country'.[38] Another example concerns the freezing of the Thames at London. During the Little Ice Age the Thames was often frozen and could be crossed on foot, the last recorded year that this took place being 1814. But in 1820 the old London Bridge with its closely set piers, the effect of which had been to jam ice floes from higher up the river and thus reduce the flow of water, was pulled down. Later in the century the Lambeth Marshes were embanked and both these events resulted in an increased rate of flow, a factor which may well have prevented the total freezing over of previous years.

Late medieval times saw a swing away from crop cultivation to sheep farming and cattle raising. The climatic deterioration may have been responsible for this shift (compare the slighting of field systems by ranch boundaries in the later Bronze Age); so too may have been the labour shortage which resulted from the Black Death. But whatever the causes, we have been left with one of the most characteristic overall features of our landscape today—enclosed fields. The fascinating story of enclosure has been described by W. G. Hoskins in *The Making of the English Landscape*.[39] The sixteenth to eighteenth centuries saw the greatest changes, although the process was taking place on a small scale as early as the thirteenth century. Literally tens of thousands of miles of artificial habitat from the simple stone wall or hawthorn hedge to the complex hedgebanks and ditches with their grassy verges and drainage gullies have been created. Nor are the implications of enclosure restricted to the immediate impact on the rural landscape. Numerous animals and plants of woodland habitats which were threatened with extinction by the ever increasing destruction of forest and other types of wilderness found homes in the newly created field boundaries.

The form taken by the enclosed fields depended on a variety of factors—soil, topography, land tenure, etc.—and we have already mentioned several types (Plate 12; Figs. 70 and 74). Often, the new boundaries were laid out irrespective of the old furlongs, denoting a complete change in the pattern of ownership. In other cases, enclosure took place along the divisions between the medieval strips; groups of strips were amalgamated, but the resulting field shape—long, with reverse-S boundaries—betrays their origin.

The construction of field boundaries goes back, of course, far beyond the Middle Ages. The later prehistoric landscape of much of Britain was essentially one of enclosed fields, a pattern which, at least on the Chalk downs, spread and persisted through the Iron Age into Romano-British times. But these fields are generally thought to have been for growing crops, and there is little to suggest direct continuity with those of the historical period whose main purpose was the enclosure of stock. In Ireland, for example, where one might have expected a link with prehistoric field boundaries due to the weak impact of the feudal system, the pattern of small hedged fields of today is largely of eighteenth and nineteenth century origin.[40] In England some of the earliest enclosures are to be found in the West Country going back perhaps 900 years. This is the one area of the Highland Zone where, according to R. Feachem, the Sub-atlantic climatic deterioration did not cause the abandonment of field systems,[41] their use continuing into Roman times; if we are searching for continuity this area might prove fruitful. Even in southern England we can recall the evidence for small forest-edge fields at Whiteparish prior to Domesday.

Walls and hedges can be dated by reference to the documentary and cartographic evidence of, for example, Anglo-Saxon land charters, tithe and later estate maps, and enclosure awards; many of our parish boundaries go back well into Saxon times.

Another interesting line of evidence, recently developed by Max Hooper, is the dating of hedges by the number of shrubs they contain.[42] Most hedges are planted originally with a single species of shrub, often hawthorn, and Hooper has argued that a further species becomes established every hundred years. A hedge which is 200 years old will contain two shrubs, one of a thousand years, ten shrubs. And for most of the areas tested there is remarkably convincing agreement between the botanical and documentary evidence. It is known, for example, that Lincolnshire was enclosed later than Kent, and Kent later than Devon. Counts from hedgerows in these three counties (Fig. 75) support this in a convincing manner. Further confirmation of what is now generally known as 'Hooper's Hedgerow Hypothesis' comes from Shropshire where the shrub counts and documentary evidence do not agree at all. But here there was a deliberate policy of planting mixed hedges.

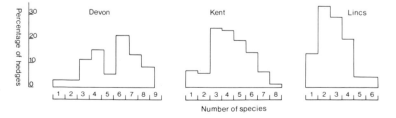

Fig. 75. Hedge counts from three counties. (After Hooper *et al.*, 1971, Fig. 8)

Enclosure was encouraged too by droving. In the eighteenth and nineteenth centuries the rising populations in London demanded meat in hitherto unprecedented proportions. This led to unnatural zoning of land-use systems epitomized by the Scottish, Welsh and Irish drove roads along which cattle from the unenclosed highland zones were driven (and from the Hebrides even swum), from their native breeding grounds and pastures, via the great cattle markets of the marcher areas, to be fattened in an artificial green belt around the metropolis as a perpetual larder-on-the-hoof for the meat-hungry Londoner. At this period, the fat acquired on these lowland pastures was not spurned as it is today, and the improved breeds of the eighteenth century resulted in the monstrous and aptly named 'Dutch-arsed' beast.

Agricultural specialization is a trend which today is becoming increasingly apparent, often at the expense of the individual small holder or tenant farmer. Its most cruel manifestation was seen in the period of Highland Clearances when hundreds, possibly thousands, of crofters in northern and western Scotland and the Western Isles were, often forcibly, removed from their homes, mainly in the eighteenth and nineteenth centuries, so that the landlords might lease their lands more profitably to sheep-farmers from the lowlands and across the border. Of course, much of the land in the area of the clearances was poor for cultivation, and Dudley Stamp has pointed out that the dispossession of farmers from marginal ground was sometimes for their own good.[43] Only the mode of eviction was inhuman. He cites, in addition to the Highland Clearances, the sacking of New Forest villages by William I to create hunting grounds on land which was totally unsuitable for agriculture (p. 165), and, more recently ,the compulsory evacuation of St Kilda in 1930. But it can also be pointed out that droving, for example, removed nitrogen, calcium and organic matter from the highland ecosystem without putting anything back (Fig. 37), thus accelerating soil degradation in an area where the balance was already delicate.

Another characteristic of medieval and later times was large-scale sheep farming. Much of the land used was never enclosed after its abandonment in the late prehistoric period, and it is only in the last decade that the Chalk, for example, has begun to lose the individual character that it has retained for centuries, largely through present-day 'plough up' policies. Monasticism saw one of the largest expansions of sheep farming ever witnessed in this country, the Cistercians, in particular, exploiting by careful management areas of marginal land such as the North York Moors. But the Cistercian movement is a prime example of how one cannot necessarily interpret back into land intake episodes a purely economic motive. The Cistercian monks required marginal land in order to exercise manual labour and to attain isolation.[44] Sheep were kept solely to provide wool for the monks in the first instance. But the finest wools are produced by sheep whose feeding grounds are least favourable for other agricultural purposes, and this was quickly realized; the deliberate policy of utilizing un-rewarding terrain in turn led to the establishment of great sheep walks. That the Cistercians were successful as cereal cultivators as well is demonstrated in the pollen record from Tregaron (Fig. 63) where a shift to arable farming in the later part of the twelfth century coincides with the establishment of the nearby monastery of Strata Florida.[45]

There is no doubt that the agricultural improvements of the eighteenth and nineteenth centuries saw sweeping landscape changes, not only in the enclosure of land already long cultivated but also in the uptake of vast tracts of wilderness. In this, drainage and manuring were key processes and both provide interesting links with environmental and archaeological events of the past. The intake of marginal land required the use of lime and phosphates. Post-glacial and Pleistocene sediments such as tufa, wind-blown sand and cave deposits rich in bone were often used, and in the extraction of these, as in the cutting of ditches for drainage, many archaeological sites have been uncovered. For example, deposits of tufa are still being worked in Flintshire, and at Prestatyn a Mesolithic site was found during extraction operations.[46] On Caldey Island off the south coast of Pembrokeshire the infilling of a Pleistocene bone cave was shipped across the Bristol Channel during the last century to be used as fertilizer in the intake of marginal land. And the discovery of the royal crannog at Lagore (p. 181), Co. Meath, in 1839 was made when 150 cartloads of bone were shipped from it to Scotland for a similar purpose.[47]

The intake of marginal land in upland areas has gone on sporadically since prehistoric times and for a variety of reasons. The North York Moors, Upper Strathdon in Abberdeenshire and Exmoor Forest are examples. The settlement of small, often remote, islands such as the Outer Hebrides, the Aran Islands, St Kilda and, until very recently, the Blasket Islands off south-west Ireland is a different aspect of the same phenomenon.

The drainage of marshland, reedswamp and bog again leads to the better use of land for farming. Such habitats, while of value to hunting communities in that they make for environmental diversity, can only be considered as wasted land to people whose essential policies entail specialization. The canalization and embankment of rivers has played an important part (p. 3). Timber revetments constructed along the sides of a river prevent erosion, and dykes prevent flooding and confine the reedswamp zone to the riverward side. This not only extends the area of pasture but keeps it well drained—essential if the liverfluke disease of sheep is to be prevented. This policy has been most successful in lowland Britain. In highland regions control is more difficult due to the swifter and less constant flow, and rivers present a more nearly natural appearance (Plate 1). The reclamation of farm land in coastal regions has been similarly brought about by the construction of sea walls. Along the south coast of England, mud flats have been colonized, at first accidentally and later deliberately, by Townsend's cordgrass, *Spartina townsendii.* This is a hybrid between the native cordgrass and an American species introduced in the nineteenth century, and its facility for stabilizing intertidal mud and initiating saltmarsh communities is now recognized as of immense importance in gaining land from the sea. Later stages in the saltmarsh succession form good sheep pasture.[48]

A further aspect of the exploitation of aquatic habitats is the construction of organized watermeadows. Meadowland was valued from early times for the production of hay which provided winter fodder for livestock (p. 109); Saxon charters of Dorset, for example, refer frequently to detached meads two to three miles from the main landholding. Organized watermeadows were probably created initially to hasten the spring growth of grass for hay, as well as for pasturing sheep and cattle. There is a magnificant series in the Frome Valley, Dorset, whose history has been described in some detail.[49] By means of a system of sluice gates to control the flow of water, and a series of channels known as carriers and drains, the former built up on ridges, a specific area of meadowland adjacent to the river could be flooded for a given length of time (Fig. 76). The warmth of the water, its manurial properties (cf p. 141) and the provision of calcium salts were key factors in the production of good hay. A further prerequisite for a successful watermeadow system was that the river should be braided and run fairly close to the top of its bank. Under these conditions, flooding could be brought about without the necessity for building up long gradients artificially. Thus the creation of a watermeadow system led to a river valley environment somewhat different from that brought about by embankment and reclamation for pasture.

Watermeadows are essentially of sixteenth/seventeenth century origin; a few may be earlier. Their primary importance was in the production of hay, but as a subsidiary function they supported cattle, often later in the year after the hay had been reaped. The meadows also played a vital role in sheep farming, the early growth of grass in February or March being particularly valuable, coming at a time when the winter downland grazing with additional hay and turnips was virtually exhausted but before the summer pastures were ready. Later on in their history, with the acceleration of land enclosure and the utilization of former downland grazing for cereal cultivation, the meadows performed an essential function in the reorganization of sheep farming. There was an emphasis away from the production of

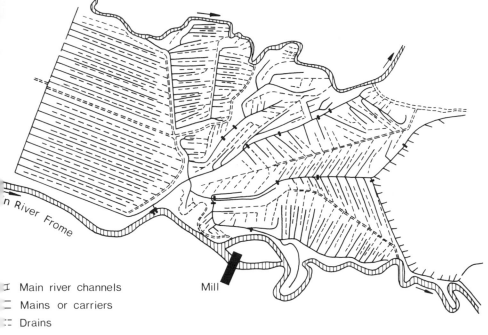

I Main river channels

= Mains or carriers

= Drains

Hatches

Mill

Fig. 76. Plan of a section of watermeadows in the Frome valley, Dorset. (After Whitehead, 1967, Fig. 4)

wool, which the downland grazing favoured, to the production of mutton favoured by the lush early grass of the meadows. In the nineteenth century the meadows were used as dairy pasture.

The maintenance of a watermeadow system depended on the manual labour of watermen with a practically inborn skill in levelling the carriers and drains. With the problem of dying labour in recent years, a mechanized system of maintenance was tried out but was not a success, and the traditional management of watermeadows has now almost everywhere lapsed. A suggestion that they be developed in relation to the use of the river—for example as fish hatcheries— emphasizes the readiness of man to adapt to environments of his own creation which have become obsolete in the face of economic and social change, a readiness which is epitomized by the whole history of the watermeadows.

The draining of lakes in Ireland and the Scottish lowlands to create farmland has led in some instances to the discovery of wooden island dwellings known as 'crannogs'. These were built either on a natural island or on one made artificially of boulders and brushwood.[50] A timber platform was then constructed and the house built on this; the entire structure was often surrounded by a palisade and linked to the

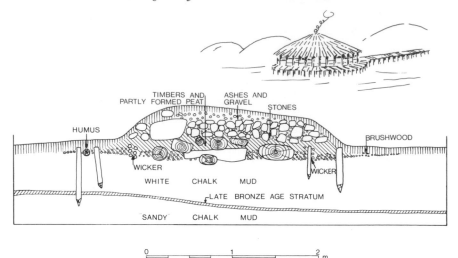

Fig. 77.   Section through a crannog, Balinderry No. 2, Co. Offaly. (After Hencken, 1942, Fig. 11)

mainland by a causeway. Crannogs date from prehistoric times, although the majority are of early Christian origin. From the environmental point of view they are important for the preservation of organic material not generally found in the aerobic conditions of terrestrial sites. At Ballinderry, Co. Offaly,[51] an Early Christian crannog was constructed on a deposit of lacustrine marl, beneath which was an earlier occupation horizon of Late Bronze Age date (Fig. 77). Pollen analysis suggests this earlier occupation to have occurred shortly after the beginning of the Sub-atlantic climatic deterioration, and the subsequent total burial of this horizon by lake muds confirms this. The construction of the crannog would then seem to have taken place in a period of climatic dryness since it rests directly on lake sediments.

Lastly a note on the exploitation of peat for fuel since peat has been with us for so much of this history. The exploitation of peat has led to many exciting archaeological discoveries and also to the creation of totally new environments. In Connemara when the blanket peat is removed the stumps of trees of former forests are exposed (Plate 8). These are sometimes used as the cores for the initial stacks of turf; later they are themselves pulled up and used for fuel. The land may then be taken over by the Forestry Commission, the original soil ploughed into channels to break up the hard pan, and conifers planted. This operation has led in some cases to the discovery of Mesolithic flints, as on the North York Moors.

The exploitation of lowland peat often resulted in the flooding of the cuttings, the most notable example being the creation of the

Norfolk Broads.[52] The main period of extraction was in the twelfth and thirteenth centuries when the peat was dug by hand. Later, in the fifteenth century, the cuttings became flooded, perhaps due in part to the climatic deterioration, and the peat was then dredged out. So the Norfolk Broads were formed, and, like the many gravel pits adjacent to our lowland rivers (p. 62), have provided new habitats for various plants and animals—in particular birds—and unrivalled conditions for recreation. Study of maps shows that some are becoming infilled as vegetation encroaches on the open water (Fig. 78).

Many further aspects could be discussed—the recent history of wild animal populations, the development of safari parks, disease, forestry, the exploitation of raw materials such as coal, iron, china clay and salt, the creation of transport networks and the development of metropolitan environments.

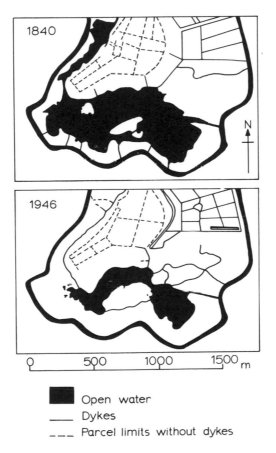

Fig. 78.   Hoveton Great Broad, Norfolk, as it appears on the 1840 Tithe Map (upper), and in 1946 (lower). (After Tansley, 1968, Fig. 10)

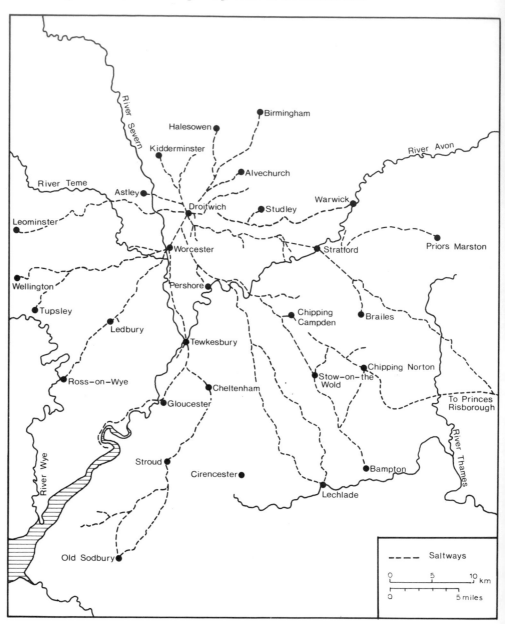

Fig. 79.   Map of saltways from Droitwich. (After Finberg, 1972, Fig. 51)

A major trend in recent years has been industrial pollution of the atmosphere, rivers and seas, and the land with smoke, chemical effluents and waste tips, causing some very striking changes. By the misuse of coal resources and the consequent production of smoke, no people has ever done more damage to the climatic environment in and around their great cities. Fortunately we have begun to recognize and redress this. The quite magnificent achievement of Manchester since 1947 stands as testimony.

We have seen salt controlling the environment since the Upton Warren Interstadial. The extraction of salt by mining and evaporation from coastal salterns has gone on at least since the Roman period. The latter process, when involving the boiling of seawater, consumed large quantities of fuel and has left its traces in the form of great volumes of reddish burnt soil and briquetage, to be seen particularly on the east coast from Lincolnshire to the Thames Estuary.[53] As early as Anglo-Saxon times the brine springs of Droitwich and Nantwich were being exploited. From these centres tracks known as 'saltways' radiated out in all directions (Fig. 79), and these are considered to have played an important part in the Anglo-Saxon road system.[54] Mining was extensively practised at Nantwich during the eighteenth and nineteenth centuries where the gradual collapse of the workings has led to remarkable subsidence effects. Today, salt is used in the chemical industry as a source of sodium and chlorine, and in the manufacture of a variety of deadly substances—e.g. hydrochloric acid.

As well as destroying agricultural land, quarries, tips and large industrial plants are seen as damaging to the aesthetic appeal of the landscape. This however is arguable. To some, the contrast between the rural and the industrial has an appeal which adds to, not detracts from, the landscape, and this is nowhere more striking than in south Wales where giant oil refineries and steel works rise up, sinister, yet magnificent, against a backcloth of moorland and bog.

The rural landscape too has been affected by its own trends of specialization and widespread change. The open-field system was among the first of these, to be followed by the enclosures which, although providing habitats for all sorts of plants and animals, add a stamp of monotony to the landscape. The use of chemical insecticides and herbicides has begun to make these habitats less favourable, and the brown withered vegetation alongside hedgerows is a not unfamiliar sight. But the most drastic change has been the total removal of hedges and walls to create larger fields in response to the use of massive agricultural machinery and the need for greater efficiency. This is specialization indeed, and its effects are far-reaching. In addition to the direct destruction of the boundaries and all the creatures which find refuge within them, there is the concomitant process of soil erosion. Hedges and walls which traverse slopes have acted in the past, and still do so today, as breaks to downhill erosion. In flat country, particularly in the east of England, wind is the main erosive force; wind-blown dust built up against hedges can be redistributed over the fields. But the removal of boundaries leads to total erosion. No lynchets or banks form, and the surface layer of land which has been created through thousands of years of Post-glacial weathering may be lost, literally in a day. We are, in effect, returning to an almost 'Late-glacial' landscape of steppe, pasture and bare ground, with processes of physical erosion—dust storms and 'solifluxion'—rife.

In the past twenty years there has developed a massive public awareness of these processes, and attempts to halt pollution, soil erosion and the destruction of plant and animal life have got underway, alongside campaigns to slow the population increase and control more strictly the exploitation of natural resources which are seen as a direct cause of many of these effects. Terms such as 'ecology', 'environment' and 'degraded landscape' have come into everyday use. A variety of documents has appeared, such as *Blueprint for Survival*,[55] putting forward schemes for landscape conservation, the control of pollution, and the wise use of raw materials, fuel and food. Nature Reserves and Sites of Special Scientific Interest have been designated, and bodies such as the Nature Conservancy and the Council for the Preservation of Rural England set up.

One may, of course, question the value of this effort. Do we have the right to lay down the requirements and attempt to mould the environment of the future? And in doing so, are we not betraying earlier, and more important, future generations of man? We cannot know what technology may achieve, nor can we predict the nature of environments to come. To view the present, as we have done, as a single episode in the long unfinished history of human environment is to awaken in us a realization of both the fleeting nature of our age and its great consequence. Man cannot control his destiny. The oscillations of Pleistocene climate, and the fact that the Post-glacial has long passed the period of maximum warmth strongly suggest that northern Europe will once more be subjected to an age of ice. In Britain the destruction of cities, towns, villages and farm land either by glacial inundation or by ice-wedging and solifluxion will ensue. The falling sea will accelerate river erosion and lead to the destruction of ports and harbours. Giant bridges will collapse in ruin. Mass migration of human population southward and the need to adapt to totally new environments and ways of life will follow.

By attempting to maintain the environmental *status quo* are we not denying ourselves and our progeny the opportunity and the ability to exploit challenging new environments both created by our own industrial and agricultural needs and by natural climatic shifts? Evolution depends on environmental stimulus, and the most successful groups of man have arisen in response to specialized simplified environments. If man had declaimed in the past at the felling of the forest he might still be at the Mesolithic stage of development. If there had been none of the specialized periglacial habitats, the brilliant Upper Palaeolithic may never have emerged. And had there been none of the rigours of a cooling Pleistocene climate, there may well have been no man.

. . . consciously or unconsciously we fear the rising tide of change and so seek to crystallize and preserve for ever . . . a particular stage in a natural evolution. But our land is clothed with a living mantle and tenanted by living creatures. All living things are born, mature, decay and die, to be replaced in due course by others which are different. However much therefore we may enjoy a particular phase of scenic evolution it is not a conservation piece to be framed and hung upon the walls of a museum . . .[56]

But the alternative view is undoubtedly more appealing to us as human beings.

The near landscape is valuable and lovable because of its nearness . . . it is where children are reared and what they take away in their minds to their long future.[57]

Notes

For full bibliographical details see Bibliography, pp. 198–209.

Preface

1. Stamp, 1969.
2. Fleure, 1971.
3. Godwin, 1956.
4. Pennington, 1969.
5. Manley, 1962; Pearsall, 1968; Sissons, 1967; Southern, 1964; Stamp, 1960; Tansley, 1968; Trueman, 1971.
6. Zeuner, 1958; 1959.
7. Higgs, 1972.
8. Clark, 1967.

Chapter 1.   The Hoxnian Interglacial

1. A good introduction to flint tools is Oakley, 1961.
2. But see Campbell and Sampson, 1971 and note 1, 34.
3. For the British Lower Palaeolithic the reader is referred to Roe, 1964, and Wymer, 1968; and for a world view, to Bordes, 1968, and Coles and Higgs, 1969.
4. For an introduction to the Pleistocene, see Butzer, 1972; Oakley, 1964; Sparks and West, 1972; West, 1968; Zeuner, 1959.
5. Ovey, 1964.
6. Kerney, 1971; Waechter et al., 1971; Wymer, 1968, 341.
7. For this and other geological terms, see p. xvi.
8. It used to be thought that a period of downcutting interrupted the aggradation of the Middle Gravels because of the presence of a 'channel' in the Lower Middle Gravel and underlying deposits. This is now interpreted as a solution hollow in the Chalk, the roof of which collapsed subsequent to the deposition of the Lower Middle Gravel (Waechter et al., 1971).
9. Chaplin, 1971; Evans, 1972b; Kurtén, 1968.
10. Kerney, 1971.
11. This is the most recent terminology, proposed by Mitchell et al., 1973. Better known but less satisfactory synonyms for the various stages are: for the Devensian—Weichselian, Wurm or Last Glaciation; for the Ipswichian—Eemian or Last Interglacial; for the Wolstonian—Gipping, Riss, Saale or Penultimate Glaciation; for the Hoxnian—Holstein or Great Interglacial; for the Anglian—Mindel, Lowestoft or Antepenultimate Glaciation.
12. Wymer, 1968, 334.

13. Waechter *et al.*, 1971.
14. Wymer, 1968, 354.
15. Pollen has recently been extracted from the Lower Loam (Waechter *et al.*, 1971, 79). Work is at an early stage and only two samples have been counted. One from the base contains 60 per cent tree pollen, mainly hazel, but with alder, pine and oak; the other from the top contains 50 per cent grasses and only 20 per cent tree pollen, mainly oak.
16. One of the best introductions to pollen analysis is Godwin, 1956, 45.
17. West, 1956; West and McBurney, 1954.
18. Turner, C., 1970.
19. Kelly, 1964.
20. Jessen *et al.*, 1959.
21. Kerney, 1971; Turner, C., 1970.
22. Oakley, 1952; Ovey, 1964.
23. West, 1956; West and McBurney, 1954.
24. Frere, 1800.
25. Bristow and Cox, 1973.
26. Turner, C., 1970, 430.
27. Oakley, 1952, 285.
28. Roe, 1964.
29. Smith, W. G., 1894.
30. Roe, 1964, Plate 27.
31. Shotton, 1968, 478.
32. Coles, 1968.
33. Campbell and Sampson, 1971.
34. Flints from a fissure at Westbury-sub-Mendip, Somerset, are also associated with a fauna which is likely to be Cromerian. Personal communication from Professor E. K. Tratman.

Chapter 2.   The Upper Pleistocene

1. Sutcliffe and Zeuner, 1962.
2. Clark, 1952, 22.
3. Sutcliffe, 1960, 21; Sutcliffe in Ovey, 1964, 104.
4. Sutcliffe, 1960, 21.
5. West, 1968.
6. West and Sparks, 1960.
7. Wilson, 1948, Fig. 27.
8. Bowen, 1973.
9. Wymer, 1968, 373.
10. Roe, 1968, 17.
11. Wymer, 1968, 354.
12. Wymer, 1968, 322.
13. Roe, 1964, Fig. 1.
14. Wymer, 1968, 19.
15. bp = 'before present', i.e. before 1950; see notes 2, 16 and 2, 31.
16. Radioactive carbon is produced in the upper atmosphere by cosmic

ray bombardment of nitrogen. This is known as carbon-14 or ^{14}C
(14 being the atomic weight), in contrast to normal, non-radioactive
carbon, ^{12}C. On being produced, ^{14}C rapidly combines with atmo-
spheric oxygen to form carbon dioxide, which then becomes mixed in
the earth's atmosphere with non-radioactive carbon dioxide in the
ratio 1 : 1,000,000,000,000. Sophisticated techniques are therefore
needed to measure radiocarbon. The two forms of carbon dioxide are
taken up by plants and converted into organic matter by photo-
synthesis; there is no discrimination against either form and the original
ratio is generally maintained. Animals, too, derive all their organic
matter from the same source through plants, and again the ratio
of the two forms of carbon in their tissues is the same. Thus all living
matter contains a known ratio of ^{14}C to ^{12}C when first formed. But
on death, the ^{14}C begins to decay. The rate of decay is expressed in terms
of the 'half-life', i.e. the time taken for half the original amount of ^{14}C
to decay, and this value is normally taken as 5568 years. Knowing this,
and by measuring the radiocarbon content of a sample of ancient
organic material, the age of the sample can be determined.

However, it has recently been discovered that radiocarbon years
are not always equivalent to calendar years. This has been shown
through the ^{14}C assay of wood dated independently by tree-ring
counting or from historical contexts—e.g. Egyptian tombs—of known
age (Renfrew, 1970). Thus a ^{14}C date in the first millennium bc may be
200 years too young; by the time the fourth millennium bc is reached the
discrepancy may be as much as 1000 years. Dates computed with
reference to ^{14}C are written as 'bp', 'bc' or 'ad' unless corrected to
calendar years.

17. Simpson and West, 1958.
18. Coope *et al.*, 1961.
19. Munro, 1879. I am grateful to George Boon for this reference.
20. Coope, 1959.
21. Coope *et al.*, 1961, 380.
22. Wymer, 1968, 356.
23. Campbell and Sampson, 1971.
24. Tratman *et al.*, 1971.
25. McBurney, 1965.
26. Wilson, 1948, Fig. 27.
27. Kerney *et al.*, 1964; Small *et al.*, 1970.
28. Kerney, 1963.
29. Kerney, 1965.
30. Evans, 1972a.
31. From this point on it is more convenient to use 'bc' rather than 'bp'
    dates; 'bp' dates are converted to 'bc' dates by subtracting 1950.
32. West, 1968, 263.
33. Kerney, 1963.
34. Kerney, 1963.
35. Godwin, 1956; Jessen and Farrington, 1938; Mitchell and Parkes, 1949;
    Smith, A. G., 1970a.
36. Garrod, 1926.

37. Campbell *et al.*, 1970; McBurney, 1965.
38. Campbell *et al.*, 1970.
39. Mellars, 1969.
40. Campbell, 1969; Campbell *et al.*, 1970.
41. Hallam *et al.*, 1973.
42. Mitchell and Parkes, 1949.
43. The radiocarbon date of $18,460 \pm 340$ bp is somewhat anomalous in falling close to the maximum of the glacial advance (Oakley, 1968). See also Bowen, 1970.
44. Tratman *et al.*, 1971.
45. e.g. Mace, 1959; Manby, 1966.
46. Clark, 1952, 25.
47. Bouchud, 1954.
48. Ucko and Rosenfeld, 1967, 91.
49. Zeuner, 1963, 112.
50. Kerney, 1963.
51. Higgs, 1972, 84.
52. Marshack, 1970.
53. Rosenfeld, 1971.

Chapter 3.   The influence of the Ice Age on the environment of Britain

1. Manley, 1962; Pearsall, 1968; Sissons, 1967; Southern, 1964; Stamp, 1960; Tansley, 1968; Trueman, 1971.
2. Gresswell, 1958a; Sparks and West, 1972.
3. Sparks and West, 1972, 24.
4. Charlesworth, 1937.
5. Wykham, 1974, 212.
6. Darbishire, 1874.
7. Mitchell, 1940.
8. Jones Hughes, 1970, Fig. 15.4; Synge, 1970, Fig. 3.1.
9. Tomlinson, 1941; Wainwright *et al.*, 1971, 228.
10. Williams, 1968.
11. Smith, A. C., 1885.
12. King, 1968.
13. Kerney *et al.*, 1964.
14. Briggs and Gilbertson, 1973; Wymer, 1968, 19.
15. Shotton, 1968.
16. Benson and Miles, 1974; *R.C.H.M.*, 1960.
17. Tamplin, 1966.
18. Wooldridge and Linton, 1933.
19. Perrin, 1956.
20. Evans, 1968.
21. These deposits should not be confused with the shell sands of the western seaboard which are of Post-glacial origin and highly fertile (p. 120).
22. Head, 1955, Maps IV and V.

23. Sparks and West, 1972, 17.
24. Two useful general works on coastlines and rivers are Gresswell, 1957 and 1958b.
25. Bibby, 1957, ch. 2.
26. West, 1968, 21.
27. Oakley, 1968.
28. Bibby, 1957; Frere, 1800.
29. Daniel, 1967.
30. West, 1968, ch. 13; Zeuner, 1959, 308.

Chapter 4.   The early Post-glacial

1. Sparks and West, 1972, 177.
2. Godwin, 1956, 27.
3. Scharff, 1907; a more up-to-date study is that of Degerbøl and Krog, 1951.
4. Praeger, 1896.
5. Pennington, 1969, 55.
6. e.g. Kerney, 1968.
7. Ritchie, 1920, 26.
8. Frenzel, 1966.
9. Walker, 1956.
10. Godwin, 1956, 330.
11. Glob, 1969a, translated from a Danish almanack of 1837.
12. Godwin, 1956, 29.
13. Conway, 1954.
14. Evans, 1972b, 297.
15. Evans, 1972b, 300.
16. Personal communication from M. P. Kerney.
17. Mackereth, 1965; Seddon, 1967.
18. Summarized in Godwin, 1956, 64 and Fig. 94.
19. Clark, 1954.
20. Clark, 1932 is the only book on the British Mesolithic.
21. Dimbleby, 1961a; 1962; Simmons, 1969a; 1969b; Smith, A. G., 1970a.
22. Pennington, 1969.
23. Dimbleby and Evans, 1974.
24. Mitchell, 1956a.
25. Pennington, 1969, 55.
26. Dimbleby and Evans, 1974.
27. Evans, 1972b.
28. West, 1968, 135.
29. Akeroyd, 1972; Jelgersma, 1966.
30. Donner, 1970. See also a special no. of *Trans. I.B.G.* no. 39 (1966) on the vertical displacement of shorelines in highland Britain.
31. Godwin, 1940.
32. Praeger, 1896.
33. Lacaille, 1954, 69, Fig. 26 ii.
34. Clark, 1947.

35. Clark, 1954.
36. Clark, 1954.
37. Degerbøl, 1961.
38. Hallam *et al.*, 1973.
39. Churchill, 1962; Wymer, 1962.
40. Hallam *et al.*, 1973.

Chapter 5. The impact of man on the environment in mid Post-glacial times

1. Davies and Rankine, 1960; Radley, 1970.
2. Radley, 1970.
3. Dimbleby, 1961b; 1962.
4. Dimbleby, 1961a.
5. Dimbleby, 1962.
6. Conway, 1954.
7. Walker, 1956.
8. Dimbleby, 1962.
9. Simmons, 1969a; 1969b.
10. Keef *et al.*, 1965.
11. Atkinson, 1957; Cornwall, 1953; Darwin, 1881.
12. Smith, A. G., 1970a.
13. Pearsall, 1968.
14. Smith, A. G., 1965.
15. Smith A. G., 1970a.
16. Harris, 1969; Waateringe, 1968.
17. Jarman, 1972.
18. Clark, 1955.
19. Evans and Smith, 1967.
20. Radley, 1969.
21. Lacaille, 1954; Movius, 1942.
22. Mitchell, 1971.
23. Clark, 1932, Map II.
24. Personal communication from Isobel Smith and Roger Jacobi.
25. Bradley, 1970; Palmer, 1970.
26. Coles, 1971; Wymer, 1962.
27. Smith, I. F., 1965.
28. Palmer, 1970.
29. Coles, 1971, 317.
30. Coles and Higgs, 1969.
31. Simmons, 1969a.
32. This was suggested to me by Pam Evans.
33. Meighan, 1969.
34. Evans, 1969.
35. Cornwall, 1964, 223.
36. Jarman, 1972; Jewell, 1963.
37. Clark, 1965; Piggott, 1965.
38. Clark, 1967.

39. Harris, 1969.
40. van Zeist, 1969.
41. Smith *et al.*, 1971.
42. Movius, 1942.
43. Stephens and Collins, 1960.
44. Liversage, 1968; Mitchell, 1956b; 1971.
45. Smith *et al.*, 1971.
46. Smith and Willis, 1962.
47. Troels-Smith, 1960.
48. Case, 1969, 3.
49. Liversage, 1968.
50. Mitchell, 1956a.
51. Pearsall, 1968.
52. Pennington, 1970.
53. Clark and Godwin, 1962.
54. Wainwright, 1972.
55. Wymer, 1970.
56. Barker *et al.*, 1969.
57. Fox, A., 1963.

Chapter 6.   Prehistoric and early farmers

1. Godwin, 1944.
2. Pennington, 1970.
3. Iversen, 1941.
4. Evidence of Neolithic 'clearance fires' in the form of extensive charcoal spreads has been recorded from beneath the blanket peat at Ballynagilly, Co. Tyrone. Personal communication from Arthur ApSimon.
5. Clark, 1952, 92.
6. Steensberg, 1957.
7. Godwin, 1944.
8. Pennington, 1969.
9. Smith, A. G., 1970a; Turner, J., 1970; Walker and West, 1970.
10. Smith, A. G., 1970b.
11. Dimbleby and Evans, 1974; Evans, 1972b.
12. Evans, 1972b, 257.
13. Fowler and Evans, 1967.
14. Evans, 1972b, 248.
15. Evans, 1972b, 230, 364.
16. Godwin, 1962.
17. Evans, 1972b, 363.
18. Evans, 1972b, 291.
19. Work in Orkney and Cornwall has been done by Penelope Spencer in the Department of Archaeology, University College, Cardiff.
20. Pennington, 1969, 72.
21. Caulfield, 1974.
22. Burleigh *et al.*, 1973.
23. Turner, J., 1970.

24. Turner, J., 1962; 1970.
25. Clark, 1952, 171; Clark and Piggott, 1933.
26. Houlder, 1961; Ritchie, 1968.
27. Evens *et al.*, 1962; Shotton, 1968.
28. Bradley, 1972.
29. Fleming, 1972.
30. Clark, 1952, 117.
31. Fowler, 1971.
32. Atkinson, 1974.
33. Elgee, 1930, 32, 77.
34. Dimbleby, 1961b, 1962.
35. Dimbleby, 1962.
36. Turner, J., 1965.
37. Dimbleby, 1962.
38. Dimbleby, 1962.
39. Fleming, 1971.
40. Feachem, 1973.
41. Taylor, J. A., 1973.
42. Fox, C., 1932, 54.
43. Wooldridge and Linton, 1933.
44. Head, 1955.
45. Grimes, 1945.
46. Scott, 1964, 136.
47. Henshall, 1963.
48. Glob, 1951, 124.
49. Pennington, 1965.
50. Pearsall, 1968, 141.
51. Praeger, 1969, 224.
52. Evans, 1972b, 277.
53. Atkinson, 1957.
54. Dimbleby and Speight, 1969.
55. Atkinson, 1960, 112.
56. Pennington, 1969, 62.
57. Coles, 1972; Coles *et al.*, 1970.
58. Cornwall, 1953.
59. Cornwall, 1953, 138.
60. Radley and Simms, 1967.
61. Godwin, 1956, 34; 1966.
62. Seddon, 1967.
63. Coles, 1972; Coles *et al.*, 1970; Godwin, 1960.
64. Coles and Hibbert, 1968.
65. Godwin, 1966.
66. Piggott, 1972.
67. Stamp, 1960, 21.
68. Evans, E., 1957.
69. Stamp, 1960, 23.
70. Feachem, 1973.
71. Fleming, 1971.
72. Dimbleby, 1962.

73. Personal communication from H. C. Bowen.
74. Fox, C., 1932.
75. Feachem, 1973, 348.
76. Personal communication from Jack Stevenson.
77. Turner, J., 1970.
78. Turner, J., 1965; 1970.
79. Bowen, H. C. 1961.
80. Fowler and Evans, 1967.
81. Megaw *et al.*, 1961.
82. Evans, 1972b, 316.
83. Evans, 1972b, 291; Megaw *et al.*, 1961.
84. Macnab, 1965.
85. Evans, 1972b, 282, 311.
86. Turner, J., 1970.
87. Turner, J., 1970.
88. Rivet, 1964, 100.
89. Anati, 1964; Bicknell, 1902; Glob, 1969b.
90. Glob, 1951.
91. Personal communication from W. H. Manning.
92. Manning, 1964.
93. Manning, 1964, 63.
94. Fox, C., 1923.
95. Wooldridge and Linton, 1933.
96. Cunliffe, 1966.
97. Applebaum, 1972, 5; Manley, 1962, 286.
98. Frenzel, 1966; Turner, J., 1965.

Chapter 7.   The historical period

1. Taylor, C. C., 1967.
2. Taylor, C. C., 1968.
3. Hoskins, 1970.
4. The problem as a whole is discussed by Beresford, 1954, 177 and Beresford and Hurst, 1971, 4.
5. Taylor, C. C., 1967, 95.
6. Mitchell, 1942; 1965; Turner, J., 1970.
7. Eyre, 1966; Hicks, 1971.
8. Seddon, in Savory, 1960, 72.
9. Evans, in Rowley, 1972, 129.
10. Pike and Biddle, 1966; Taylor, E. L., 1955.
11. Exhibited in the National Museum, Dublin.
12. Stamp, 1969.
13. Stenton, 1951, 99.
14. Head, 1955, 88.
15. Mead, 1954.
16. Bowen, H. C., 1961, 10.
17. Finberg, 1972, 418.
18. Bowen, H. C., 1961, 47.

19. Taylor, C. C., 1972.
20. Glasscock, 1970; Hurst and Hurst, 1957.
21. Buchanan, 1970.
22. Aalen, 1970.
23. Proudfoot, 1961.
24. Mitchell, 1965.
25. Evans, E., 1957.
26. Buchanan, 1970.
27. Evans, E., 1957.
28. Alcock, 1964.
29. Jones Hughes, 1970, Fig. 15.4; Synge, 1970, Fig. 3.1.
30. Aalen, 1970.
31. For the climate of the historical period see especially Lamb, 1972, and Manley, 1962, ch. 12.
32. Manley, 1965.
33. Personal communication from M. G. Jarrett.
34. Schove and Lowther, 1957.
35. Manley, 1962, 289.
36. Ladurie, 1972; Manley, 1962.
37. Manley, 1962.
38. Manley, 1962, 373.
39. Hoskins, 1970.
40. Evans, E., 1957, 20.
41. Feachem, 1973.
42. Hooper *et al.*, 1971.
43. Stamp, 1969, 51.
44. Knowles, 1969.
45. Turner, J., 1965.
46. Clark, 1938.
47. Evans, E., 1966, 170.
48. Tansley, 1968, 258.
49. Whitehead, 1966.
50. Evans, E., 1966; Feachem, 1963; Piggott, 1952-3.
51. Hencken, 1942.
52. Tansley, 1968, 245.
53. Clark, 1952, 127.
54. Finberg, 1972.
55. *Blueprint for Survival*, 1972.
56. Stamp, 1969, xiii.
57. Darling, 1970, 87.

Bibliography

The following abbreviations have been used:

Ag. Hist. Rev.—Agricultural History Review
Ant. J.—Antiquaries Journal
Arch. Camb.—Archaeologia Cambrensis
Geog. J.—Geographical Journal
J. Arch. Ass.—Journal of the Archaeological Association
J. Arch. Sci.—Journal of Archaeological Science
J.R.S.—Journal of Roman Studies
J.R.S.A.I.—Journal of the Royal Society of Antiquaries of Ireland
J. Soil Sci.—Journal of Soil Science
Med. Arch.—Medieval Archaeology
New Phyt.—New Phytologist
P.D.A.E.S.—Proceedings of the Devon Archaeological and Exploration Society
P.D.N.H.S.—Proceedings of the Dorset Natural History and Archaeological Society
P.G.A.—Proceedings of the Geologists Association
Phil. Trans.—Philosophical Transactions of the Royal Society
P.P.S.—Proceedings of the Prehistoric Society
P.R.I.A.—Proceedings of the Royal Irish Academy
P.S.A.S.—Proceedings of the Society of Antiquaries of Scotland
P.W.C.F.C.—Proceedings of the West Cornwall Field Club
Q.J.G.S.—Quarterly Journal of the Geological Society
R.C.H.M.—Royal Commission on Historical Monuments
S.A.F.—Scottish Archaeological Forum
Trans. I.B.G.—Transactions of the Institute of British Geographers
T.T.N.H.S.—Transactions of the Torquay Natural History Society
U.J.A.—Ulster Journal of Archaeology
W.A.M.—Wiltshire Archaeological and Natural History Magazine
Y.A.J.—Yorkshire Archaeological Journal

Otherwise, abbreviations are those given in the *World List of Scientific Periodicals*.

Aalen, F. H. A., 1970. The origin of enclosures in eastern Ireland, in Stephens, N., and Glasscock, R. E. (Eds.), *Irish Geographical Studies*. Department of Geography, Queen's University, Belfast, 209–23.

Agassiz, J. L. R., 1840. *Études sur les Glaciers*.

Agassiz, J. L. R. 1847. *Système Glaciaire*.

Akeroyd, A. V. 1972. Archaeological and historical evidence for subsidence in southern Britain, *Phil. Trans.* A **272,** 151–69.

Alcock, L. 1964. Some reflections on early Welsh society and economy, *The Welsh History Review* **2,** 1–7.

Anati, E. 1964. *Camonica Valley*. Cape, London.

Applebaum, S. 1972. Roman Britain, in Finberg, H. P. R. (Ed.), *The Agrarian History of England and Wales. I, ii. AD 43–1042*. Cambridge University Press.

Arkell, W. J. 1947. *The Geology of Oxford*. Clarendon Press, Oxford.

Atkinson, R. J. C. 1957. Worms and weathering, *Antiquity* **31**, 219–33.

Atkinson, R. J. C. 1960. *Stonehenge*. Penguin, Harmondsworth.

Atkinson, R. J. C. 1974. Neolithic science and technology, *Phil. Trans.* A **276**, 123–31.

Barker, H., Burleigh, R., and Meeks, N. 1969. British Museum natural radiocarbon measurements VI, *Radiocarbon* **11**, 278–94.

Benson, D. G., and Miles, D. 1974. *The Upper Thames Valley: An Archaeological Survey of the River Gravels*. Oxfordshire Archaeological Unit, Survey no. 2, Oxford.

Beresford, M. 1954. *The Lost Villages of England*. Lutterworth, London.

Beresford, M., and Hurst, J. G. 1971. *Deserted Medieval Villages*. Lutterworth, London.

Bibby, G. 1957. *The Testimony of the Spade*. Collins, London.

Bicknell, C. 1902. *The Prehistoric Rock Engravings in the Italian Maritime Alps*. Bordighera.

Blueprint for Survival, Ecologist **2** (ii). January 1972.

Blytt, A. 1876. *Essay on the Immigration of the Norwegian Flora during Alternating Rainy and Dry Periods*. Cammermeyer, Christiania.

Bordes, F. 1968. *The Old Stone Age*. Weidenfeld and Nicolson, London.

Bouchud, J. 1954. Le renne et le problème des migrations, *L'Anthropologie* **58**, 79–85.

Bowen, D. Q. 1970. The palaeoenvironment of the 'Red Lady' of Paviland, *Antiquity* **44**, 134–6.

Bowen, D. Q. 1973. The Pleistocene succession of the Irish Sea, *P.G.A.* **84**, 249–72.

Bowen, H. C. 1961. *Ancient Fields*. British Association, London.

Bradley, R. 1970. *A Mesolithic Assemblage from East Sussex*. Sussex Archaeological Society, Occasional Paper 2.

Bradley, R. 1972. Prehistorians and pastoralists in Neolithic and Bronze Age England, *World Archaeology* **4**, 192–204.

Briggs, D. J., and Gilbertson, D. D. 1973. The age of the Hanborough terrace of the River Evenlode, Oxfordshire, *P.G.A.* **84**, 155–73.

Bristow, C. R., and Cox, F. C. 1973. The Gipping Till: a reappraisal of East Anglian glacial stratigraphy, *Journal of the Geological Society* **129**, 1–37.

Buchanan, R. H. 1970. Rural settlement in Ireland, in Stephens, N., and Glasscock, R. E. (Eds.), *Irish Geographical Studies*. Department of Geography, Queen's University, Belfast, 146–61.

Buckland, W. 1823. *Reliquae Diluvianae, or Observations on Organic Remains Attesting to the Action of a Universal Deluge*. Murray, London.

Burleigh, R., Evans, J. G., and Simpson, D. D. A. 1973. Radiocarbon dates for Northton, Outer Hebrides, *Antiquity* **47**, 61–4.

Butzer, K. W. 1972. *Environment and Archaeology*. Methuen, London.

Campbell, J. B. 1969. Excavations at Creswell Crags, *Derbyshire Archaeological Journal* **89**, 47–58.

Campbell, J. B., Elkington, D., Fowler, P., and Grinsell, L. 1970. *The Mendip Hills in Prehistoric and Roman Times.* Bristol Archaeological Research Group, Bristol City Museum.

Campbell, J. B., and Sampson, C. G. 1971. A new analysis of Kent's Cavern, Devonshire, England, *University of Oregon Anthropological Papers* **3**, 1–40.

Case, H. 1969. Settlement patterns in the north Irish Neolithic, *U.J.A.* **32**, 3–27.

Caulfield, S. 1974. Agriculture and settlement in ancient Mayo, in Blake, I. (Ed.), Archaeology in Ireland Today, *The Irish Times*, 23 April, 3.

Chaplin, R. E. 1971. *The Study of Animal Bones from Archaeological Sites.* Seminar Press, London.

Charlesworth, J. K. 1937. A map of the glacier-lakes and the local glaciers of the Wicklow Hills, *P.R.I.A.* B **46**, 29–36.

Churchill, D. M. 1962. The stratigraphy of Mesolithic Sites III and IV at Thatcham, Berkshire, England, *P.P.S.* **28**, 362–70.

Clark, J. G. D. 1932. *The Mesolithic Age in Britain.* Cambridge University Press, London.

Clark, J. G. D. 1938. Microlithic industries from tufa deposits at Prestatyn, Flintshire and Blashenwell, Dorset, *P.P.S.* **4**, 330–4.

Clark, J. G. D. 1947. Whales as an economic factor in prehistoric Europe, *Antiquity* **21**, 84–104.

Clark, J. G. D. 1952. *Prehistoric Europe: The Economic Basis.* Methuen, London.

Clark, J. G. D. 1954. *Excavations at Star Carr.* Cambridge University Press, London.

Clark, J. G. D. 1955. A microlithic industry from the Cambridgeshire fenland and other industries of Sauveterrian affinities from Britain, *P.P.S.* **21**, 3–20.

Clark, J. G. D. 1965. Radiocarbon dating and the expansion of farming culture, *P.P.S.* **31**, 58–73.

Clark, J. G. D. 1967. *The Stone Age Hunters.* Thames and Hudson, London.

Clark, J. G. D., and Godwin, H. 1962. The Neolithic in the Cambridgeshire Fens, *Antiquity* **36**, 10–23.

Clark, J. G. D., and Piggott, S. 1933. The age of the British flint mines, *Antiquity* **7**, 166–83.

Coles, J. M. 1968. Ancient man in Europe, in Coles, J. M., and Simpson, D. D. A. (Eds.), *Studies in Ancient Europe.* Leicester University Press, 17–43.

Coles, J. M. 1971. The early settlement of Scotland: excavations at Morton, Fife, *P.P.S.* **37** (ii), 284–366.

Coles, J. M. 1972. Later Bronze Age activity in the Somerset Levels, *Ant. J.* **52**, 269–75.

Coles, J. M., and Hibbert, F. A. 1968. Prehistoric roads and tracks in Somerset, England: 1. Neolithic, *P.P.S.* **34**, 238–58.

Coles, J. M., Hibbert, F. A., and Clements, C. F. 1970. Prehistoric roads and tracks in Somerset, England: 2. Neolithic, *P.P.S.* **36**, 125–51.

Coles, J. M., and Higgs, E. S. 1969. *The Archaeology of Early Man.* Faber and Faber, London.

Conway, V. M. 1954. Stratigraphy and pollen analysis of southern Pennine blanket peats, *J. Ecol.* **42**, 117–47.

Coope, G. R. 1959. A late-Pleistocene insect fauna from Chelford, Cheshire, *Proc. R. Soc.* B **151**, 70–86.

Coope, G. R., Shotton, F. W., and Strachan, I. 1961. A late Pleistocene fauna and flora from Upton Warren, Worcestershire, *Phil. Trans.* B **244**, 379–421.

Cornwall, I. W. 1953. Soil science and archaeology with illustrations from some British Bronze Age monuments, *P.P.S.* **19**, 129–47.

Cornwall, I. W. 1964. *The World of Ancient Man.* Phoenix House, London.

Cunliffe, B. 1966. The Somerset Levels in the Roman period, in Thomas, C. (Ed.), *Rural Settlement in Roman Britain.* Council for British Archaeology, Research Report 7, London, 68–73.

Daniel, G. 1967. *The Origins and Growth of Archaeology.* Penguin, Harmondsworth.

Darbishire, R. D. 1874. Notes on discoveries in Ehenside Tarn, Cumberland, *Archaeologia* **44**, 273–92.

Darling, F. F. 1970. *Wilderness and Plenty: The Reith Lectures 1969.* BBC, London.

Darwin, C. 1859. *The Origin of Species by Means of Natural Selection.* Murray, London.

Darwin, C. 1881. *The Formation of Vegetable Mould through the Action of Worms with Observations of their Habits.* Murray, London.

Davies, J., and Rankine, W. F. 1960. Mesolithic flint axes from the West Riding of Yorkshire, *Y.A.J.* no. 158, 209–14.

Degerbøl, M. 1961. On a find of a Preboreal domestic dog (*Canis familiaris* L.) from Star Carr, Yorkshire, with remarks on other Mesolithic dogs, *P.P.S.* **27**, 35–55.

Degerbøl, M., and Krog, H. 1951. Den europaeiske Sumpskildpadde (*Emys orbicularis* L.) i Danmark, *Danm. geol. Unders.* II Rk. Nr. 78.

Dimbleby, G. W. 1961a. Soil pollen analysis, *J. Soil Sci.* **12**, 1–11.

Dimbleby, G. W. 1961b. The ancient forest of Blackamore, *Antiquity* **35**, 123–8.

Dimbleby, G. W. 1962. *The Development of British Heathlands and their Soils.* Oxford Forestry Memoir, no. 23, Oxford.

Dimbleby, G. W., and Evans, J. G. 1974. Pollen and land-snail analysis of calcareous soils, *J. Arch. Sci.* **1**, 117–33.

Dimbleby, G. W., and Speight, M. C. D. 1969. Buried soils, *Advancement of Science* **26**, 203–5.

Donner, J. J. 1970. Land/sea level changes in Scotland, in Walker, D., and West, R. G. (Ed.), *Studies in the Vegetational History of the British Isles.* Cambridge University Press, London, 23–39.

Elgee, F. 1930. *Early Man in North-east Yorkshire.* Bellows, Gloucester.

Evans, E. E. 1957. *Irish Folk Ways.* Routledge and Kegan Paul, London.

Evans, E. E. 1966. *Prehistoric and Early Christian Ireland: A Guide.* Batsford, London.

Evans, J. G. 1968. Periglacial deposits on the Chalk of Wiltshire, *W.A.M.* **63**, 12–26.

Evans, J. G. 1969. The exploitation of molluscs, in Ucko, P. J., and Dimbleby,

G. W. (Eds.), *The Domestication and Exploitation of Plants and Animals.* Duckworth, London, 477–84.

Evans, J. G. 1972a. Ice-wedge casts at Broome Heath, Norfolk, in Wainwright, G. W. The excavation of a Neolithic settlement on Broome Heath, Ditchingham, Norfolk, England, *P.P.S.* **38,** 77–86.

Evans, J. G. 1972b. *Land Snails in Archaeology.* Seminar Press, London.

Evans, J. G., and Smith, I. F. 1967. Cherhill, *Archaeological Review* (Dept. of Extra-mural Studies, University of Bristol) no. 2, 8–9.

Evens, E. D., Grinsell, L. V., Piggott, S., and Wallis, F. S. 1962. Fourth report of the sub-committee of the south-western group of museums and art galleries on the petrological identification of stone axes, *P.P.S.* **28,** 209–66.

Eyre, S. R. 1966. The vegetation of a south Pennine upland, in Eyre, S., and Jones, G. (Eds.), *Geography as Human Ecology.* London.

Feachem, R. W. 1963. *A Guide to Prehistoric Scotland.* Batsford, London.

Feachem, R. W. 1973. Ancient agriculture in the highland of Britain, *P.P.S.* **39,** 332–53.

Finberg, H. P. R. (Ed.), 1972. *The Agrarian History of England and Wales. I, ii. AD 43–1042.* Cambridge University Press, Cambridge.

Fleming, A. 1971. Bronze Age agriculture on the marginal lands of north-east Yorkshire, *Ag. Hist. Rev.* **19,** 1–24.

Fleming, A. 1972. The genesis of pastoralism in European prehistory, *World Archaeology* **4,** 179–91.

Fleure, H. J. 1951 (2nd ed. fully revised by M. Davies, 1971). *A Natural History of Man in Britain.* Collins, London.

Fowler, P. J. 1971. Early prehistoric agriculture in western Europe: some archaeological evidence, in Simpson, D. D. A. (Ed.), *Economy and Settlement in Neolithic and Early Bronze Age Britain and Europe.* Leicester University Press, 153–82.

Fowler, P. J., and Evans, J. G. 1967. Plough-marks, lynchets and early fields, *Antiquity* **41,** 289–301.

Fox, A. 1963. Neolithic charcoal from Hembury, *Antiquity* **37,** 228–9.

Fox, C. 1923. *Archaeology of the Cambridge Region.* Cambridge University Press, London.

Fox, C. 1932. *The Personality of Britain.* Cardiff National Museum and University of Wales.

Frenzel, B. 1966. Climatic change in the Atlantic/Sub-boreal transition on the Northern Hemisphere: botanical evidence, in *World Climate from 8000 to 0 BC* Royal Meteorological Society, London, 99–123.

Frere, J. 1800. Account of flint weapons discovered at Hoxne in Suffolk, *Archaeologia* **13,** 204–5.

Garrod, D. A. E. 1926. *The Upper Palaeolithic Age in Britain.* Clarendon Press, Oxford.

Glasscock, R. E. 1970. Moated sites, and deserted boroughs and villages: two neglected aspects of Anglo-Norman settlement in Ireland, in Stephens, N., and Glasscock, R. E. (Eds.), *Irish Geographical Studies.* Department of Geography, Queen's University, Belfast, 162–77.

Glob, P. V. 1951. *Ard og Plov i Nordens Oldtid.* Universitetsforlaget, Aarhus.

Glob, P. V. 1969a. *The Bog People: Iron-Age Man Preserved.* Faber, London.

Glob, P. V. 1969b. *Helleristninger i Danmark*. Jutland Archaeological Society Publication 7, Copenhagen.

Godwin, H. 1940. A Boreal transgression of the sea in Swansea Bay, *New Phyt.* **39**, 308.

Godwin, H. 1944. Age and origin of the 'Breckland' heaths of East Anglia, *Nature* **154**, 6.

Godwin, H. 1956. *The History of the British Flora*. Cambridge University Press, London.

Godwin, H. 1960. Prehistoric wooden trackways of the Somerset Levels: their construction, age and relation to climatic change, *P.P.S.* **26**, 1–36.

Godwin, H. 1962. Vegetational history of the Kentish chalk downs as seen at Wingham and Frogholt, *Veröff. geobot. Inst., Zürich* **37**, 83–99.

Godwin, H. 1966. Introductory address, in *World Climate from 8000 to 0 BC*. Royal Meteorological Society, London, 3–14.

Gresswell, R. K. 1957. *The Physical Geography of Beaches and Coastlines*. Hutton, London.

Gresswell, R. K. 1958a. *The Physical Geography of Glaciers and Glaciation*. Hutton, London.

Gresswell, R. K. 1958b. *The Physical Geography of Rivers and Valleys*. Hutton, London.

Grimes, W. F. 1945. Early man and the soils of Anglesey, *Antiquity* **19**, 169–74.

Hallam, J. S., Edwards, B. J. N., Barnes, B., and Stuart, A. J. 1973. A Late Glacial elk with associated barbed points from High Furlong, Lancashire, *P.P.S.* **39**, 100–28.

Harris, D. R. 1969. Agricultural systems, ecosystems and the origins of agriculture, in Ucko, P. J., and Dimbleby, G. W. (Eds.), *The Domestication and Exploitation of Plants and Animals*. Duckworth, London, 3–15.

Head, J. F. 1955. *Early Man in South Buckinghamshire*. Wright, Bristol.

Hencken, H. O'N. 1942. Ballinderry Crannog no. 2, *P.R.I.A.* C **47**, 1–43.

Henshall, A. S. 1963. *The Chambered Tombs of Scotland. Vol. I*. Edinburgh University Press.

Hicks, S. P. 1971. Pollen-analytical evidence for the effect of prehistoric agriculture on the vegetation of north Derbyshire, *New Phyt.* **70**, 647–67.

Higgs, E. S. (Ed.), 1972. *Papers in Economic Prehistory*. Cambridge University Press, London.

Hooper, M. D. *et al.* 1971. *Hedges and Local History*. National Council of Social Service, London.

Hoskins, W. G. 1970. *The Making of the English Landscape*. Penguin, Harmondsworth.

Houlder, C. H. 1961. The excavation of a Neolithic stone implement factory on Mynydd Rhiw in Caernarvonshire, *P.P.S.* **27**, 108–43.

Hurst, D. G., and Hurst, J. G. 1957. Excavation of two moated sites: Milton, Hampshire and Ashwell, Hertfordshire, *J. Arch. Ass.* **30**, 83–6.

Iversen, J. 1941. Landnam i Danmarks Stenalder, *Danm. geol. Unders.* II Rk. Nr. 66, 1–68.

Jarman, M. R. 1972. European deer economies and the advent of the Neolithic, in Higgs, E. S. (Ed.), *Papers in Economic Prehistory*. Cambridge University Press, London, 125–49.

Jelgersma, S. 1966. Sea-level changes during the last 10,000 years, in *World Climate from 8000 to 0 BC*. Royal Meteorological Society, London, 54–71.

Jessen, K. and Farrington, A. 1938. The bogs at Ballybetagh, near Dublin, with remarks on Late-glacial conditions in Ireland, *P.R.I.A.* B **46**, 205–60.

Jessen, K., Farrington, A., and Andersen, S. J. 1959. The interglacial deposit near Gort, Co. Galway, Ireland, *P.R.I.A.* B **60**, 1–77.

Jewell, P. 1963. Cattle from British archaeological sites, *Royal Anthropological Institute*, Occasional Paper No. 18, 80–101.

Jones Hughes, T. 1970. Town and baile in Irish place-names, in Stephens, N., and Glasscock, R. E. (Eds.), *Irish Geographical Studies*. Department of Geography, Queen's University, Belfast, 244–58.

Keef, P. A. M., Wymer, J. J., and Dimbleby, G. W. 1965. A Mesolithic site on Iping Common, Sussex, England, *P.P.S.* **31**, 85–92.

Kelly, M. R. 1964. The Middle Pleistocene of North Birmingham, *Phil. Trans.* B **247**, 533–92.

Kerney, M. P. 1963. Late-glacial deposits on the Chalk of south-east England, *Phil. Trans.* B **246**, 203–54.

Kerney, M. P. 1965. Weichselian deposits in the Isle of Thanet, East Kent, *P.G.A.* **76**, 269–74.

Kerney, M. P. 1968. Britain's fauna of land Mollusca and its relation to the Post-glacial thermal optimum, *Symp. zool. Soc. Lond.* No. 22, 273–91.

Kerney, M. P. 1971. Interglacial deposits in Barnfield Pit, Swanscombe, and their molluscan fauna, *J. Geol. Soc.* **127**, 69–93.

Kerney, M. P., Brown, E. H., and Chandler, T. J. 1964. The Late-glacial and Post-glacial history of the Chalk escarpment near Brook, Kent, *Phil. Trans.* B **248**, 135–204.

King, N. E. 1968. The Kennet Valley sarsen industry, *W.A.M.* **63**, 83–93.

Knowles, D. 1969. *Christian Monasticism*. Weidenfeld and Nicolson, London.

Kurtén, B. 1968. *The Pleistocene Mammals of Europe*. Weidenfeld and Nicolson, London.

Lacaille, A. D. 1954. *The Stone Age in Scotland*. Oxford University Press, Oxford.

Ladurie, E. Le Roy, 1972. *Times of Feast, Times of Famine: A History of Climate Since the Year 1000*. Allen and Unwin, London.

Lamb, H. H. 1972. *The Changing Climate*. Methuen, London.

Le Patourel, J. 1972. Moated sites of Yorkshire: a survey and its implications, *Chateau Gaillard* **5**, 121–32.

Liversage, G. D. 1968. Excavations at Dalkey Island, Co. Dublin, 1956–9, *P.R.I.A.* C **66**, 53–233.

Lyell, C. 1830–3. *Principles of Geology*. Murray, London.

Mace, A. 1959. An Upper Palaeolithic open-site at Hengistbury Head, Christchurch, Hants, *P.P.S.* **25**, 233–59.

Mackereth, F. J. H. 1966. Some chemical observations on Post-glacial lake sediments, *Phil. Trans.* B **250**, 165–213.

Macnab, J. W. 1965. British strip lynchets, *Antiquity* **39**, 279–90.

Manby, T. G. 1966. Creswellian site at Brigham, East Yorkshire, *Ant. J.* **46**, 211–28.

Manley, G. 1962. *Climate and the British Scene*. Collins, London.

Manley, G. 1965. Possible climatic agencies in the development of Post-glacial habitats, *Proc. R. Soc.* B **161,** 363–75.

Manning, W. H. 1964. The plough in Roman Britain, *J.R.S.* **54,** 54–65.

Manning, W. H. 1971. The Piercebridge plough group, *The British Museum Quarterly* **35,** 125–36.

Marshack, A. 1970. *Notation dans les gravures du Paléolithique Supérieur*. Publications de l'Institute de Prehistoire de l'Université de Bordeaux, no. 8. Bordeaux.

McBurney, C. B. M. 1965. The Old Stone Age in Wales, in Foster, I. Ll., and Daniel, I. G. (Eds.). *Prehistoric and Early Wales*. Routledge and Kegan Paul, London.

Mead, W. R. 1954. Ridge-and-furrow in Buckinghamshire, *Geog. J.* **120**.

Megaw, J. V. S. *et al.*, 1961. The Bronze Age settlement at Gwithian, Cornwall, *P.W.C.F.C.* **2,** 200–15.

Meighan, C. W. 1969. Molluscs as food remains in archaeological sites, in Brothwell, D., and Higgs, E. S. (Eds.), *Science in Archaeology*. Thames and Hudson, London, 415–22.

Mellars, P. A. 1969. Radiocarbon dates for a new Creswellian site, *Antiquity* **43,** 308–10.

Mitchell, G. F. 1940. Studies in Irish Quaternary deposits: some lacustrine deposits near Dunshaughlin, Co. Meath, *P.R.I.A.* B **46,** 13–37.

Mitchell, G. F. 1942. A composite pollen diagram from Co. Meath, Ireland, *New Phyt*, **41,** 257–61.

Mitchell, G. F. 1956a. Post-Boreal pollen diagrams from Irish raised bogs, *P.R.I.A.* B **57,** 185–251.

Mitchell, G. F. 1956b. An early kitchen-midden at Sutton, Co. Dublin, *J.R.S.A.I.* **86,** 1–26.

Mitchell, G. F. 1965. Littleton Bog, Tipperary: an Irish agricultural record, *J.R.S.A.I.* **95,** 121–32.

Mitchell, G. F. 1971. The Larnian Culture: a minimal view, *P.P.S.* **37** (ii), 274–83.

Mitchell, G. F., and Parkes, H. M. 1949. The giant deer in Ireland, *P.R.I.A.* B **52,** 291–314.

Mitchell, G. F., Penny, L. F., Shotton, F. W., and West, R. G. 1973. *The correlation of Quaternary deposits in the British Isles*. Geological Society Special Paper no. 4, London.

Movius, H. J. 1942. *The Irish Stone Age*. Cambridge University Press, London.

Munro, R. 1879. Lochlee Crannog, *P.S.A.S.* **13,** 241.

Oakley, K. P. 1952. Swanscombe Man, *P.G.A.* **63,** 271.

Oakley, K. P. 1961. *Man the Toolmaker*. British Museum, London.

Oakley, K. P. 1964. *Frameworks for Dating Fossil Man*. Weidenfeld and Nicolson, London.

Oakley, K. P. 1968. The date of the 'Red Lady' of Paviland, *Antiquity* **42,** 306–7.

Ovey, C. D. (Ed.), 1964. The Swanscombe Skull. A survey of Research on a Pleistocene Site. *Royal Anthropological Institute*, Occasional Paper no. 20.

Palmer, S. 1970. The stone age industries of the Isle of Portland, Dorset and the utilisation of Portland Chert as artificial material in southern England, *P.P.S.* **36,** 82–115.

Pearsall, W. H. 1950 (revised W. Pennington, 1968). *Mountains and Moorlands.* Collins, London.

Pennington, W. 1965. The interpretation of some Post-glacial vegetation diversities at different Lake District sites, *Proc. R. Soc.* B **161,** 310–23.

Pennington, W. 1969. *The History of British Vegetation.* Unibooks, London.

Pennington, W. 1970. Vegetation history in the north-west of England: a regional synthesis, in Walker, D., and West, R. G. (Eds.), *Studies in the Vegetational History of the British Isles.* Cambridge University Press, London, 41–79.

Perrin, R. M. S. 1956. Nature of 'Chalk Heath' soils, *Nature* **178,** 31–2.

Piggott, C. M. 1952–3. Milton Loch Crannog I. A native house of the 2nd century AD in Kirkcudbrightshire, *P.S.A.S.* **87,** 134–52.

Piggott, S. 1965. *Ancient Europe.* Edinburgh University Press, Edinburgh.

Piggott, S. 1972. A note on climatic deterioration in the first millennium BC in Britain, *S.A.F.* **4,** 109–13.

Pike, A. W., and Biddle, M. 1966. Parasitic eggs in medieval Winchester, *Antiquity* **40,** 293–6.

Pilcher, J. R. 1968. Some applications of scanning electron microscopy to the study of modern and fossil pollen, *U.J.A.* **31,** 87–91.

Praeger, R. L. 1896. Report upon the raised beaches of the north-east of Ireland, with special reference to their fauna, *P.R.I.A.* **4,** 30–54.

Praeger, R. L. 1969. *The Way that I Went.* Allen Figgis, Dublin.

Proudfoot, V. B. 1961. The economy of the Irish rath, *Med. Arch.* **5,** 94–122.

Radley, J. 1969. An archaeological survey and policy for Wiltshire, Part II: Mesolithic, *W.A.M.* **64,** 18–20.

Radley, J. 1970. The Mesolithic period in north-east Yorkshire, *Y.A.J.*, 314–27.

Radley, J., and Simms, C. 1967. Wind erosion in east Yorkshire, *Nature* **216,** 20–2.

R.C.H.M. 1960. *A Matter of Time.* HMSO, London.

Renfrew, C. 1970. The tree-ring calibration of radiocarbon: an archaeological evaluation, *P.P.S.* **36,** 280–311.

Ritchie, J. 1920. *The Influence of Man on Animal Life in Scotland.* Cambridge University Press, London.

Ritchie, P. R. 1968. The stone implement trade in third-millennium Scotland, in Coles, J. M., and Simpson, D. D. A. (Eds.), *Studies in Ancient Europe.* Leicester University Press, 117–36.

Rivet, A. L. F. 1964. *Town and Country in Roman Britain.* Hutchinson, London.

Roe, D. A. 1964. The British Lower and Middle Palaeolithic: some problems, methods of study and preliminary results, *P.P.S.* **30,** 245–67.

Roe, D. A. 1968. British Lower and Middle Palaeolithic handaxe groups, *P.P.S.* **34,** 1–82.

Rosenfeld, A. 1971. Review of Marshack, 1970, *Antiquity* **45,** 317–19.

Rowley, T. 1972. First report on the excavations at Middleton Stoney Castle, Oxfordshire, 1970–1, *Oxoniensia* **37,** 109–36.

Savory, H. N. 1960. Excavations at Dinas Emrys, Beddgelert (Caern.), 1954–6, *Arch. Camb.* **109,** 13–77.

Scharff, R. F. 1907. *European Animals: Their Geological History and Geographical Distribution*. Constable, London.

Schove, D. J., and Lowther, A. W. G. 1957. Tree rings and medieval archaeology, *Med. Arch.* **1,** 78–95.

Scott, J. G. 1964. The chambered cairn at Beacharra, Kintyre, Argyll, *P.P.S.* **30,** 134–58.

Seddon, B. 1967. Prehistoric climate and agriculture: a review of recent paleo-ecological investigations, in Taylor, J. A. (Ed.), *Weather and Agriculture*, Oxford University Press, Oxford, 173–85.

Sernander, R. 1908. On the evidence of Post-glacial changes of climate furnished by the peat mosses of northern Europe, *Geol. Fören. Förh.* **30,** 465–78.

Shotton, F. W. 1968. Prehistoric man's use of stone in Britain, *P.G.A.* **79,** 477–91.

Simmons, I. G. 1969a. Evidence for vegetation changes associated with Mesolithic man in Britain, in Ucko, P. J., and Dimbleby, G. W. (Eds.), *The Domestication and Exploitation of Plants and Animals*. Duckworth, London, 110–19.

Simmons, I. G. 1969b. Environment and early man on Dartmoor, Devon, England, *P.P.S.* **35,** 203–19.

Simpson, I. M., and West, R. G. 1958. On the stratigraphy and palaeobotany of a late-Pleistocene organic deposit at Chelford, Cheshire, *New Phyt.* **57,** 239–50.

Sissons, J. B. 1967. *The Evolution of Scotland's Scenery*. Oliver and Boyd, Edinburgh.

Small, R. J., Clark, M. J., and Lewin, J. 1970. The periglacial rock-stream at Clatford Bottom, Marlborough Downs, Wiltshire, *P.G.A.* **81,** 87–98.

Smith, A. C. 1885. *British and Roman Antiquities of North Wiltshire*. Wiltshire Archaeological and Natural History Society.

Smith, A. G. 1965. Problems of inertia and threshold related to Post-glacial habitat changes, *Proc. R. Soc. B* **161,** 331–42.

Smith, A. G. 1970a. The influence of Mesolithic and Neolithic man on British vegetation: a discussion, in Walker, D., and West, R. G. (Eds.), *Studies in the Vegetational History of the British Isles*. Cambridge University Press, London, 81–96.

Smith, A. G. 1970b. Late- and Post-glacial vegetational and climatic history of Ireland: a review, in Stephens, N., and Glasscock, R. E. (Eds.), *Irish Geographical Studies*. Department of Geography, Queen's University, Belfast, 65–88.

Smith, A. G., Pilcher, J. R., and Pearson, G. W. 1971. New radiocarbon dates from Ireland, *Antiquity* **45,** 97–102.

Smith, A. G., and Willis, E. H. 1962. Radiocarbon dating and the Fallahogy landnam phase, *U.J.A.* **24–5,** 16–24.

Smith, I. F. 1965. *Windmill Hill and Avebury: Excavations by Alexander Keiller, 1925–1939*. Oxford University Press, Oxford.

Smith, W. G. 1894. *Man the Primeval Savage*. Stanford, London.

Southern, H. N. (Ed.), 1964. *The Handbook of British Mammals*. Blackwells, Oxford.

Sparks, B. W., and West, R. G. 1972. *The Ice Age in Britain*. Methuen, London.

Stamp, L. D. 1960. *Britain's Structure and Scenery*. Collins, London.

Stamp, L. D. 1969. *Man and the Land*. Collins, London.

Steensberg, A. 1957. Some recent Danish experiments in Neolithic agriculture, *Ag. Hist. Rev.* **5,** 66–73.

Stenton, D. M. 1951. *English Society in the Early Middle Ages*. Penguin, Harmondsworth.

Stephens, N., and Collins, A. E. P. 1960. The Quaternary deposits at Ringneill Quay and Ardmillan, Co. Down, *P.R.I.A.* C **61,** 41–77.

Stephens, N., and Glasscock, R. E. (Eds.), 1970. *Irish Geographical Studies*. Department of Geography, Queen's University, Belfast.

Stukeley, W. 1740. *Stonehenge and Abury*. Innys and Manby, London.

Sutcliffe, A. J. 1960. Joint Mitnor Cave, Buckfastleigh, *T.T.N.H.S.* **13,** 3–28.

Sutcliffe, A. J., and Zeuner, F. E. 1962. Excavations in the Torbryan Caves, Devonshire. 1. Tornewton Cave, *P.D.A.E.S.* **5,** 127–45.

Synge, F. M. 1970. The Irish Quaternary: current views 1969, in Stephens, N., and Glasscock, R. E. (Eds.), *Irish Geographical Studies*. Department of Geography, Queen's University, Belfast, 244–58.

Tamplin, M. J. 1966. *The Middle Thames Brickearths: Their Nature, Stratigraphy and Archaeology*. M.Sc. thesis. Institute of Archaeology, London.

Tansley, A. G. 1968. *Britain's Green Mantle: Past, Present and Future*. Allen and Unwin, London.

Taylor, C. C. 1967. Whiteparish: a study of the development of a forest-edge parish, *W.A.M.* **62,** 79–102.

Taylor, C. C. 1968. Three deserted medieval settlements in Whiteparish, *W.A.M.* **63,** 39–45.

Taylor, C. C. 1972. Medieval moats in Cambridgeshire, in Fowler, P. J. (Ed.). *Archaeology and the Landscape*. John Baker, London, 241.

Taylor, E. L. 1955. Parasitic helminths in medieval remains, *The Veterinary Record* **67,** 216–18.

Taylor, J. A. 1973. Chronometers and chronicles: a study of palaeo-environments in west central Wales, *Progress in Geography, International Reviews of Current Research*, **5,** 247–334.

Tomlinson, M. E. 1941. Pleistocene gravels of the Cotswold sub-edge plain from Mickleton to the Frome Valley, *Q.J.G.S.* **96,** 385.

Tratman, E. K., Donovan, D. T., and Campbell, J. B. 1971. The Hyena Den (Wookey Hole), Mendip Hills, Somerset, *Proc. speleol. Soc.* **12,** 245–79.

Troels-Smith, J. 1960. Ivy, mistletoe and elm: climatic indicators—fodder plants, *Danm. geol. Unders.*, IV Rk. Nr. 4, 1–32.

Trueman, A. E. 1971. *Geology and Scenery in England and Wales*. Penguin, Harmondsworth.

Turner, C. 1970. The Middle Pleistocene deposits at Marks Tey, Essex. *Phil. Trans.* B **257,** 373–437.

Turner, J. 1962. The *Tilia* decline: an anthropogenic interpretation, *New Phytol.* **61,** 328–41.

Turner, J. 1965. A contribution to the history of forest clearance, *Proc. R. Soc.* B **161,** 343–53.

Turner, J. 1970. Post-Neolithic disturbance of British vegetation, in Walker, D., and West, R. G. (Eds.), *Studies in the Vegetational History of the British Isles*. Cambridge University Press, Cambridge, 97–116.

Ucko, P. J., and Rosenfeld, A. 1967. *Palaeolithic Cave Art*. Weidenfeld and Nicolson, London.

van Waateringe, W. G. 1968. The elm decline and the first appearance of *Plantago maior*, *Vegetatio* **15**, 292–6.

van Zeist, W. 1969. Reflections on prehistoric environments in the Near East, in Ucko, P. J., and Dimbleby, G. W. (Eds.), *The Domestication and Exploitation of Plants and Animals*. Duckworth, London, 35–46.

Waechter, J. d'A., Hubbard, R. N. L. B., and Conway, B. W. 1971. Swanscombe 1971, *Proceedings of the Royal Anthropological Institute*, 73–85.

Wainwright, G. J. 1972. The excavation of a Neolithic settlement on Broome Heath, Ditchingham, Norfolk, *P.P.S.* **38**, 1–97.

Wainwright, G. J., Evans, J. G., and Longworth, I. H. 1971. The excavation of a Late Neolithic enclosure at Marden, Wiltshire, *Ant. J.* **51**, 177–239.

Walker, D. 1956. A site at Stump Cross, near Grassington, Yorkshire, and the age of the Pennine microlithic industry, *P.P.S.* **22**, 23–8.

Walker, D., and West, R. G. (Eds.), 1970. *Studies in the Vegetational History of the British Isles*. Cambridge University Press, London.

West, R. G. 1956. The Quaternary deposits at Hoxne, Suffolk, *Phil. Trans.* B **239**, 265–356.

West, R. G. 1968. *Pleistocene Geology and Biology with especial Reference to the British Isles*. Longmans, London.

West, R. G., and McBurney, C. B. M. 1954. The Quaternary deposits at Hoxne, Suffolk, and their archaeology, *P.P.S.* **20**, 131–54.

West, R. G., and Sparks, B. W. 1960. Coastal interglacial deposits of the English Channel, *Phil. Trans.* B **243**, 95–133.

Whitehead, B. J. 1966. The management and land-use of water meadows in the Frome Valley, Dorset, *P.D.N.H.S.* **89**, 257–81.

Williams, R. B. G. 1968. Some estimates of periglacial erosion in southern and eastern England, *Biuletyn Peryglacjalny* no. 17, 311–35.

Wilson, V. 1948. *British Regional Geology: East Yorkshire and Lincolnshire*. HMSO, London.

Wooldridge, S. W., and Linton, D. L. 1933. The loam-terrains of south-east England and their relation to its early history, *Antiquity* **7**, 297–310.

Wykham, H. 1974. *Ribstone Pippins*. Allen Figgis/Calder and Boyars, London.

Wymer, J. 1962. Excavations at the Maglemosian sites at Thatcham, Berkshire, England, *P.P.S.* **28**, 329–61.

Wymer, J. 1968. *Lower Palaeolithic Archaeology in Britain*. John Baker, London.

Wymer, J. 1970. Radiocarbon date for the Lambourn Long Barrow, *Antiquity* **44**, 144.

Zeuner, F. E. 1958. *Dating the Past*. Methuen, London.

Zeuner, F. E. 1959. *The Pleistocene Period*. Hutchinson, London.

Zeuner, F. E. 1963. *A History of Domesticated Animals*. Hutchinson, London.

Index